Orang-Utans
in Borneo

Gisela Kaplan
and
Lesley Rogers

Photography by Gisela Kaplan

UNIVERSITY OF NEW ENGLAND PRESS

First published in 1994 by
University of New England Press
(a division of University Partnerships Pty Ltd, the commercial company of the
University of New England, Armidale)
1st Floor, Richardsons Arcade, Beardy Street
Armidale NSW 2350
Tel: (067) 71 1097   Fax: (067) 72 5230

National Library of Australia
Cataloguing-in-Publication data:

Kaplan, Gisela.
  Orang-Utans in Borneo.

  Bibliography.
  Includes index.
  ISBN 1 875821 13 9.

  1. Orangutan – Borneo I. Rogers, Lesley J. (Lesley Joy), 1943-   . II. Title.

599.8842095983

Photography by Gisela Kaplan
Produced and typeset by University Partnerships
Printed by Griffin Press Pty Ltd

Contents

List of tables/illustrations

Tables

Figures/maps

Foreword

It is a pleasure to write a foreword to this erudite and accessible book on orang-utans. Orang-utans, by and large, have been the least understood, recognisable and appreciated of the great apes. Indeed, they have suffered a scientific and popular identity crisis, for although Hollywood has taken a fancy to them, few people can accurately picture them as they are in real life — fruit-eating, brachiating, solitary (or semi-solitary) primates living high in the rainforest canopy. The public and the conservation community have been slow to comprehend the plight of this 'person of the forest'. Numbers have dwindled so drastically in the past decade that the term 'pongicide' might not be inappropriate to describe the effects that the illegal pet trade has had in South East Asia. Due to the latter and to other reasons discussed in the book, the numbers of wild Bornean orang-utans may be as few as 10 000 – 12 000.

In the past, public attention has been focused on chimpanzees and gorillas, rather than orang-utans. A number of recent events has begun to change some of these perceptual inequities. In 1991, the Second International Great Ape Conference was held in one of the orang-utan's home nations, Indonesia. During the conference, field scientists and organisers were able to put more of a face on the species within that country's interested media community. In 1994, an International Orang-Utan Conference was held at California State University, Fullerton, attracting over 200 scholars, conservationists and wildlife managers. The subtitle of the conference was 'Orang-Utan: the Neglected Ape'.

In the literature, the gaps in our knowledge of orang-utans are now beginning to be filled. There is for instance Dr Jeffrey Schwartz's book, *The Red Ape,* published in 1987 and Dr Biruté Galdikas' book, *Reflections of Eden,* is to be released in 1995. Now Drs Gisela Kaplan and Lesley Rogers have written a significant volume which focuses on the Bornean subspecies and the Malaysian program. *Orang-Utans in Borneo* represents the most comprehensive book-length behavioural work to be published so far. This book offers timely information and an improved understanding of the orang-utan as a species.

One of the undoubted strengths of this book is that the behaviour described is based on field work observations by the authors, as well as incorporating all previous field work results in the areas covered by the book. This is not to say that the authors have neglected to present information on orang-utans derived from laboratory studies. Much of the available information on orang-utan mentality has come from the laboratory where controlled training and tests can be performed. However, a growing body of information has come from the field. It is in the field where detailed observation has revealed the adaptive nature of intelligence within the ecological context. While orang-utans are known for their creative ability to disassemble items in captivity (including their cages), their wild cousins appear to learn spatio-temporal relationships regarding food, individual arboreal pathways, and other resources. They also learn complex extractive foraging and food processing techniques that are food and food-type specific. But orang-utans do not appear to employ the highest levels of intelligence while performing extractive foraging. Rather, their intelligence is put to the test up in the treetops. Techniques that enable the largest arboreal mammal to locomote from tree to tree are amongst the most challenging. Young orang-utans spend years learning tensile strengths of various woody materials. As they grow larger, they must learn how to distribute and transfer their weight to thin branches which might not support them individually as they pole-swing or brachiate from tree to tree.

Orang-utan communication abilities have also been examined in both the laboratory and field environments. While their natural communication system serves them well in the wild, they can also be taught referential communication systems (symbols and sign language). Not surprisingly, orang-utans use the systems to request edibles and contact. They also can produce strings of symbols or signs in combinations that appear to appropriately convey meaning. All of this information is covered in this book.

Orang-utans are a fascinating species. This book provides welcome and pertinent discussions regarding the orang-utan and its evolutionary relationship to humans and the other great apes. Furthermore, it provides a very extensive and comprehensive bibliography on orang-utans which will allow readers easy access to the dispersed orang-utan literature. This is a book written with empathy and compassion, containing a plea for the orang-utan's right to survival in the wild. The book will help to promote the perceptual transformation of the orang-utan to a species which will be appreciated, protected and admired as the arboreal primate that it is.

Dr Gary Shapiro, Vice President, Orangutan Foundation International

Acknowledgments

We wish to gratefully acknowledge the financial and personal support received for this project. It began in 1989 as a personal initiative. In 1991 the University of New England supported the project by awarding an internal research grant to Lesley Rogers thus ensuring its continuation. In 1992 the Queensland University of Technology granted leave of absence and some financial support to Gisela Kaplan in pursuit of further field work within its framework of a competitive 'professional development' program. Although there are some excellent primatologists in Australia, internationally Australia is not in the forefront of primate research and we are most grateful to both institutions for their indulgence in what must have at first appeared a flamboyant project.

We further thank Norman Rosen, Department of Anthropology, California State University, Fullerton, and his team for getting together the first international conference on orang-utans, conducted in March 1994. This gave us a timely opportunity for debate just before submission of the book. And we thank Professor Biruté Galdikas and the Orangutan Foundation for their inspirational contribution to this project.

Locally, at the University of New England in Armidale, we particularly wish to thank Mr Gavin A. Krebs for his astutely reliable and valuable research assistance, particularly in securing literature searches, library material, producing some of the figures and ensuring the completion of a number of the figures in the text; and Michelle Hodgkinson for a brief but important involvement with this manuscript in the checking of references. We warmly thank Jill and Brian Chetwynd of Crystal Colour for their astute, patient and professional advice on all matters related to photography and filming, as well as for their record keeping of the large number of negatives, a service which considerably simplified accessing the material. Our thanks go to Dr Ian Metcalfe, geologist and expert for the South East Asian region, for the production of the maps. Any errors in them are entirely our responsibility. We are very grateful to Associate Professor Amarjit Kaur, economic historian and specialist in Sabah and Sarawak, also at the University of New England, for her expert advice on the region and her bibliographical assistance. Associate Professor Kaur's personal library contains material we were unable to find ourselves or obtain elsewhere. Associate Professor Kaur furthermore read a section of the manuscript and offered extremely valuable advice. Further, our thanks go to Professor Clive Kessler, School of Sociology, University of New South Wales (Sydney), who has advised us and functioned as an intermediary in important ways on a number of occasions. We are especially indebted to Professor Mike Cullen, Department of Ecology and Evolutionary Biology, Monash University (Melbourne), for reading the entire manuscript, and offering much stimulating and helpful advice.

Within Malaysia, we wish to thank particularly Dr Norani Othman in the Department of Anthropology and Sociology at the Universiti Kebangsaan Malaysia, Bangi Selangor, for supplying material and employing some research assistance in Kuala Lumpur on our behalf. We are particularly grateful to the staff at Sepilok, for their endless patience in providing us with the names of individual orang-utans and for useful advice from the veterinarian, Dr Rika Akamatsu of Minato, Okayama City, Japan, who was then stationed at the Sepilok Rehabilitation Centre. We are also most grateful to the Sarawak Museum in Kuching for assistance in referencing and supplying copies of papers.

Introduction

This book discusses the behaviour of orang-utans in the broad context of their habitat and their particular socio-political environment. It enters into the current debates about their evolution, cognitive abilities and survival. It presents a comparative assessment with human and other non-human primate development and characteristics and incorporates past and present knowledge about the species, including the results of our own field work on orang-utans. The elusiveness of this great ape and its unique lifestyle have puzzled researchers for a long time. Too few studies are available. There are still substantial gaps in knowledge, for instance of the orang-utan's behaviour and perception, with resulting misconceptions. This book is an attempt to fill a gap and foster further debate and research.

At the first international conference on orang-utans, held in California in 1994, several conservation activists expressed the view that field research was no longer useful. Action, not research, was needed to save the orang-utan. There is no doubt that action is needed. In our view, such action must first and foremost concentrate on negotiations for habitat preservation. Beyond that, we continue to believe that research is vital. First, in many instances it can be shown that where teams of researchers have descended into wildlife areas, there have been some immediate benefits to their sites. In Africa, the presence of researchers resulted in substantial changes in the conditions for primates. Now well-known areas, such as Gombe and Mahale, Tanzania, have been declared reserves or national parks where no such status existed before. Changes in legislation of a specific country for the protection of primates were often a consequence of researcher presence, as they recorded and advised the wider community of specific problems. Second, if orang-utans are to be saved we have to be able to advise ways of doing so effectively. We agree with Kevin Hunt ('Primate-talk' network information, 21 February 1994) that one of the best ways to maintain hope for primates, and for great apes in particular, is more and more field research.

The great apes include the gorilla (*Gorilla gorilla*), the orang-utan (*Pongo pygmaeus*) and the two types of chimpanzee, the common chimpanzee (*Pan troglodytes*) and the pygmy chimpanzee, also known as the bonobo (*Pan paniscus*). In some classifications, humans (*Homo sapiens*) are considered to be great apes. The survival of all the great apes, except humans, is threatened by a host of events and processes. One important factor contributing to their demise is the human population explosion of the last 150

1

years, which has led human societies to claim more and more space for themselves, pushing back and raiding wildernesses. Over and above this phenomenon, general economic development and human greed have done their part.

From the later nineteenth and throughout the twentieth century, laboratory research (pharmaceutical and medical) has required live animals and this has grown into extremely large-scale activities. Primates have been used as research animals for the last 100 years. They have been prized because of their similarity to humans and demand for them has forever increased. For example, by the 1950s the USA imported about 2 000 rhesus monkeys a year. Between 1967 and 1972 at least 530 000 wild primates were imported to the USA alone. Furthermore, an estimated two to three million primates died during trapping and shipping before getting to the laboratories (Koebner 1984). The Humane Society of the USA (HSUS) in conjunction with the Humane Society International (HSI) discovered that for every ten primates taken from the wild only two survived. Indonesia alone used to export 10 000 primates a year, being a supplier of about 30 percent of the world primate market (Telecky 1994).

Zoo populations of primates have increased since the 1930s when apes became part of a regular zoo repertoire. In the 1950s there were 284 orang-utans held in zoos worldwide (Harrisson 1961). In the 1990s, the figure has tripled to over 900 (Western 1994). Some of that increase occurred through reproduction within the captive environments but much of it continued through imports. A large number of primates, including orang-utans, continue to be poached for illegal trafficking into other countries where they are used as pets, in circuses, as sideline attractions in shows, or even as food or ornamental items.

Quite a number of countries are known to be recipients of illegally imported wildlife. The full extent is not known but the range and numerical strength of the primate smuggling organisations worldwide is alarming. To give just one example, it is estimated that in the last five years up to 3 000 orang-utans have been smuggled to Taiwan alone (Eudy 1994). In all these smuggling records, the extent of the damage to wildlife populations can only be ascertained from live samples. It is known, however, that the majority of wildlife does not survive the smuggling transportation conditions (hidden in suitcases or other containers, without sufficient oxygen, often in freezing or extremely hot temperatures, without food and water etc). Present estimates for live orang-utans held captive in Taiwan vary between 400 and 800. In 1978, the Convention on International Trade in Endangered Species (CITIES) declared all primates 'endangered'.

In the wild, orang-utan populations, like other wildlife, are chiefly threatened by the expansion of agriculture and general economic 'development', and through logging and poaching. The risks are enormous because any of these interventions can result in the fragmentation of populations to a point where the remaining individuals are cut off from territory and from other orang-utans for reproduction. Despite legal protection, laws remain difficult to enforce. Poaching has continued in all areas. It might be stressed that illegal capture of orang-utans is particularly objectionable because they are so similar to us. As a rule, only infant or juvenile orang-utans are caught which invariably means killing the mother. Hence, for every live orang-utan at least one has died at the time of capture. Transportation kills another 80 percent of the live cargo. Even if young live orang-utans are kept locally and not shipped or flown elsewhere, their chances of survival may be poor. However, generally, methods of confiscation and notification have improved. In a research site in Bali Kapan, East Kalimantan, 100 confiscated orang-utans have so far been received. Of those, 90 percent were said to have been seriously ill (Smits & Herlyanto 1994).

Estimates of the actual number of surviving orang-utans range widely, and population studies continue (Payne & Andau 1994). In a recent BBC report it was claimed that the world's wild population in 1993 stood at 20 000 on Sumatra and Borneo combined, having dropped by a drastic 50 percent in a mere decade (Western 1994). Other estimates claim that the total world population of orang-utans has dropped even more sharply: from about 80 000 in the 1980s to 20 000 in the early 1990s (Sugardjito 1994). It is difficult to estimate their numbers because of their elusive nature. Hence, for large terrains, aerial surveying and counting of nests is the only method that so far has been and can be used. This is a notoriously unreliable method, as orang-utans may build up to 365 nests a year, possibly even more, and nest tangles may survive longer in trees than the orang-utans who built them. Also, there may be evidence of orang-utan nests but the population has either moved, been poached off or died out. The age of the nest can be judged only roughly from aerial surveys and some of them may be built too far below the canopy to be visible from a plane. Although checking the number of nests counted by aerial surveying against that obtained by counting from ground level in sample regions allows correction factors to be used, Payne agrees that it is more difficult to assess numbers on slopes where some orang-utan groups are now surviving.

In zoos there are now extensive breeding programs. These breeding programs are selective and offer a spectrum of further ethical issues and problems, some of which will be discussed in Chapter 5. Currently, the European Breeding Program for orang-utans (EEP) has decided to enforce a ban on all forms of hybrid breeding between the Sumatran and Bornean orang-utans by introducing castration and sterilisation requirements when appropriate partners cannot be found (Vancatova 1994). However, breeding programs undertaken under the banner of species diversity and later re-stocking of the wild are based on the assumption that there will still be areas which can be re-stocked with wildlife. Increasingly, a question worth pondering is: will there be any habitat left for them?

We have called this book *Orang-Utans in Borneo* and it is fitting for an introduction to explain why we use the word Borneo. Borneo refers here not to a political entity but to a geographical unit. For the species name the following can be said. There are two main subspecies of the orang-utan. One subspecies lives exclusively on Borneo and the other exclusively on Sumatra. It has recently been suggested that there may even be a third subspecies in the Crocker Range of Sabah (Payne 1994, personal communication). The Sumatran and Bornean orang-utans can interbreed in captivity to produce hybrids. The taxa names are still not fully agreed upon internationally. In non-English speaking countries the Bornean orang-utan is at times called *Pongo satyrus borneensi* after Wurmb's classification of 1784 and the Sumatran one *Pongo satyrus satyrus*, after Linnaeus' classification of 1758 (cf. Röhrer-Ertl 1989). In English-speaking countries, the most often used nomenclature is *Pongo pygmaeus pygmaeus* for the Bornean subspecies after Linnaeus (1760) and *Pongo pygmaeus abelii* for the Sumatran one after Lesson (1827). Both populations belong to the same genus (*Pongo*) and species (*pygmaeus*), meaning that they can interbreed, but they have been categorised as different subspecies (*pygmaeus* and *abelii*). The Sumatran subspecies is slightly different from its Bornean cousin in that males do not develop such pronounced cheek pads, and both male and female Sumatran orang-utans are smaller. In Sumatran orang-utans the phenotypical characteristics have also been deemed more variable than those of the Bornean species and it has therefore been suggested that the Sumatran orang-utan is closer to the ancestral form than the orang-utan of Borneo (Röhrer-Ertl 1989). Recent analysis of subspecific variation in the orang-utan has shown that even within Borneo there are substantial morphological differences between groups. Hence, the morphological distance of orang-utans between Sabah and Sarawak is said to be greater than between Sarawak and the whole south-west of Borneo, and between the latter and Sumatra. In terms of the genetic diversity, this recent finding has a number of extremely important implications. Evidently, the orang-utan diversity is greater than first thought and this raises questions for conservation and for further study (Shapiro 1993). Our book focuses on the Bornean *Pongo pygmaeus pygmaeus* and within the diverse but fragmented populations of Borneo it focuses on the orang-utans of Sabah. Reference will also be made to studies undertaken in Kalimantan Tengah, Sarawak and Sumatra.

It is worth saying a few words on Borneo itself. The name Borneo has all but disappeared except in geographical contexts. What we hear instead is East Malaysia and Kalimantan. East Malaysia refers to the two provinces Sarawak and Sabah which joined Malaysia's Federation in 1963. The area of this political conglomerate covers less than a quarter of the landmass of Borneo. The vast majority of the landmass belongs to Indonesia under the name of Kalimantan. Orang-utans are less concerned with borders and are found in both countries, the largest number of them on the Indonesian side.

Borneo is an island and possesses one of the richest and most diverse flora and fauna on earth. Borneo is also large. Indeed, it is the third largest island on the planet, after Australia and Greenland. In area, Borneo is as large as the United Kingdom and France put together, or, to compare it with a different region in the world, the size of Turkey or Pakistan. The seemingly small area of Sabah, where we conducted most of our observations, is the size of Austria or of Belgium and the Netherlands combined. It represents, however, a vast expanse of relatively sparsely populated land. In terms of conservation all of Borneo is of great importance to the world.

Finally, a word on the organisation of the book and the material itself. The book is purposely multidisciplinary and because both authors come from different but interrelated fields, it was possible to put such an ambitious project into practice. We have chosen to place the orang-utan debates, and our work on orang-utan behaviour, in the context of the wider world and wider issues. Chapters 1 and 2 concentrate on background information, such as the philosophical, socio-economic and ecological context of and attitudes to the orang-utan. We begin with western attitudes to primates through the ages because we believe it is vital to expose our own blindspots and prejudices in order to address the magnitude of the orang-utan's plight appropriately. We do so as part of our deep commitment and concern for the survival of this magnificent close relative of ours. We then switch from western nations to the localities where orang-utans are found. Too often, western debates on endangered species or on the rainforest in general are discussed with a blatant disregard for the views, role and rights of the nations under whose charge the particular endangered species happens to live or wherever rainforests happen to be. This is, of course, not necessarily true for activists in the various fields. We wanted to ensure that the socio-political and even the diplomatic aspects of such debates will not get lost amongst the enthusiasms and justified concerns. Readers who are less interested in these issues might want to begin the book at Chapter 2.

Chapter 2 provides more than just details on the actual habitat of the orang-utan. It gives an overview of where orang-utans now occur and what islands of survival, in the form of reserves, rehabilitation centres and national parks, currently exist. Chapter 2 introduces field work on orang-utans by discussing the conditions that all field researchers face. In Chapter 5 the specific details of our own field work are addressed.

The main sections of the book (Chapters 3 to 6) deal with orang-utan behaviour, and the detailed discussions and information we have developed in these chapters were inspired by the field work of colleagues and by our own observations in the field. The orang-utan's behaviour raises many intriguing theoretical questions that concern our own history and evolution.

We cannot even begin to express our views on how we feel about this species other than to say that the orang-utan is a fascinating being. If we are able to convey anything of their subtlety, complexity and sensitivity that will lead one to feel a deep respect for their right to be, then the book will have done its most important work. If, over and above this, readers are able to read this book for enjoyment, we would be tremendously pleased. It was our distinct aim to write a book that was neither technical nor incomprehensible because of jargonistic or scientific and highly specialised vocabulary. This book was written as much for the serious researcher in the primate field (especially Chapters 3, 4 and 6), for zoo personnel dealing with orang-utans, for conservationists and other interest groups, as it was written for the general reader. It raises, and in a number of novel ways answers, some very complex issues but it attempts to do so by remaining accessible to a wider audience. It is up to the reader to decide whether or not in this presentation we have succeeded in straddling the fence between the research insider and the larger world outside.

Gisela Kaplan and Lesley Rogers, June 1994

1

The cultural context

We know a great deal more about orang-utans now than 100 years ago but the pace of discovery has quickened just in the last 30 years. Only in the last five years has the orang-utan reached popular interest, be this through television, magazine publications, wildlife photography, documentaries or travel bureaus throughout the world.

Such interest coincides with the stunned realisation that the orang-utan is on the list of endangered species. One of the many questions that such a realisation raises is simple to pose: how could it get to this? Larger conservation questions can only be alluded to in this book devoted to one particular species but we should broach the issue at least with respect to the orang-utan. Let us ask the hypothetical and simple question: 'What have orang-utans done to us that we have driven them to near extinction?'. The answer to this is easy (as indeed for most other species in this predicament) and there would be few who could quarrel with the answer: nothing, absolutely nothing.

Orang-utans are known to mind their own business. They are not predatory or aggressive and rarely have there been verified stories of orang-utans interfering with or threatening human life. In the case of the latter, Galdikas (1994, personal communication) has emphasised that instances of orang-utans having caused damage to humans are not only rare but they are usually a consequence of *human* provocation (including causing injury) and attack. Galdikas's judgment needs to be trusted in these matters because she has lived with and near orang-utans for over 20 years now (Gallardo 1993). Our own observations would support her views in this and in many other respects (more of this later).

There is also another simple answer to the question: what has the orang-utan done to us? The simple answer is that we never meant to harm it but that population pressures and human needs have had this unintended consequence. The problem, not so much with simple questions but with simple answers, is that they hide more than they reveal. The matter is and remains more complicated and refers to traditions, aspirations and attitudes which have accumulatively and collectively shaped and informed our consciousness and our actions. In this chapter we refer to two of the most important areas of impact that we consider highly relevant to our appreciation of the orang-utan's predicament today: those shaped in the history of ideas in western countries on the one hand, and the socio-economic aspirations of the political nations which control orang-utan territory on the other.

The history of western attitudes is of more than marginal importance, even though orang-utans are an Asian species. The western world has exported its ideas mainly via four routes: exploration and trade, conquering and subjugation, and religion represent three routes. The fourth has been by creating a world economy and international market that has seen the wholesale adoption of its model and the tumbling and ruin of any other. Those countries that have resisted its application have ultimately all suffered severely and those that have not restructured their economy and thinking in the past are now in a desperate battle to imitate that model. They have begun to compete for their own niche in this world system — a system which many in western nations have begun to question on every level.

In our context, it is important to stop and think: What does an orang-utan mean to us today? Where do our attitudes come from and by what kind of forces have these been shaped? We ask those questions far too little, even though our actions, views and behaviour depend on these attitudes and values, whether they be formulated clearly or at a subliminal level.

Attitudes to orang-utans

The question of how it could come to this, must lead us to consider the context in which any debate about orang-utans, primates or any other species might have been raised. Where, in our view, do they belong and how can we begin a story on the way attitudes were formed? Inevitably, a search for an answer leads to a broad and ambivalent concept of 'nature'.

Over the centuries, the orang-utan has fared badly at the hands and in the minds of western countries, except for a brief spell during the period of the European Enlightenment in the eighteenth century. Even in this period, attitudes to the newly discovered apes were not concerned with the species in its own right and for its own merits but rather sparked off debates about how close humans could be placed to orang-utans. In other words, the theoretical and practical interest and curiosity did not derive from an interest in the species *per se* but from questioning where humans stood in relation to nature (Kaplan & Rogers 1994; Kaplan & Rogers 1995).

One of the proponents of the enlightenment, French philosopher Jean Jacques Rousseau, for instance, argued in his widely debated work that humanity had drifted far away from its origin in nature. Accordingly, we had gone from natural being to social citizen and, as citizens, we had become corrupted, putting people in chains and morally depleting institutions. It was time to listen to one's emotions and turn back to a harmonious 'natural' state. In his view there were two ways for rediscovery: journeys to other places and cultures, in the hope of discovering people and life forms which were as yet not corrupted and 'overcivilised', and a journey into self. In a romantic move, Rousseau suggested retiring to the woods to 'behold your history … not in books written by your fellow creatures, who are liars, but in nature, which never lies' (cf. Hendel 1937).

Rousseau accepted the concept of the 'noble savage', derived from discoveries of the New World. Steeped in misconceptions and prejudices, the 'noble savage' of 'primitive' society was nevertheless set as a paradigm for the natural life. It was this construct of the 'noble savage', which permitted a pre-Darwinian evolutionary benevolence. If 'savages' could live (allegedly) without laws (ie only by their instincts), then those half-men half-beasts might also deserve our attention. Daniel Beeckman is said to be one of the first westerners to have visited orang-utan territory. His account in *A Voyage to and from the Island of Borneo* (1714) suggests an ambivalence:

> *The Monkeys, Apes, and Baboons are of many different Sorts and Shapes; but the most remarkable are those they call Oran-ootans, which in their Language signifies Men of the Woods: these grow up to be six Foot high; they walk upright, have longer Arms than Men, tolerable good Faces (handsomer I am sure than some Hottentots that I have seen), large Teeth, no Tails nor Hair, but on those Parts where it grows on humane Bodies … The Natives do really believe that these were formerly Men, but Meta-morphosed into Beasts for their Blasphemy.*

(cited in Harrisson 1987)

Similarly, and at about the same time, a Frenchman by the name of Benoît de Maillet wrote in *Telliamed* (1702) that '[orang-utans have] the whole of the human form, and like us walked upon two legs' and in captivity to be 'very melancholy, gentle, and peaceable' (cited in Schwartz 1987). In 1774, Lord Monboddo published the first of six volumes called *Of the Origin and Progress of Language*. Monboddo's sense of where to put the boundaries between humans and animals had been blurred by his experiences and study of orang-utans. He wrote: 'I still maintain, that this [the orang-utan] being possessed of the capacity of acquiring it [language], by having both the human intelligence and the organs of pronunciation, joined to the dispositions and affections of his mind, mild, gentle, and humane, is sufficient to denominate him a man' (Monboddo 1774).

Hence, in the spirit of the enlightenment, the ape was accorded a status of humanness and an anthropomorphic interpretation, commencing a tradition that might well be evoked under the new banner of the 'Great Ape Project' (Cavalieri & Singer 1993). This tradition accords equality to those who lack it and human status to those who are denied such status. At the basis of these arguments were not just certain social convictions but, embedded in these, a romantic view of nature as benign and noble, or as a symbol for paradise. The idea of a 'noble savage' and of a paradisiacal nature vanished altogether at the time of the Industrial Revolution in the early nineteenth century.

There is a vast literature on the early scientific history of anthropoidology. In summary, it may be said that underlying that literature two discrete views of nature can be detected. Both of these are still flourishing today in one form or another. One of them is based on competition: nature is something to be feared and that fear is managed by attempting to assume control. Humankind is the highest form of creation and hence master of the earth. This attitude allows us, as a species, to continue the plundering of the earth and it allows us to do so without the slightest moral discomfort. On the other hand, there is a pragmatic, economic model: nature is simply a resource in a utilitarian pragmatic sense. We can take anything from it, whatever we need. It offers us our subsistence and, with some labour, it can be made to extract its riches. These riches are boundless and exist for our sake. Again, moral questions do not arise in this context or, if they do, they function as a justification for *our* species: it is moral to take what we need if this ensures our wellbeing as humans and our survival.

The view that nature is something negative and to be feared has probably been the most prevalent one, at least since the beginnings of Christianity. It re-emerged in a new garb and received a new boost with the onset of the Industrial Revolution, which occurred in England in the early 1800s and in the 1830s in France. In the literature, there is a notable change in attitude towards apes and orang-utans, for the worse, around this time. In 1838 Rennie, in his observation of orang-utans, condemned them as slovenly and useless creatures:

> *Their deportment is grave and melancholy, their disposition apathetic, their motions slow and heavy, and their habits so sluggish and lazy, that it is only the cravings of appetite, or the approach of imminent danger, that can rouse them from their habitual lethargy, or force them to active exertion.*

(cited in Yerkes & Yerkes 1945)

The change in attitude can be ascribed to the new value given to two words: competition and work. Theories of the nature and value of competition were expounded just as eloquently in the evolutionary theories of Charles Darwin and Alfred Wallace as they were by the social and economic theorists of the nineteenth century. Darwin's theory of evolution was not accidentally coeval with *laissez-faire* capitalism. The idea of a survival of the fittest also had an old religious moral value attached to it: those that do survive *are* better (or, at least, better adapted) and those that die deserve to die because they are weak. Not 'the meek shall inherit the earth', but whoever can push harder, fight harder, be more cunning and more self-centred shall be the carrier to the future. Human adaptation and its strengthening position as a species on this globe was yet another sign of human superiority and seemed to confirm the view expounded in Judaeo-Christian religions of the human being as the pinnacle of creation. Animals became devalued in a wholesale fashion.

Ironically, despite, or because of, the discovery of evolutionary theory, it was considered necessary to delineate humans from animals even further by creating a large moral and biological gulf between the two. This became particularly necessary in the case of apes, which had now advanced to the status of a human relative and its closest forerunner. It was important to guard the human condition from any further encroachment by claims of a natural link, be this by constantly pointing to evolutionary 'disjunctions' (ie we can do things they cannot do; we have things biologically that they do not) or by disinheriting animal species from the creative process. The latter refers to a theological position in the Judaeo–Christian tradition that, broadly speaking, argues that all living things are God's creation and creatures. This pantheistic position, argued by Spinoza and others, states that animals are not only God's creation but that they carry within them a divine spark. It was postulated that this should mean that animals were capable of wisdom, of altruism, of love and perhaps even of moral judgment. The processes of the nineteenth century changed all this dramatically. What we generally refer to as a progressive 'secularisation' is, amongst many other things, a break with creationism. Ironically, scientific advances in unravelling the mysteries of human evolution, indeed, of life on earth, at first did not lead to a greater closeness to or respect for other living things. Rather it led to a deterioration of that relationship, with human attitudes ranging from an anxious defence of human superiority to a militant and aggressive condemnation of animals. Once divested of any positive values, assessment of animals switched from wise, gentle and loving to dumb, dirty and lazy.

Hand in hand with the divide created between apes and humans went another set of theories, such as those of Chamberlain and Gobineau, intent on declaring the supremacy of certain human 'races' over others, of some peoples over others and of man over woman. Hence, blacks, and at one time also Jews, were considered closer to apes. In addition women, if not considered closer to apes, were at least considered an 'immature' version of the full human status of (white) males. Racism and imperialism based on white western supremacy became the order of the day and it is still defended vigorously in some quarters to this day. Evolutionary theory had provided a welcome framework for creating a totally imaginary ladder of evolution within the human species itself (Kaplan 1994; Kaplan & Rogers 1994). Although entirely incorrect, these deterministic and racist theories took hold so well that it needed the horrendous wholesale slaughter of millions of people by the Nazis for most people to realise the extent of the untenability of these theories. Nevertheless, even that did not suffice to persuade enough people to rescue blacks and a host of indigenous populations from genocide or mistreatment, nor women from their inferior status and oppression. Such changes needed to be wrought in the 1960s and 1970s in the largest socio-political international protest movement ever staged in the history of humanity.

In terms of the history of ideas, one must classify the continued displacement, misuse, cruel treatment and extinction of countless species as the last vestiges of a view formed in the period of the Industrial Revolution. The problem is that neither orang-utans nor the other great apes, nor tigers, elephants, whales nor a host of other species, are able to stage their protests effectively on human terms. They need protection from humans by humans and, while they continue to need this protection, we know that the pernicious attitudes formed in the last century have not died.

A way of justifying one's own competitive interests was also to resurrect the view that nature was dangerous and had to be fought. The travel literature of the nineteenth century was dominated by science and by adventurers (often both combined in one). This was the era of the big game hunters, of men whose one aim was to shoot and bring home trophies. It was in the interest of such adventurers to proclaim whatever they found as truly awesome and dangerous. Hence Schlegel and Müller, in an expedition to Borneo in 1839–44, described the orang-utan thus:

> *His penetrating sharp glance and wild features, indicated him to be a more than untractable animal. Moreover, the long rough hair of his head and the heavy red beard under the chin gave him a wild appearance. Add to all this his terrible strength, of which he sometimes made use in a violent way, whenever one would torment him with a stick.*

(cited in Yerkes & Yerkes 1945)

The term 'wild' then did not imply 'free' and unfettered by human control but brutish, dangerous and terrifyingly uncompromising. This new paradigm was something qualitatively different from the long-standing traditions in which supra-human beings were thought to appear in animal garb. For instance, there is a long Christian tradition in representing the devil as a goat. Not unconnected with it was the earlier Greek and Roman belief in satyrs, which were thought to be woodland deities in human form that grew tails and horns. The satyrs were sometimes applied to other species. For example, the chimpanzee was first called satyrus, and still in the 1969 edition of *The Concise Oxford Dictionary* the orang-utan is listed as a (rare) synonym for satyr. William Golding's novel, *The Inheritors,* ends with the image of a 'red devil' almost as if Golding suggested that religious belief in the devil might have started with an orang-utan.

The new paradigm arises from developments after the Industrial Revolution. It is characteristic of a new perception that is not inspired by religious sentiments adjudging certain animals *selectively* as devilish but by a wholesale reassessment of *all* living things in the wild as being untractable, terrible and violent. We find an unbroken chain of films, literature, posters and drawings from the nineteenth and especially the twentieth century portraying beasts coming out of swamps, horrible prehistoric birds attacking and carrying away humans, rats and mice infesting human quarters and eating human flesh. Other variations intended to evoke fear and nausea are images of insects (ants, bees) that attack in the thousands and fall upon the human skin to devour it. In the ape world, one of the first epithets of the new horrible monster ape image was created by Edgar Rice Burroughs in 1912 with his publication of *Tarzan of the Apes.* Scattered through the pages of this work is an imagery that was later used in King Kong, and we quote some excerpts from it.

> *At last he saw it, the thing the little monkeys so feared — the man-brute of which the Claytons had caught occasional fleeting glimpses [p.21]. The ape was a great bull, weighing probably three hundred pounds. His nasty, close-set eyes gleamed hatred from beneath his shaggy brows, while his great canine fangs were bared in a horrible snarl as he paused a moment before his prey [p.22]. The man swung his axe with all*

his mighty strength, but the powerful brute seized it in those terrible hands, and tearing it from Clayton's grasp hurled it far to one side [p.23]. The other males scattered in all directions, but not before the infuriated brute had felt the vertebra of one snap between his great, foaming jaws … With a wild scream he was upon her, tearing a great piece from her side with his mighty teeth, and striking her viciously upon her head and shoulders with a broken tree limb until her skull was crushed to a jelly [p.27]. Standing erect he threw his head far back and looking fully into the eye of the rising moon he beat upon his breast with his great hairy paws and emitted his fearful roaring shriek. Once-twice-thrice that terrifying cry rang out across the teeming solitude of that unspeakably quick, yet unthinkably dead, world.

(Burroughs 1912, p.53)

The orang-utan has never quite had the reception of the gorilla or been cast into similar lead roles of terror but, both in literature and drawings, some attempts were made to develop a similar story line for the orang-utan. Stories were told of orang-utan males who had abducted fragile English ladies and raped them in a tree. Likewise, drawings of awesome and/or ugly faces were no doubt intended to generate dislike and fear. Moreover, the orang-utan exemplified what Thomas Hobbes (1588–1679) had described as the ultimate outcast image of 'man' devoid of ordered social existence, namely a *solitary* life, short, nasty and brutish [our emphasis]. The orang-utan was a mirror to humans, reflecting what they might be but ought not to be and it therefore had to be smashed. Reading the travelling accounts of men such as Beccari, Shelford, Hornaday or even Wallace, it is clear that they felt not the slightest twinge of pity when they aimed at and shot orang-utans, even when the orang-utans were looking directly at their attackers from a tree, peacefully feeding.

By the time the nineteenth century came to a close, the utopian image of harmonious human societies and the idea of a paradise and nobility in nature had moved very far from view. Nature, as depicted in H.G. Wells' novel, *The Time Machine* (1894), no longer led to the utopian and benign anarchy that John Locke (1623–1704), a noted English philosopher, had proposed two centuries earlier. Wells' book portrayed the *fin de siècle* feeling that such harmony was false and that in the process of a rapacious industrial capitalism hopes of progress towards a more humane and perfect world were in vain. Instead of innocence, the time traveller finds only ignorance. Instead of peace, he finds humanity in the distant future to be collapsed back on itself into prehistoric origins and back into two species: one, the Eloi, a beautiful peaceful people, ignorant and disinterested victims, apparently living in paradise and feeding from the fruits of nature; and the other, the Morlocks.

We discovered an interesting piece of atavism in H.G. Wells' novel, suggesting strongly that this novelist had read widely in the scientific literature about evolution and apes. His 'Morlocks' were fashioned in detail on the description of Linnaeus' classification that we find in the tenth edition of his *System of Nature* (1758). In it Linnaeus described a humanoid in addition to *Homo sapiens* which he called *Homo nocturnus* or *Homo sylvestris orang-outang*. This strange being refers, on the one hand, to lemurs and, on the other, to elements of orang-utan mythology (more on this later):

Body white, walks erect, less than half our size. Hair white, frizzled. Eyes orbicular; iris and pupils golden. Vision lateral, nocturnal. Lifespan 25 years. By day hides; by night it sees, goes out, forages. Speaks in a hiss. Thinks, believes that the earth was made for it, and that sometime it will be master again [our emphasis], if we may believe the traveller.

(Wells 1894)

The time traveller in H.G. Wells' novel notes that the Morlocks were small, white and about half human size, 'apelike creatures' that were like a 'second species of man'. They looked and sounded like Linnaeus creatures. 'These whitened Lemurs' were 'whispering odd sounds to each other' and 'those pale, chinless faces and great, lidless, pinkish-grey eyes' frightened him in the dark, for the creatures were nocturnal and occupied an underworld. They had turned carnivorous and were feeding on the beautiful people living above them. In Wells' novel, evolution had turned on itself and what we thought was going to be greater refinement became a relapse into ignorance and barbarism. This cultural pessimism, not uncommon in Europe around the turn of the century, occasionally even challenged the supremacy of human beings.

In all, there is a tradition that has experienced nature as trauma which, in turn, has led to views and actions of plundering and fighting it. Denial of fear can take several forms, such as aggression, hatred, revenge or exploitation. There are examples of all forms of action in human conduct. The most prevalent since the Industrial Revolution is exploitation. Exploitation has been most widely practised and accepted by inadvertently or openly declaring all of nature simply as a supermarket for human needs. We pluck and pick what we like and as much as we like. Indeed, much of modern technology is aimed at making the exploitation faster, more efficient and on an ever increasing scale.

The problem is how we respond when some 'article' in this natural supermarket does not strike our fancy. It is clear from the many accounts of the nineteenth century that no particular value could be ascribed to an orang-utan. The orang-utan was considered to be good for nothing — it grows too large and strong for a pet, it is only of limited use as a domestic helper (in 1892 Garner records that an orang-utan worked as his 'domestic', performing chores like other 'domestics', cf. Yerkes & Yerkes 1945). It does not have the same entertainment value as a chimpanzee, nor has it any immediate medical or research value. It is hard to observe, allegedly boring to watch because of its 'sluggish' behaviour and difficult to keep confined. It is, if anything, superfluous within the scheme of human development. Since the Industrial Revolution this attitude has run parallel with a confronting posture. We may gain a view of this attitude from Mrs Pryer's diary entry of 15 August 1894, where she records an incident with an orang–utan:

Later Mr. H. went, and after $2^1/2$ hours absence arrived saying the Sooloos had got the poor beast but it was not dead so they brought it bound hand and foot and placed it before the house. I felt so sorry for it; for it had been shot and had also had a fall from a tree, but it was very brave and patient not making a sound altho' it must have been suffering severely.

W. said it was a female of the large species. As it was tremendously powerful and too large to keep in captivity and was wounded and also they thought had an arm broken it was the most merciful thing to kill it, but it would not die, they had to shoot it three times before they succeeded in dispatching it. A horrid affair but orang-utans can't be allowed to roam about at will devouring the sugar cane.

(Tarling 1989)

The death of this female orang-utan was pragmatically dismissed as a necessity. There was literally no place for it. Upon that realisation Mrs Pryer closed the matter, even though she had felt sorry for the 'poor beast'.

The attitude that orang-utans were really not very interesting because one could allegedly 'do' so little with them was echoed in 1924 in a scientific paper by Sonntag, who then proclaimed that 'The Orang is the least interesting of the Apes. It lacks the grace and agility of the Gibbon, the intelligence of the Chimpanzee and the brutality of the Gorilla' (cited in Yerkes & Yerkes 1945). That prejudice was still present in the 1960s when Reynolds (1967) said of the orang-utan that there was 'nothing very spectacular about them'. The orang-utan was thought to be less suitable for experiments (Drescher & Trendelenburg 1927; Yerkes & Yerkes 1929), less capable of problem solving (Köhler 1921, cf. responses to Köhler: Lethmate 1977; Rogers & Kaplan 1993) and less skilled in manipulation than other apes, especially the chimpanzee. More recent research has shown that this is not so (see Chapter 6).

There has only been one way in which the orang-utan has been 'marketed' positively and this has been when demystifying it as a little toy. Recent articles, such as 'Born to be mild' (Williams 1991) or reports of the cruel transport details of orang-utan babies, have roused the sympathy of many. Williams dubbed the orang-utan as being 'trusting' and 'inquisitive', as 'endearing, loyal pets' and 'one of the world's most delightful and rare animals'. Travel magazines now advertise the orang-utan as a major tourist attraction, as a 'sight not to be missed' because they are endangered and so 'lovable' (Scantlebury 1994). Whether the imagery is terrifying or cute, grossly exaggerated or belittling, these depictions of the orang-utan and those of the past have nothing to do with real life but a good deal to do with our commercial world of marketing. Use of such symbolism reveals an attitude to nature which is, at least, alien, if not hostile.

It took up to the 1960s and 1970s before more positive and sober voices were heard. These can be found in the works of Barbara Harrisson, the American primatologist Rumbaugh, and the German primatologist Jürgen Lethmate, whose behavioural studies from 1974 to 1977 conclusively proved Rumbaugh's point, that the chimpanzee's intellectual superiority over the orang-utan was a myth.

There are signs of change. The environmental movement from the 1970s onwards has created a discourse for examining our view of nature on a wide scale. A fourth and new way of viewing nature has slowly emerged which we like to call the dialectic model. The dialectic model argues for a two-way interaction between us and nature: our relationship to it is complex (in a sense, entailing all views of nature described above) and human society is a development out of the natural world. By recognising that nature has its own laws and rules for survival, it is possible to live with nature and use it by maintaining it and by putting something back. In other words, we can use nature but it does not solely exist for us or only in relation to us. Words like 'sustainable growth' have appeared in our vocabulary and amidst economic rationalism. Non-renewable resources are classified as such and the battle for the maintenance of rainforests has begun in earnest, but most likely too late.

We begin our book then with a recognition that we are bound by views and attitudes to nature which in turn determine the way in which we think of orang-utans or any other species. There is also evidence that, at least at the formal and international level, the western world has gone into damage-control mode. The various institutions and organisations that we have already mentioned (see also Appendix 4) have taken some steps, albeit in our view not always correct ones and not always forcefully enough, to halt the avalanche of destruction that we have wreaked. Animal liberation activities have resulted in animal welfare structures and organisations and

Figure 1: Map of South East Asia

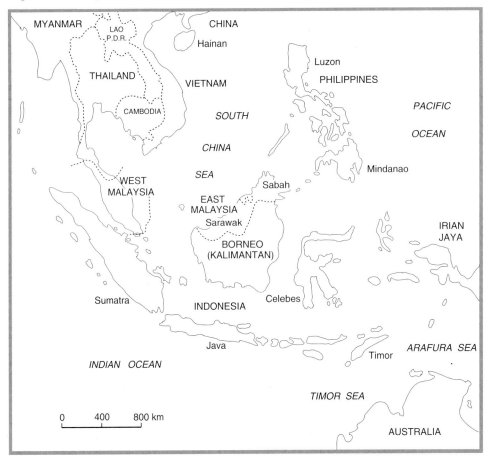

many of their views and requirements are compulsorily embedded now into institutions and organisations. Even the medical profession, by definition interested in human welfare for which animals can be sacrificed at whim, has felt that it needs to curtail some of its appetite for an unlimited supply of living species. This move became evident in 1977 with the formation of the US Interagency Primate Steering Committee, which assesses the needs of primates by the medical community (Koebner 1984).

We believe that the dialectic model for viewing nature holds much promise. In the contemporary world, support for it is growing substantially, with an emphasis on putting things right before it is too late. It is not often clear, however, how we define 'right' and there are fundamental disagreements between environmentalists and zoo personnel (see epilogue) but the fact that even these debates take place is a step in the right direction.

Malaysia

Our personal exposure to and experiences with orang-utans have been exclusively in the Malaysian part of Borneo. One of the first important realisations for members of the western industrialised world must be that most of the world's concerns for flora and fauna and for rainforests lie outside western national, political and cultural boundaries. The guardians of most tropical rainforests and species are countries in South America, Africa and South East Asia.

Recent comments on South East Asia have described Singapore, Hong Kong, Taiwan and Korea as the region's four 'mini-dragons'. The reference was made with respect to their living standards, their growth and general levels of productivity. Malaysia, Thailand and Indonesia are not far behind and have become, or will soon be, major economic forces.

Table 1: Measure of national income by per capita GNP (values in US$)

Singapore	11 160	Philippines	730
Brunei	9 600	Indonesia	570
Taiwan	8 026	Vietnam	215
Korea/South	6 265	Myanmar (Burma)	250
Malaysia	2 320	Laos	200
Thailand	1 420	Cambodia	130
Korea/North	1 240		

Source: *Aktuell 94*. For comparative purposes these data rely on 1990 statistics and show the relative position of Malaysia. By the year 2000, some of these orders may have changed. Malaysia is predicted to show a sharp increase in GNP. Compared to the rest of the world on the same measure (in rounded figures): most western European countries (except three) are above 15 000 and up to 32 000, Japan 25 500, North America around 22 000, oil countries in the Middle East between 7 000 and 20 000, Australia 17 000, eastern European countries around 2 000–3 000 (except Albania 200), South America between 1 160 (Peru) and 3 000 (Surinam), Africa between 80 (Mozambique) and 3 000, mostly under 1 000, and the rest of Asia under 500, including India and China, except for Mongolia (660).

Some years ago Malaysia started an international advertising campaign to put itself 'on the map' of the world economically. One reason for this campaign was to get its international flight company, Malaysia Airline, entrenched in the international air traffic; another, more generally, to foster tourism and economic growth via the tourist industry. Malaysia's promotion of itself, its country and people, is noteworthy for one fact: there is hardly a travel brochure that does not list the orang-utan. Orchids amongst flowers and orang-utans amongst all animal species have been singled out to represent the uniqueness of Malaysia. Irrespective of the fact that orang-utans also live in Indonesia and are found on the 500 rupiah note, the orang-utan has become known internationally as an emblem of Malaysia, just as the koala or kangaroo are of Australia or the giant panda of China. To elevate orang-utans to the status of a quasi-national emblem and to allow it publicly to be called 'Malaysia's Mascot' (Payne & Andau 1989) suggests to us that Malaysia considers them worthy of protection.

Malaysia became a Federation in 1963, including West Malaysia (also known as Peninsular Malaysia), East Malaysia and initially also Singapore. Singapore, however, was expelled from the Federation in 1965. Since Malaysia became an independent Federation, it has been dedicated to a policy of growth and development. Its explicit program for the 1990s is a concerted effort 'towards a better quality of life for all Malaysians' (*The Star* 1991, p.8). There is a spirit of optimism and assertiveness in the official press that is not only matched by the economic facts of Malaysia but by the East Asian region in general. Such optimism, if borne out in practice, could and should ultimately contribute to how much time, money and effort will be expended on social, health and environmental issues, including the preservation of the orang-utan and its natural habitat, the tropical rainforests of East Malaysia (North Borneo).

Economic predictions for the immediate future of Asian countries are extremely favourable. Growth rates are predicted to remain high at five to eight percent per annum. Gross Domestic Product in the East Asian region is estimated to run at 112 percent, as against 80 percent in the European communities. The growing importance of the new industrialised East Asian economies will be further enhanced by the intended economic integration of the region. Talks began in the early 1990s, under the leadership of Malaysia, to form an East Asia Economic Group, much along the lines of the original European Economic Communities. Its aim is to promote free trade amongst its members and 'to strengthen its bargaining position in dealing with other regional trade blocs as a group' (*The Star* 1991, p.8). Malaysia has devised a New Development Policy (NDP) and, within it, has conceived of various 'outline perspective plans' with timeframes for target developments in the next five to ten years. The focus of the latest outline perspective plan OPP2 (Malaysian Government 1991) is to focus on: 1) the eradication of hardcore poverty and the reduction of relative poverty, 2) the rapid development of an effective 'Bumiputera' (Malay) commercial and industrial community, and 3) human resource development as a fundamental requirement to achieve the objectives of growth and distribution. In the foreword to the new OPP2, Prime Minister Datuk Seri Dr Mahathir wrote:

The government envisions that by the year 2020, Malaysia will be a united nation with a confident Malaysian society, infused by strong moral and ethical values, living in a society that is democratic, liberal, tolerant, caring, economically just and equitable, progressive and prosperous, and in full possession of an economy that is competitive, dynamic, robust, resilient and socially just.

Thus far, the hopes for the future. The present, despite its clear economic achievements, remains beset by problems of some magnitude. The population explosion and the enormous problems with poverty, racial tensions, refugees, political and religious struggles have barely eased, even though for some there are very clear signs of positive change.

The health of Malaysians is improving, life expectancy rising and infant mortality is on the decline. Some of these changes have been dramatic indeed. If one can believe the figures on poverty, given that there are many remote rural areas, the overall incidence of acute poverty on Peninsular Malaysia has declined from nearly 50 percent in 1970 to 15 percent in 1990. In parts of West Malaysia, the standard of living has increased drastically, often five to tenfold, as measured by the number of television sets, telephones and motorcars, although all these indices are still very low compared to the 'mini-dragons' or to poorer western countries.

There have been several politico-economic landmarks for federal Malaysia which are worth mentioning here. First, in 1967, there was the formation of the Association of South East Asia (ASEAN), consisting of Thailand, Malaysia, Singapore, the Philippines and Indonesia. The second landmark was set by the inauguration of the 'New Economic Policy' in 1971. This was important in so far as it set out economic and social policy until 1990. Since the 1960s, the Malaysian Government, in its social policy in particular, has embarked upon policies overtly favouring ethnic Malays. The

Table 2: Structural data for Malaysia 1960–1990

	1960	**1970**	**1982**	**1990**
population (in millions)	6.90	10.70	14.40	16.10
population growth (%)	3.60	2.80	2.70	2.70
urban population (%)	25.00	28.00	30.00	38.00
employed in rural sector (%)	62.00	60.00	51.00	
employed in industry (%)	23.00	25.00	33.00	
illiteracy (%)	47.00	45.00	40.00	20.00
life expectancy (years)				
female		65.50		73.50
male		61.60		69.00
birth rate (per 100 population)		3.24		2.71
infant mortality (% of 100 live births)		3.94		1.35
death rate (per 100 population)		0.67		0.47

Source: Malaysian Government OPP2, *The Star*, 1991

New Economic Policy of 1971 made it clear that Malaysia was going to continue to support its population selectively by giving Malays privileged access to public sector housing, university entrance, civil service employment and allocation of commercial licenses (Kaur 1993). The current definition of a Malay (or Bumiputera) is a person who habitually speaks Malay and is Muslim (Kaur 1993).

As the Malay government sees it, there are strong inter-ethnic imbalances in favour of ethnic groups such as Chinese, Indian and others of Malayan citizenship, leaving the indigenous Bumiputeras in the lowest positions and income brackets. The 1980 census counted 55.3 percent of the population as Malays in West Malaysia. The Malaysian government has decreed that 68.4 percent of all new employment recruitments into the professions and technical categories will be taken up by Bumiputeras. To achieve these ends, the government will continue to uphold entry quotas for ethnic groups to institutes of higher learning (universities and colleges). It has outlined training and re-training help for Bumiputeras as one of its measures to restructure the ethnic composition of employment in the various sectors of the economy and at all occupational levels.

Racial tensions remain apparent and, in a sense, ambivalences and new tensions have been created by direct government intervention and social engineering. It is important to mention this here as it pertains strongly to East Malaysia. The employment restructuring process will eventually mean that professions, academic institutions and leadership positions in the service sector and industry will be dominated by Muslim Bumiputeras. It will affect selection and recruitment procedures, job opportunities in every walk of life and at every occupational level. At present, despite the restrictions often keenly felt by all ethnic minorities, there now exists in practice an ethnic and religious pluralism that allows for some diversity of lifestyles and views. Some may perceive a contradiction in the government's aims of creating a political environment that is 'liberal, tolerant, caring, and socially just' (as quoted above), and in its direct discrimination against Malaysians of ethnic backgrounds other than Malay. The government would like to argue that it is the Malay population that is discriminated against and disadvantaged and therefore needs additional incentives and assistance to bring it into line with other ethnic groups.

These government policies raise issues of nationality versus ethnicity. Moreover they resurrect debates about what 'social justice' and 'equality of treatment' mean, particularly in the context of a revival of fundamentalist Islam and the overt signs of encouragement for and propagation of Islam in Malaya as a whole. One of the side effects of these policies and attitudes has been a constant brain-drain of Malaysia's intellectuals and professionals of Indian and Chinese descent to other countries. Such people have felt discouraged by the lack of career opportunities and occupational rewards for them.

Malaysia's ambition to play a leading economic role in the world will no doubt modify some of the irrational elements of social planning. Daily newspapers continue to report and propagate the idea that Malaysia can match the best economic powers in the world. Indeed, in July 1991, the then Deputy Prime Minister Abdul Ghafar

Baba announced that within the next 30 years Malaysia could easily manage to match the economic achievements of Japan and of Germany (*The Star,* 1 July 1991). He wanted to see Malaysia fully industrialised within the next decade. The catchwords have been: work harder, export more and industrialise. In the West Malaysian States of Selangor, Johor and Penang, the mushrooming of electronic factories promises to see these goals fulfilled within the next decade but other, less developed States on the Peninsula, such as Pahang, Negri Sembilan, Perak, Malacca, as well as Sabah and Sarawak in East Malaysia will continue to lag behind even though they are showing economic growth rates similar to the most developed States. Uneven development will remain a feature within the Malaysian Federation, as such States as Kedah, Perlis and Kelantan show poor per capita GNP of US$1 700 to US$2 800 as against US$7 000 in Selangor (*The Star,* 1 July 1991).

East Malaysia

What does the development mean for Sabah and Sarawak? And more importantly, what does this mean for orang-utans? To do justice to the complexities and history of East Malaysia would far exceed the purpose and format of this book. However, we wish to relate at least a few facts which may convey those complexities and current issues of East Malaysia.

First, a geographical point. Considering the whole of Borneo, East Malaysia is just a small strip in the north, indented by the independent Sultanate of Brunei. Sarawak runs along the northern shores of Borneo. Sabah, its only other province, occupies the north-eastern tip of the island. Those two States alone, which make up less than a quarter of the landmass of Borneo, amount to sizeable areas of land. As mentioned earlier, Sabah is the size of Belgium and the Netherlands combined and Sarawak is even larger.

Sabah and Sarawak joined the Federation in 1963 but they were initially reluctant to do so. Only two years later, Sabah and Sarawak leaders made an unsuccessful bid for State autonomy. Rising ethnic nationalism in Sabah led to the formation of a political party, the Parti Bersatu Sabah (PBS), which has retained government since 1986. This party was re-elected in 1990 for a five-year period. Kaur points out that relationships between the Federal and State governments have not been 'altogether cordial' (Kaur 1993).

Ethnic considerations and religious affiliations in East Malaysia are different from those of the Peninsula. Today, Sabah has a population of about 1.5 million. One third are of Kadazan origin, consisting of the Rungus, the Orang Sungai and another four or five groups. Most of them are Christian and some Muslim. Another third consists of Chinese who migrated in the nineteenth and twentieth centuries to Sabah, also with different religious affiliations. The remaining third is subdivided between Indians, Eurasians, Europeans and a mix of indigenous people of no less than 12 different ethnic groups, each with their different languages or dialects. In 1980, at the time of the census, the total Muslim population in Sabah was just 38 percent. We recall that the definition of a Malay was to speak Malay habitually and to be Muslim.

Sarawak has a population of approximately 1.2 million, again a conglomerate of people from indigenous and immigrant backgrounds. Half of Sarawak's population is indigenous and collectively called Dayak, a summary term for a dozen indigenous groups. Among the best known of these are the Iban (Sandin 1967), the Kenyah, Kayan and the Penan. The Penan, of whom we heard much in the international media some years ago, number about 7 600 to 10 000 and they are the only remaining group

Figure 2: Map of Borneo (political boundaries)

to have retained a semi-nomadic lifestyle (Davis & Henley 1990). According to the 1980 census, the percentage of Muslims in Sarawak was even smaller than in Sabah, just 25.4 percent, while the non-Muslim indigenous population accounted for 44 percent and Chinese for about 30 percent (Kaur 1993).

Geographically and ethnically, and at times also politically, East Malaysia is far away from the mainland. Except for tourism, especially in and around the capital cities of Kota Kinabalu and Kuching, East Malaysia reaps little visible benefit from the mainland's economic success. Kuala Lumpur is far away — over 1 600 km by plane, a four-hour trip into a different world. The border with the Philippines, on the other hand, is just a mere 28 km away, connected by a trail of islands. The dust from the active volcano that erupted recently in the Philippines settled on cars and buildings in Sandakan. From Labuan and many other islands, such as 'Turtle Island' (Selingan) out of Sandakan Bay, heavily armed soldiers guard the East Malaysian borders against the never-ending stream of illegal immigrants pouring into Sabah.

Malaysia may be far away geographically, separated by a vast sea, but its distance is much better expressed as that of a cultural and ethnic distance. Repeatedly, there have been rumours of secessionist ambitions by East Malaysia, especially by Sabah. As we pointed out, the Kadazan population is largely Christian. There are also pagan religions and a vast variety of ethnically different splinter groups. Malaysia's racial policy to redress the balance in favour of Muslim Bumiputeras is a difficult and complex issue in the case of Sabah and Sarawak because here the population largely consists of non-Muslim Dayak and Kadazan groups. Our impression obtained in casual conversations with East Malaysians was one of deep resentment against the Federal Government for imposing its wishes on the local population on one hand, while exploiting it on the other. By its own (mainland government) admission, Sabah is overall the poorest State in the Malaysian Federation in terms of income (Malaysian Government 1991). Kadazans who have spoken to us particularly resent having officials from mainland West Malaysia placed in leading positions so as to keep the 'locals' in check.

Mainland West Malaysia appears to be acutely aware of what some have described as its tenuous hold in East Malaysia and especially Sabah throughout the last 30 years of a shared national flag. When logging operations led to a series of local strikes in Sarawak in 1987, the Malaysian Prime Minister invoked the ISA *(Internal Security Act of 1960),* as has been done on several other occasions in regard to dissenting groups, and had 91 protesters imprisoned. Any criticism of the regime, we were told, was quickly thwarted.

Over the years that we have travelled to Sabah, we have noticed changes in Sabah's daily life. For instance, the difference in cultural imagery between the 1980s and the 1990s in Kota Kinabalu is profound. In the 1990s we saw for the first time a noticeable number of veiled women and men in obvious Muslim attire. On every available television monitor at the airport, Muslim religious services were aired and its music dominated the place. No such displays of Muslim presence had ever existed before, despite a local Muslim population. These are demonstrations of mainland values that partly clash with local interests and mentality.

Meanwhile, the slums (Kampongs) of illegal immigrants from the Philippines and from Indonesia continue to grow. Heavily armed, unemployed, uneducated and hungry people pour into and stay in Sabah. They cannot get educated and do not receive any benefits. Severe overcrowding in near-permanent temporary Kampongs over the water, housing at times 15 people to a small room, exacerbates already existing social and health problems and contributes to severe levels of community stress, both psychologically and financially. Illegal immigration is viewed ambiguously by the Federal Government; it is not entirely averse to it because most of the immigrants are Muslims.

However, the influence of Peninsular Malaysia is not structurally provided for in all areas. Mainland Malaysia is not necessarily central to the forest industry debacle that has occupied locals and the minds of international conservation groups for so long and in such a futile manner. The Federal Government of Malaysia has full control over taxes, defence, security and petroleum, the latter being of great importance due to huge oil and petroleum reserves off the shores of East Malaysia. Affairs pertaining to forests and local flora and fauna, however, are the exclusive responsibility of the local State governments of Sabah and Sarawak. The Sabah Foundation alone owns 36 percent of Sabah's remaining 'commercial' forests. In Sarawak, two very senior government officials at one time or another between them controlled 2.9 million hectares of logging concessions (Davis & Henley 1990).

Logging in any form is certainly big business, as long as the forests last. The increase in exports is shown in Table 3 below. Between 1975 and 1980, forest revenue in Sabah alone increased tenfold from M$152 million to over one billion Malaysian dollars (Udarbe 1982). These figures speak for themselves. Yet the Sarawak Timber Industry Development Corporation seriously suggested at one point that the destruction of rainforest was due to illegal immigrants, 300 families in all, who practised shifting cultivation and had thereby destroyed the forest (Sarawak Timber Industry Development Corporation 1978; see also comment by Pearce 1990).

Payne said that in the logging boom of the 1970s and 1980s, there were more millionaires per square metre in Sandakan than anywhere else in the world (Teo 1990).

Table 3: Amount and value of timber exports from Sabah 1959–1987

	1959	1969	1979	1987
Amount (m³)				
Plywood	Nil	6 155	43 903	129 955
Veneer	Nil	17 167	25 260	142 376
Sawn timber	30 063	10 016	77 075	838 694
Logs	1 386 107	6 187 654	10 332 238	9 449 206
Export value (M$)				
Sawn timber	3 670 662	935 541	25 029 472	382 797 077
Logs	57 393 045	374 422 613	2 179 194 409	2 198 990 200

Source: Adapted from Appendices 4, 6 and 8, *Forestry in Sabah* 1989.

In 1979, forest revenue accounted for 77 percent of the total State revenue for Sabah. Copper and petroleum amounted to less than a tenth of forest revenue (just six percent of total revenue), not because of a lack of income in this field but because the Federal Government located in West Malaysia collects nearly all revenue from mineral resources. If the Federal Government were to renegotiate a deal more favourable to the East Malaysian provinces concerning petroleum, Sabah and Sarawak would not need to use their forests as their main form of revenue (Udarbe 1982).

The simple and well-known fact is that the rainforest is disappearing at a very rapid rate. As we write, according to the World Resource Institute, forests are being decimated at the rate of 100 000 km^2 per year. In Sabah and Sarawak the Bornean rainforest may disappear almost entirely within the next five years. There are reforestation and afforestation programs in Sarawak and Sabah but these tend to suffer from a lack of diversity and a futile race against time. Forests simply are being cut at a much faster (and accelerating) rate than new trees can grow. For the orang-utans the year 2000 holds no large celebratory events. There may be nothing left for them to live on or in.

Many of the States' logging activities are linked with giant Japanese and some Korean companies who have obtained the right to log from local government. So deep is Japan's involvement that at one time it had repercussions in Japan itself. In 1987 a scandal erupted when it was discovered that 200 million yen of foreign aid funds had been given to the Limbang Trading Company in Sarawak for the building of logging roads (Davis & Henley 1990, p.132). Each day, 850 hectares are being cleared in Sarawak alone so that even the International Timber Trade Organization (ITTO) agrees that no primary forest will be left in Sarawak by the year 2000. The rapacious exploitation of local rainforest (for the cost of a lease and very little local employment) has incensed local populations, particularly the Penan and the Iban, who have seen their forest, and livelihood, being bulldozed down. Within the Baram and Limbang districts of Sarawak the Penan, Kayan and Kelabit protested bitterly throughout 1987 in a series of logging blockades staged by local environmentalists and activists. At that time, the Penan people issued a declaration of their political anger. It read:

We, the Penan people of the Tutoh, Limbang, and Patah rivers regions, declare: Stop destroying the forest or we will be forced to protect it. The forest is our livelihood. We have lived here before any of you outsiders came. We fished in clean rivers and hunted in the jungle. We made our sago meat and ate the fruit of trees. Our life was not easy but we lived it contentedly. Now the logging companies turn rivers to muddy streams and the jungle into devastation. Fish cannot survive in dirty rivers and wild animals will not live in devastated forest. You took advantage of our trusting nature and cheated us into unfair deals. By your doings you take away our livelihood and threaten our very lives. You make our people discontent. We want our ancestral land, the land we live off, back. We can use it in a wiser way. When you come to us, come as guests with respect.

We, the representatives of the Penan people, urge you: Stop the destruction now. Stop all logging activities in the Limbang, Tutoh, and Patah. Give back to us what is properly ours. Save our lives, have respect for our culture. If you decide not to heed our request, we will protect our livelihood. We are a peace-loving people, but when our lives are in danger, we will fight back. This is our message.

(cited in Davis & Henley 1990, p.134)

The Penans never received a reply and the blockades ended by the incarceration of its most vocal leaders. Yet the local population had not given up and a further series of blockades were put in place, eventually also involving Iban communities. The strikes spread and continued for almost two years causing brief damage to the logging industry but ultimately, by the end of 1989, the local groups were beaten by imprisonment and harsh treatment.

It remains our impression, therefore, that except for a small ruling elite of Sabah and Sarawak, the people of those two States are powerless to shape their own destiny. This is not so noticeable in everyday life in towns, but when it comes to issues of the forest, as we have seen, it is a highly political matter and repeatedly demonstrates where and by whom the political muscle is flexed.

What does all this mean for the orang-utan? First, we would like to suggest that the economic goals of Malaysia as a whole have fostered general attitudes to the environment which are inimical to conservation. Sabah and Sarawak have been gripped by the national fervour just as much as Peninsular Malaysia. Strategies of parcelling out all of Sabah for human settlement, for expansion of monocultural agriculture and logging exemplify these emphases well enough. We have mentioned the Sabah Foundation and other powerful stakeholders in these developments.

Second, the tensions that have persisted between Sabah and Peninsular Malaysia, both in terms of the racial and/or denominational policies as well as in terms of controlling the finances of the State of Sabah, have not augured well for habitat conservation and thereby for the orang-utan. One wishes that Malaysia's economic success would be fuelled by the oil and gas reserves, not the timbers of Sabah and Sarawak. The independent Sultanate of Brunei, nestled in between Sarawak and Sabah, is now one of the richest nations in Asia and compares well with the living standards of most Middle Eastern oil countries, such as Saudi Arabia and Kuwait (see Table 1); but it has barely any rainforest and no orang-utans.

Local orang-utan stories

The indigenous populations of Sarawak and Sabah have created their own attitudes to orang-utans. Much of that is reflected in stories told by locals and in their lifestyle. There are apparently local stories describing women being carried off by amorous male orang-utans and views that orang-utans decided not to talk for fear that they would be put to work (Woods 1989). There were stories mentioned to Beccari about orang-utans who had successfully fought with bears, crocodiles and with the python (Beccari 1904).

Charles Hose recorded in 1926 that the Kenyahs, and other groups such as the Kayans 'are more or less afraid of offending the orang-utan (Maias) or the long-nosed proboscis *Nasalis* monkey, and are very careful not to look one straight in the face, or to laugh at its antics' (Hose 1988). It was also a taboo in Kayan culture for pregnant women to look at an orang-utan. Nevertheless, there are records available showing that Kenyah and other groups also ate Maias (local name for orang-utan). Tom Harrisson, for instance, obtained evidence of a killing of a large male orang-utan. When he investigated, Harrisson found that the skin had been fashioned into a dancing coat and the flesh had been eaten (T. Harrisson 1960). We have seen artifacts by the Iban people which use the stylised head of an orang-utan as a motif. This may be placed on food bowls, on drinking vessels or on sticks. We have not found any religious/spiritual explanation for the presence of these orang-utan skulls, although it has been suggested that some of the skulls collected by head-hunters and said to represent humans were, in fact, those of orang-utans. A research program has recently been undertaken to ascertain traditional Iban attitudes to orang-utans. Bennett has so far found out that hunting taboos may have spared the orang-utan in a number of areas in Sarawak. Her work will be amongst the few to establish to what extent orang-utans form part of the stock of mythologies recorded in Borneo (Bennett 1993). Stories about birds, rocks, creation, are plentiful but to our knowledge very few are known or recorded specifically about the orang-utan (Rutter 1985). As we mentioned earlier, Linnaeus had heard travellers' reports which told of the large ape as a species fallen from grace and as former rulers, ie they had really been human once and were still hoping to return as masters of the earth. H.G. Wells exploited this for his novel.

However, there are a few stories available which were collected and supplied by Gaun Anak Sureng (1960). These stories express either fear of the orang-utan, mentioning their strength and, in one case, their invulnerability, or the stories are reports of attacks by orang-utans when provoked. One orang-utan was said to have killed a dog and to have attacked several people (cf. also Payne & Andau 1989). The most violent community response was recorded when an orang-utan had approached a woman, seemingly with bad intent.

MacKinnon (1971) claimed that there were many stories in Bornean folklore which tell of male orang-utans taking women and keeping them as lovers/brides. These stories often cross the divide of deep taboos. Here a male orang-utan interbreeds with a human female. In one of them, the offspring of the involuntary union (involuntary from the point of view of the female human) was half ape half human in such a way that each half divided the body equally and horizontally. When she left him and ran to escape, she left the child behind and the orang-utan male ripped the child into its two halves, hurling the human half in the direction of the woman and the other back into the forest. We are not sure why MacKinnon argues that we cannot learn anything from this account simply because the baseline story of a male ape stealing a female human is such an old one. It seems to us that the issue of interbreeding, brought up in a number of Bornean stories, goes far beyond the themes of the kidnapping or the rape of a maiden. One is a matter of raising the taboo question of interspecies sexuality. The other, quite rarely told other than in English Gothic novels, is the tabooed idea of successfully interbreeding two different species, of a woman giving birth to a being whose origin may be less/other than human. The fear of atavism was strongly expressed in early fascist writing all over western Europe in the 1920s and 1930s as a fear that interbreeding *might* indeed be successful (Kaplan 1994). Many local Bornean stories spell out in detail the fantasy of human and orang-utan interbreeding. The most unusual twist in these legends is that they also tell of female orang-utans abducting male humans. As MacKinnon rightly observed, these versions were not without some basis of truth because the orang-utan female also has a say in matters of sexuality (see Chapter 4).

A small but systematic account of orang-utan stories and folklore, however, was compiled by T. Harrisson (1955a). It contains a beautiful Dayak story of the 'Ape Rajah and his Human Associates' — well worth reading. It is too long to do it justice here. Its main storyline is that a male orang-utan helped a forsaken woman and she bore a child which was raised in the jungle by her and two orang-utans. The offspring of the orang-utans in turn became the playmate for the young son of the forsaken woman. It shows an intertwining of both worlds which allows for a variety of interpretations. One would be to suggest that both the orang-utans and the woman (who had fallen pregnant without being married) were outcasts of human society and had to make their living quite outside that context. Another interpretation is that Dayaks made no clear distinction between human and ape, at least not one that was hostile and created barriers between the two groups. Indeed, Harrisson (1955a) argues that this kind of story was rather typical of Dayak folklore and belief, and that the orang-utan was not just embedded in their belief system but it was even intertwined with local genealogies. According to Iban belief and mythology, orang-utans were often viewed as their forest cousins.

2

Orang-utan habitat

The rainforest

Over time, orang-utans have experienced a substantial reduction of their habitat. The estimated range of orang-utans 10 000 years ago included almost all of China (up to Beijing), the entire Indo-Chinese peninsula as far north as Bhutan and extended as far south as Java. Their range also spread throughout Sumatra, Java and Borneo. They have long since disappeared from the mainland areas (cf. Linden, 1992). Even for the last island populations of Sumatra and Borneo, their habitat has been increasingly under threat from human populations. In the last few hundred years they have experienced further habitat reduction and are now found in Sumatra only in the north of the island. They have also vanished from a number of recorded sites in Borneo (Yoshiba 1964; Rijksen 1978). They have adapted to living in the rainforest over evolutionary time and now their only habitats are in the jungles of Borneo and Sumatra.

The rainforests of Borneo are thought to be the oldest remaining on earth, older even than those of the Congo and the Amazon. For botanists, Borneo is part of a network of islands in South East Asia which have such strong floristic similarities, so sharply delineated from the flora northwards and southwards (referred to as a 'disjunct' between mainland Asiatic flora and the islands) that the entire region has been called 'Malesia', see map page 33.

Rainfall and temperature ranges within this equatorial region are by and large similar. Rainfall tends to be high, ensuring constant levels of high humidity. Among the native plants of this area are a number of tree species which give the jungle its special appearance. One of these families includes the dipterocarps, *Dipterocarpaceae* (deriving from Greek and meaning 'two-winged seeds'), which used to be sprinkled throughout the lowlands of the Bornean forests. Unfortunately their timber is very good and too many have given way to chainsaws. As far as we know, dipterocarps

▲ *The forest is rich in diverse subtlety and beauty.*
▼ *The forest floor is littered with debris that vitalises the soil. Pitcher plants in Sarawak, growing naturally even if they appear to be arranged for the camera.*

▲ *The proboscis monkey, coming to the edge of the mangrove swamp to settle for the night on a tree overlooking a small tributary of the Kinabatangan River. This is a large male. Note the distinct markings and the nose. The nose of the female is much smaller.*

◄*Early morning at the Kinabatangan River near Sukau.*

have no essential food value for orang-utans but the bark of some dipterocarps is eaten quite regularly by orang-utans. Additionally, because of the structure of their branches and access to the canopy, they provide shelter and excellent sites for nests. Of the approximately 500 species, 380 are exclusive to Malesia (Veevers-Carter 1991) and the dipterocarp forest in Borneo is usually associated with the highest densities of orang-utans.

Of Sabah's 7.3 million hectares of land, a total of 4.7 million hectares were under forest cover in a 1989 count. Four percent of this consisted of mangrove, 2.5 percent of transitional beach and swamp forest, nearly 10 percent was montane forest and nearly 25 percent was immature, disturbed and regenerating forest. Only 17 percent consisted of undisturbed lowland and highland dipterocarp forest (*Forestry in Sabah* 1989). In Sarawak's forested areas peatswamp and dipterocarp dominate (Napier & Napier 1967). Shallow peatswamp (27 percent of cover) is also found on the south-western side of the island, in the area of Tanjung Puting (Galdikas 1984).

There still exist some serious misconceptions about the nature of rainforests in the tropics. It is often believed that the lushness of the rainforest indicates fertility of the soil and a fast rate of growth. Nothing could be further from the facts. The soil of Borneo and most tropical islands in the region is extremely poor and rates of growth are mostly excessively slow. The dipterocarps actually thrive on this poor soil and by dropping leaves and adding to the fungal and bacterial culture of the forest floor, they provide essential nutrients from the surface that the soil lacks. Nevertheless, it is as if time stood still on these islands. The poor soil, the similarity of temperature all year round, the lack of wind or other forces (south of the typhoon belt) and the lack of competition from the mainland of South East Asia seems to have adapted plants to a slow growth rate and long lifespan.

The ironwood tree is a case in point. It is part of the *Lauraceae* family to which the mango and avocado belong and it is coveted for its insect-impervious hardwood. Ironwoods are amongst the slowest growing trees on earth. Incidentally they also contain the largest seeds in the world (about 12 cm long and 4 cm in diameter). Ironwoods (the Bornean ironwood *Eusideroxylon zwageri*) grow 15–30 metres high but in order to gain a diameter of just one metre they may need 200 years. Dipterocarps also grow excessively slowly and may be fully mature for reproduction (dropping of seeds) only after 60 years of growth. Sixty years until the first flowering! Veevers-Carter points out that the logging cycles, imposing a 35-year ban on trees before cutting, or 25 years in Sarawak (*Sarawak Timber Industry* 1978), are absolute nonsense in the case of these tree families. Their genetic material is lost whether they are cut after 10 or after 40 years of growth (Veevers-Carter 1991). Furthermore, no regrowth can be expected nearby as their seeds are not airborne further afield, have no pollination or cross-breeding or other intermediary help via droppings from birds or orang-utans. New trees can only grow near the mature ones because the seeds drop from the canopy straight to the ground. Assuming that these trees are left growing for 60 years, it is still a rather risky undertaking to cut them even then. One flowering does not necessarily produce results and the next flowering may be as far as 10 years hence. For instance, the various species of the dipterocarp family seem to have an arrangement that no two species must flower at the same time. So they take it in turns, according to climatic conditions.

Irregularity, even an erratic cycle of flowering and fruiting, is a characteristic of the tropical rainforest and it is one of the reasons why frugivorous species, such as orang-utans, need to forage over large terrains. The lack of regularity in flowering and sparse dispersal of each species of plant is compensated by an enormous variety of species. In 'Malesia' there are no less than 700 species of *Eugenia*, to which the clove tree belongs, and 35 species of rambutan, of which 25 are found in Borneo alone. In Borneo, the durian, considered one of the favourite foods of the orang-utan, is represented by 14 varieties.

The flora and fauna of Borneo are astounding. There are 1 200 species of orchids, including the largest (*Raffensis*), and the largest pitcher plant in the world. There are over 500 bird species, many of them extremely shy and difficult to see, a range of rare and common small animals such as the squirrel, flying fox, barking deer, mouse deer, leopard, mongoose, slow loris and the tree-shrew. Large animals include wild pigs, elephants and a range of primates. Among the larger primate species are the rare proboscis monkey, the gibbon, leaf monkeys and a variety of macaques (pig-tailed and long-tailed). The Bornean rhinoceros is all but extinct but there are attempts to breed from the few remaining individuals. The entire ecosystem is diverse and interdependent but this diversity is not a consequence of good soil conditions.

It may take 15 minutes to cut a tree that has needed 200 years to grow to full height. With the degraded soil conditions that follow logging, such growth may take

Figure 3: Map of Botanic 'Malesia'

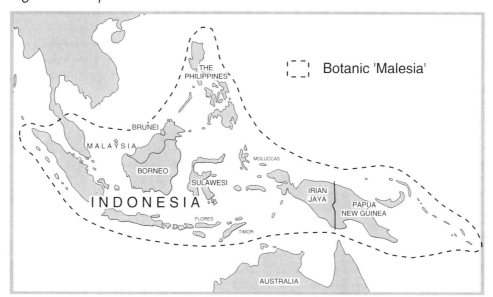

Source: Veevers-Carter 1991

even longer in future. Logging and monocultures are therefore exceptionally damaging to the region as a whole and make the idea of successful reforestation a difficult, if not impossible, task. Even if the latter were partly achieved by cultivating fast-growing and a less diverse flora, the problem remains that not all plants may come back and the animals will have become extinct.

Climate and conditions for research

Travel brochures continue to praise Borneo's climate as even (rarely below 25°C or above 32°C). This may well be so and it sounds good as long as one does not consider the humidity. Locals or people from hot and humid climates may have no difficulties at all. Coming from moderate climates, such as prevail in Europe, the USA and large parts of Australia, perceptions of and opinions about the allegedly ideal climate may conjure up very different images. At least for us and for some others (cf. O'Hanlon 1984), ie the unacclimatised, Borneo's climate is mostly unpleasantly hot and sticky, except in the hills where it can get relatively cool at night. For several months per year it is also constantly wet and throughout the year the humidity is extremely high (92–98 percent). Inland or in the forest there is no wind, no air movement at all to help soothe the overheating body and face. There is no relief from the stillness of this sauna. Anyone who has lived or even just been in climate zones of this kind knows that there is no way to stay dry or even just reasonably comfortable. Indeed, it takes about 20 minutes for dry and fresh clothes to become as soaked as if one had gone through a torrential shower. Camera equipment rapidly becomes dysfunctional. Overheated automatic zoom lenses have trouble focusing, especially at crucial moments. Gisela has spent more time in the jungle fanning the video camera than her face. Her hat usually rested on the camera to ensure that at times when the video camera was not in use, it was shaded from the sun's rays. The viewing window fogs up after about two minutes. Binoculars, so essential for observing behaviour in the wild, go equally fuzzy. Even the batteries, which are meant to last for an hour each, discharge in the humidity and give the user about a 20-minute lifespan. Sensitive films need to be kept in plastic bags together with moisture absorbing particles.

In addition, there are certain inconveniences which one learns to take in one's stride. These have been described in detail in travel logbooks by such writers as O'Hanlon and MacKinnon (cf. also Western 1994). There may be ants, spiders or a range of other inconvenient insects. First and foremost, however, enemy number one on the forest floor and lower canopy are the blood-sucking parasites, such as ticks, mosquitoes, elephant flies, sandflies and leeches. The mosquito in these regions is capable of passing on dangerous and potentially fatal diseases. Insect repellents that we draw on freely in temperate zones are entirely useless in the jungle. Perspiration, even on the backs of one's hands, washes off the repellent within minutes. Anti-malarial pills are of only limited use. Prolonged use can have dangerous side effects (such as developing cancer) but worst of all is the fact that anti-malarial protection can, and in the case of the fatal variety of malaria (*Plasmodium falciparum*) does, inhibit its symptoms. Because the symptoms are suppressed, the person infected by this disease may not seek medical help quickly enough to escape certain death. The recent death of an Australian on appropriate anti-malarial medication in another South East Asian country occurred within four days of the traveller noticing a sense of general ill health but with no other symptoms. A recent tourist brochure issued by the Malaysian Ministry of Culture and Tourism reported that the World Health Organisation had declared Malaysia a malaria-free zone. Such optimism by an international organisation seems inappropriate to us, unless the fine print excluded East Malaysia. Every surgery in Sandakan was set up to deal with malaria very swiftly and efficiently and we had occasion to learn this first-hand when one of us contracted a Borneo flu, a very vicious and sudden flu with similar symptoms to malaria.

A less dangerous but very unpleasant companion in the Bornean jungle is the leech. It gets easily into clothes and then proceeds with its quiet work of injecting anti-coagulants and feeding on its victim's blood. By the time one notices the burning sensation, the head of the leech is firmly anchored under the skin. We always carried a small bottle of tea-tree oil with us. A few drops of that on the body of the leech and it will let go of its victim. Tearing it off, as one is tempted to do on any such discovery, will tear the skin further and cause heavy bleeding and at times infections.

Apart from these two quiet companions, there are no others of immediate and grave concern. Usually one can avoid larger animals by spotting them well before an encounter. This sounds a little braver than we are and were. There are several poisonous snakes in Borneo but most remain hidden and very few would attack unless provoked. Orang-utans are said to have moved above ground into the trees partly in order to avoid the now nearly extinct python. In all the many months of visits to Sabah we saw only one cobra, one large silky black snake (about 6 cm in diameter) with narrow yellow stripes in a tree near the Kinabatangan River and a ground-dwelling slim pale green snake which was a little harder to spot because it looked just like a liana. We were told they were poisonous and informed about their names but failed to take notes of our 'discoveries' or their names.

We were a little uncertain about what we would do in the case of an attack by wild pigs or an unfriendly greeting by elephants. In the lower swamp forest none of the tree stems were large enough to afford protection from an angry pig or elephant. We spotted footprints in the Sukau area. The soil had been freshly dug over by pigs and relatively recent footprints indicated the presence of a small elephant herd nearby. Needless to say that we carried no weapons on our expedition to locate wild orang-utans and hopefully to catch a glimpse of several subspecies of hornbills which were known to breed in that area.

Some troops of macaques can be unfriendly, with some trying to bite or snatch at passers-by or their equipment. We found that standing quietly, exposing one's teeth and hissing was sufficient to discourage further advances. We were told locally that some macaques appear to respond very aggressively to bright colours, but these were not part of our wardrobe.

Apart from considerations of terrain and climate, the orang-utans themselves are not necessarily easy to study. First, they do not live in groups; second, they are hard to find. They tend to be nomadic or at least they may travel a considerable number of kilometres per day to find food. They occur in low density throughout the forest and keep changing position. Finally, when they travel and feel observed or threatened or both, they tend to move higher into the canopy, sometimes up to 20 metres high. From the forest floor, observation at an angle, which requires constantly tilting the head back, is not a particularly relaxing posture. Galdikas overcame the problem by taking a mat with her and lying on the forest floor (Woods 1989). In addition, filming or photographing from the shadow of the forest floor into and against the dappled and moving light at the tree crowns goes against all basic instructions in photography.

In other words, the habitat is such that work on orang-utans is generally difficult and observation times can be unrewardingly low. This risk alone, if one works within time constraints of several weeks, can be extremely frustrating and makes field work on orang-utans a risk for anyone who wants fast data and promotion. Hence, proportionately, field studies on orang-utans have remained far lower than studies on chimpanzees and gorillas.

Dressing sensibly in the jungle is a difficult feat. We wore army jungle clothes, unattractive khaki green shirts and pants made of thick cotton. The thick cotton prevents mosquitoes from penetrating the cloth, and therefore the skin, but long shirts and long pants in 30°C heat and high humidity are not ideal for the wearer. This outfit is complemented by woollen socks and heavy army boots. The ground can get very sloshy and slippery and good walking shoes are essential. Strangely, wearing woollen socks in this heat never caused any discomfort. Throughout all our work our feet remained the only part of our bodies that was totally comfortable. The clothing also provided some welcome but not perfect protection against leeches. Local employees in the rehabilitation centres or in the forestry commissions wore more or less the same clothes as we did (but short-sleeved shirts). We also always had to wear a small towel around the back of our necks, just as if we were in a sauna. This helped to absorb perspiration from the head and the tips could be used to free eyelashes from stinging sweat droplets and wipe the face free of moisture. Interestingly, regular wiping of the face gave at least the illusion of a cooling effect and prevented immediate overheating.

For our recording purposes we had a number of essential pieces of equipment. Lesley's task was to score behaviour continuously for which she needed binoculars, while Gisela's task was to film and follow individuals that Lesley could not score. We wore photographer's vests, equipped with countless pockets of relatively small size, big opening slits in the back and net-meshed material to allow skin to breathe. The vests were equipped with zips rather than tear-off self-sticking fibre, which is essential for field work with orang-utans familiar with humans. Although most orang-utans had no difficulty at all in operating a zip as efficiently as a tear-off contraption, it took a little longer in fingering and gave us just enough time to foil the intended pick-pocketing. The disadvantage of the pockets for all intending photography enthusiasts is the proximity of some of the front pockets to the skin. For extra video films in plastic hard covers this proved no shortcoming, but for the battery packs it created a continuous problem. The batteries heated up near the skin and got wet so that they discharged even before use. The battery packs finally found a place in loose side pockets in the trousers, where they dangled with every step up and down the territory and made one feel like a convict in transport, but they were safe.

We carried three cameras, a video camera and a tripod. Lesley had one camera just in case a good opportunity arose. Gisela carried two cameras and the video camera and tripod. One camera contained light-sensitive film and a large zoom lens that was set up for continuous frames. Another camera, more manageable and set for high speed, enabled snapshots to be taken at close range (no flashlights). The video camera was to complement our scoring activity. Only some researchers (cf. Bard 1992) mention video cameras as a tool for behavioural research on orang-utans. After using the camera for a while, we found that its use paid off in many unexpected and beneficial ways. More than once we saw behaviours on playback that we had been unable to watch or had not noticed during the day. The camera was able to move a good deal closer than our eyes. In other instances, we were able to make novel interpretative assessments of scenes only through several replays. Finally, as most field workers on orang-utans have commented, orang-utans are extraordinarily well camouflaged. We were surprised to see how the bright orange of the coat that can light up to a stunning fiery display of extraordinary power and beauty would strangely hide the individual within the speckled light and shadows of the forest. Often we could not distinguish faces and movements but the video camera managed to transform scenes of candlelight quality into the brightest and clearest images on the screen. There is no doubt that one travels far more comfortably, lighter and freer without all this equipment but despite the inconvenience, weight and restriction in movement, we found the technological assistance to our observations invaluable.

The field researchers and the researched (distribution of orang-utans)

If we invited all researchers who had undertaken extensive and/or systematic behavioural research on wild or semi-wild orang-utans in Borneo and Sumatra, we would not fill a high school assembly hall. However, most, if not all, people involved in such research would be able to attend that meeting because this field research is less than 30 years old. There were a few isolated studies earlier, such as by Carpenter (1938), Stott and Selsor (1961) or Schaller (1961), which were more concerned with population density and distribution. In the 1960s, the Harrisson team was one of the first to spend longer periods in the jungle and with orang-utans. Barbara Harrisson's work in particular, we believe, has been underrated to date. The Harrissons were appalled by the state of neglect and sheer lack of interest in the orang-utan. They derided the fact

▲ Excellent camouflage. Find the orang-utans! ▼

that so little published material was available, so little known and appreciated about the orang-utan and that so much misuse was continuing under cover of the law. In 1961, Barbara Harrisson wrote that it was still legally possible in the then British Borneo (Sabah) to obtain a license to keep orang-utans while it was already forbidden in Sarawak. Further, her plea, published in 1960, was explicit enough:

> It is a remarkable fact that although many scientists, naturalists and collectors have seen and shot the wild Orang, from Alfred Russel Wallace, Count Beccari and William Hornaday of the Smithsonian onward, no serious attempt has been made to carry out systematic field observations of Orang living in the wild. There is no reliable, first-hand, scientific information whatever on daily journeys, arboreal/terrestrial movement, natural groups, food gathering, effect on vegetation habitat, calls and sounds, other than what we have gathered here in recent years.

(B. Harrisson 1960)

A decade later, her plea began to be answered. The 1970s saw the beginnings of a trickle, if not a steady stream, of genuine scientific interest. A sense of continuity of observation and reporting is only gained by looking at the results of the last two decades. In the 1970s researchers, such as Rodman (1973, 1977, 1979), MacKinnon (1971, 1972, 1974a, 1974b) and Horr (1972), released the results of their field work and this entirely unstudied ape was finally on track for regular and extensive field work (Mitani 1985a; Rodman 1984). Others came to stay much longer. Galdikas arrived in Tanjung Puting in Borneo in 1971. About the same time Rijksen and Schürmann went to Sumatra. Such a new wave of interest was essential. Galdikas has now observed Bornean orang-utans for over two decades, providing researchers and zoos with invaluable information. This includes details in the life history of specific individuals over time, and of their offspring. In other words, for the first time in the history of the only Asian great ape, we have a body of knowledge based on three populations of orang-utans outside zoos: 1) wildlife observations on orang-utans without any direct human contact, 2) semi-wild orang-utans with brief or more extended contacts with humans, often referred to as habituated orang-utans, and 3) orang-utans once kept as pets who have undergone substantial re-training in order to cope with independent living in the forest, sometimes referred to as ex-captives.

It is of importance that all these studies have been carried out in the natural habitat of the orang-utan. By 'natural' we refer to the climatic conditions, to the indigenous flora and fauna and related local food sources, and to the customary seasonal variation and ecological conditions. It was recognised quite early that zoo conditions for orang-utans were imposing severely circumscribed conditions on the orang-utan. It was further recognised that the change of climate and flora and fauna alone had serious effects on the health and wellbeing of the orang-utan (Yerkes & Yerkes 1945).

The tragedy is that interest in and knowledge of the orang-utan has come at a time when the orang-utan is at the brink of extinction. There is strong evidence of ever-decreasing numbers and corresponding shrinkage of their distribution range. In the nineteenth century, Borneo was still an exotic goal for adventurers and big game hunters: out in the jungle they sought to shoot whatever seemed of interest, and this included the orang-utans. Some made some scientific use of their rampant killings but others just left the carcasses to rot or for use by indigenous populations.

Within a mere few weeks Wallace (1890) had obtained a large number of orang-utans and Hornaday had shot forty-five. Davenport, on the other hand, coming with very peaceful intentions 100 years later, encountered just 16 in seven months of his study (Davenport 1967). Some of the descriptions of orang-utans in Sarawak by the Harrisson team in the 1960s are now history. There are no more orang-utans where they conducted their research. When we visited areas outside Kuching (in Sarawak) in 1992, we were told that any orang-utans had long gone from the area. Beccari reported in 1904 that while orang-utans were rare around Kuching, they abounded in Sadong and in the Batang Lupar region (Beccari 1904). In 1960, when Sarawak commissioners undertook a detailed habitat survey of Sarawak they concluded that:

> With a stretch of the imagination one might get a total figure of a thousand Maias [orang-utans] now living in Sarawak. Yet only 100 years ago, some two hundred of these animals were exported to Europe and Hornaday alone took away forty-five specimens in 1878.

(cited in Harrisson 1961)

The 'Maias Report' also established comparative maps for the earlier period (1850s to 1910) and one for the decade from 1950 to 1960. The maps, adapted from the originals, illustrate the point clearly enough (see Figure 4).

Reports of dense populations of orang-utan (Davenport 1967; MacKinnon 1971; Horr 1972) had led to recommendations for reserves in those areas but these recommendations were not followed up. The areas in which MacKinnon and Horr undertook their work, the Ulu Segama Reserve and the Lokan sites respectively, have all been cleared completely and half of the Kutai Reserve has been logged and cleared (Rodman & Mitani 1987). Payne and Francis reported in 1985 that, in three substantial regions, there had been no sightings of orang-utans in many years (see Figure 5 for 1986 distribution). On the Malaysian side of Borneo, these concerned the Tawau region in Sabah and the lowlands between S. Rajang in Sarawak and S. Padas in south-western Sabah. In the latter region there are still bone deposits of orang-utans found especially near and in the Niah caves (Harrisson 1957; Hooijer 1960). The decrease of distribution in these areas has been attributed by Payne largely to three factors: hunting in the nineteeth and early twentieth centuries, malaria and deforestation (Payne & Francis 1985).

The density of orang-utans varies to some extent according to habitat availability and altitude (see Figure 6). There are few, if any, records of Bornean orang-utans above 1 500 metres, with the exception of Mt Kinabalu. Orang-utans are found in a variety of habitats, such as montane, secondary and swamp forests but it is in the tall lowland dipterocarp forests that we still find densities of four individuals or more within an area of two square kilometres. By contrast, in hill forests the density is at best one individual per two square kilometres (Payne & Francis 1985). Yet it is in the lowlands

Figure 4: Map of orang-utan distribution 1850–1960 in Sarawak

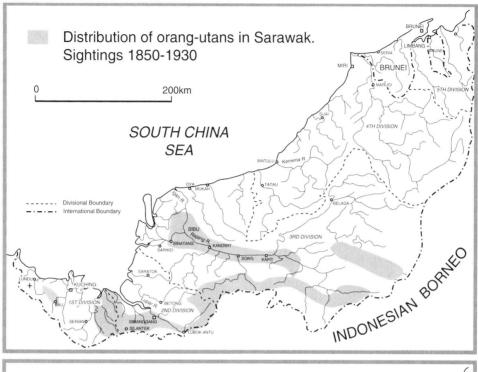

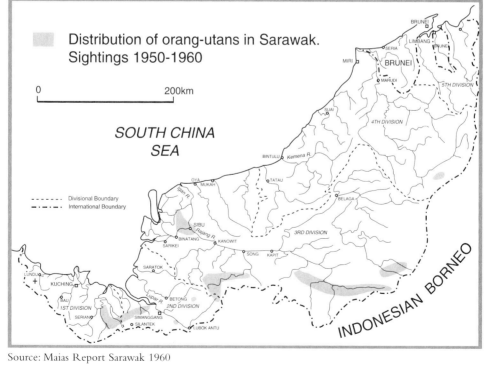

Source: Maias Report Sarawak 1960

that most human development and forest clearing takes place and in the hill forests that the government is willing to relent and to declare some areas as national parks and reserves for the orang-utan, such as the Tabin Wildlife Reserve, an area which no longer had any wild population of orang-utans.

The current distribution of orang-utans is still wider in Borneo than in Sumatra, where they are confined to the very northern end of the island. In Sumatra, the Gunung Leuser Park is now virtually the only Sumatran habitat for orang-utans and their higher density (five per square kilometre) compared to Bornean orang-utans probably relates as much to habitat availability as to the greater concentration of fig trees in that region, which form a major food source for orang-utans.

Figure 5: Map of distribution of wild orang-utans in Sabah (1986 data)

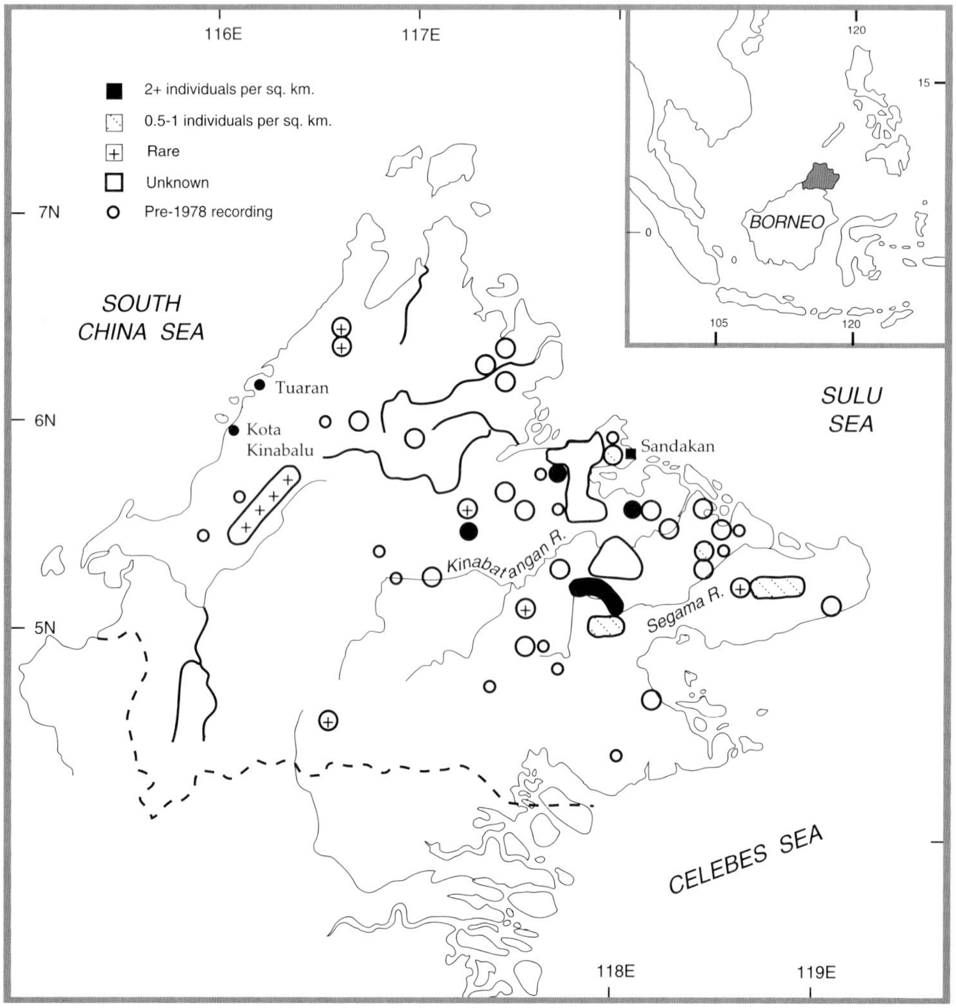

Source: Adapted from Davies, 1986

Studies have shown that even selective logging has a detrimental effect on orang-utans (Johns 1983). Here we are not speaking about activities that somehow lie in the future. Much of the total clearing has already been done. What is left is only a small percentage of the rainforest that once was. In 1992, there was less than one third of Sabah's original primary rainforest still under cover. In areas where logging is occurring some orang-utans may be killed during felling but, as Davies reports, most travel to an undisturbed area with the result of overcrowding (Davies 1986). This kind of migration is not in any way helpful for maintaining orang-utan numbers because, as MacKinnon argued as early as 1971 (MacKinnon 1971), the result of overcrowding is a decline in fertility. In other words, orang-utans adapt to their requirements in such a way that they lower their numbers through reduced progeny. It is a form of self-culling that helps reduce the total population even further.

Figure 6: Density of orang-utan distribution by altitude

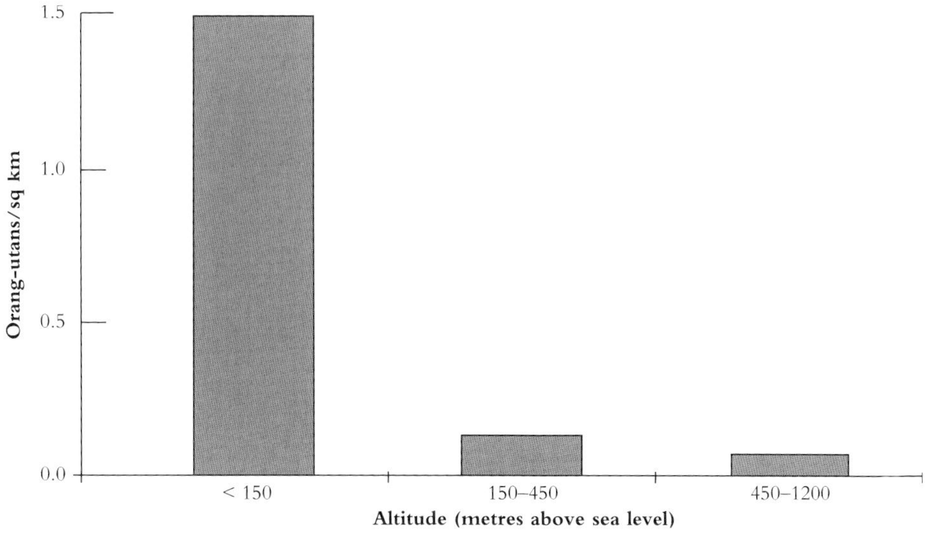

Source: Adapted from Davies 1986, p.41.

Rehabilitation centres, national parks, reserves

The map shown in Figure 7 indicates the current distribution of national parks and reserves. By 1986 it was already clear that there was a mismatch between the planning of protected areas for orang-utans and the designation of areas for national parks (Davies 1986). There are national parks where there is no known or only a sparse presence of orang-utans, and there are others where a healthy density of orang-utans is not supported by adequate policy measures. The small number of gazetted reserves in Sabah reveals that there are indeed very few areas where the orang-utan is truly protected. One of them is the 100 square kilometre Tabin Wildlife Reserve into which orang-utans are now being restocked by translocation from high-risk zones (Andau 1993). Another recommendation that has been long standing, evident since MacKinnon's field work in 1971, concerns the Danum Valley area which is within the Ulu Segama Forest Reserve. The reluctance here may be explained by pointing out that this reserve is a part of the Sabah Foundation timber concession area and most of that area has now been logged selectively.

Contrary to what one might hope and think, it is not always reassuring to have any area declared as unsuitable for agriculture, since this has often meant that it is considered wasted unless it is logged. Logging has become so important because it is seen as a commercial alternative to agricultural exploitation. The entire land of Sabah has been mapped out in terms of its short-term, immediate cash, *commercial* value. For a long time little, if any, consideration was given to the thought that an intact forest might prevent many fiscal and social problems that would result without it. It is much like killing the golden goose.

Nevertheless, unlike other endangered species, the orang-utan has actually been singled out for special protection and rehabilitation. The care and protection of the orang-utan in the wild now falls exclusively to two governments, Malaysia and Indonesia. Both countries have taken a number of steps to safeguard the orang-utan. In Indonesia these occurred before World War II whilst still under Dutch rule. The original Faunal Protection Ordinance was inaugurated in 1925 and amended in 1931 and 1936. It explicitly forbade the killing, trade or ownership of orang-utans (Shapiro 1992). Malaysia followed suit after federation. We know, of course, that these laws have been difficult if not impossible to police, given the nature and the size of the terrain but these laws have possibly made trade a little more difficult. However, many orang-utans get killed in illegal trade which requires concealed transport in horrific conditions. Until 1993, Indonesia supplied about a third of the world's demand for wild-caught primates. It remains to be seen what effect Indonesia's new 1994 legislation on banning export of all primates will have on the subversive export of macaques.

The very first Bornean rehabilitation program was put in place by Barbara Harrisson in Sarawak in the late 1950s and early 1960s and the first centre was established at Sepilok near Sandakan in Sabah. It was opened in 1964. From its humble beginnings and its simple accommodation and hospital facilities it has grown into an attractive tourist park, complete with reception area, cafeteria, signposts and guides. Semengoh in Sarawak near Kuching was opened in 1975. It commands a much smaller area. It is surrounded by human population, is generally less accessible and has a far smaller orang-utan population.

On the Indonesian side of Borneo, which is known as Kalimantan, there is the notable Tanjung Puting National Park which was previously a reserve (Galdikas & Shapiro 1994). This centre, despite its initial physical isolation, has managed the Orang-Utan Research and Conservation Project and has gained a name through the singular efforts of Biruté Galdikas, her family and team, both locally and through extensive publications in international journals. Sumatra boasts two rehabilitation centres in the north of the island, one in Ketambe and the other in Bohorok. Ketambe was established in 1971 and Bohorok in 1973. The latter was started by two Swiss women and it, too, has become a major tourist attraction (cf. Freeman 1979).

In addition to these centres there are a number of national parks in Indonesia and East Malaysia in which orang-utans are also more numerous than elsewhere. On Sumatra, there is the Gunung Leuser National Park from which many studies on the Sumatran orang-utan (*Pongo pygmaeus abelii*) have originated since 1971 (Rijksen 1974, 1978; Aveling 1982; Sugardjito 1983, Sugardjito & van Hooff 1986). In East Kalimantan there is the Kutai National Park, a small area of just three square kilometres and in West Kalimantan there is the Gunung Palung Nature Reserve with the Cabang Panti Research Station, covering five square kilometres. In Sabah, there are still some isolated areas where wild orang-utans can be found outside any reserves and at last count they were particularly numerous at the upper end of the Segama River (Danum Valley) which has its own research station accommodation. There are additional national parks, most of which are no longer inhabited by orang-utans, such as the Kota Kinabalu National Park, the Tunku Abdul Rahman National Park, the Gunung Mulu National Park as well as the Niah National Park (see Figure 7). Apparently other smaller protected areas are also being planned, eg one along the Kinabatangan River (Payne 1994, personal communication).

Hayes (1992) argues that rehabilitation centres provide a crucial contribution to conservation. There are several reasons why one may feel uneasy or ambivalent about rehabilitation centres and we cannot entirely agree with Hayes. First, it depends on the definition and expectation of what a rehabilitation centre means. Second, it is already known that rehabilitation as a goal is a very difficult undertaking (De Silva 1970; Aveling & Mitchell 1982). Third, without effective monitoring of the released individuals, ie of those which have been considered 'rehabilitated' sufficiently well to go back into the forest, the entire program is on very shaky ground. For instance, a recent survey of the success of rehabilitation of gibbons in Sarawak established that 90 percent of the confiscated or found gibbons died shortly after release from the rehabilitation centre (Bennett 1992). Fourth, another aspect of these problems is the question of what options there are in general for discarded and unwanted primates (cf. Harcourt 1987).

Several models of rehabilitation are available. There is at least one rehabilitation centre that even in the early 1990s was still run more like a zoo than a rehabilitation centre, or how we would perceive a rehabilitation centre to function. It contained caged animals — not because they were ill and had to be prevented from leaving before the treatment was concluded — but because the particular individuals were considered dangerous. The area is too small, or rather the hinterland too circumscribed, to allow any free movement by orang-utans. The food source in that hinterland is insufficient to entice orang-utans outside the reserve. Even were this not so, for orang-utans to have freedom of movement, this hinterland would need national parks and reserves to be interlinked by corridors. This is not the case. Indeed, as the map in

Figure 5 above, shows, there is no longer even a 'bridge' between the north-eastern populations of orang-utans near the Sepilok/Sukau. The fragmentation between south-east and central Borneo was already fact by the 1960s.

Another model for a rehabilitation centre is the highly efficient medical model, which limits contact between orang-utans and humans to an absolute minimum, allowing only medical services to be provided. In preparation for release back into the forest, such individuals are housed in cages and do not get to communicate or interact much with the human carers. Our personal experiences suggest that orang-utans may be as traumatised by 'hospitalisation' as humans are and are in need of special warmth, care and attention to minimise trauma. The clinical approach that argues for minimal contact with humans is no doubt a laudable corollary for any wildlife. But when, out of a sense of concern, we *have* interfered with an animal's life by trying to heal it or to cure it of disease, we *have* taken an active step of intervention that cannot be cancelled out by

Figure 7: Locations of national parks, reserves and rehabilitation centres on the island of Borneo (approximations only)

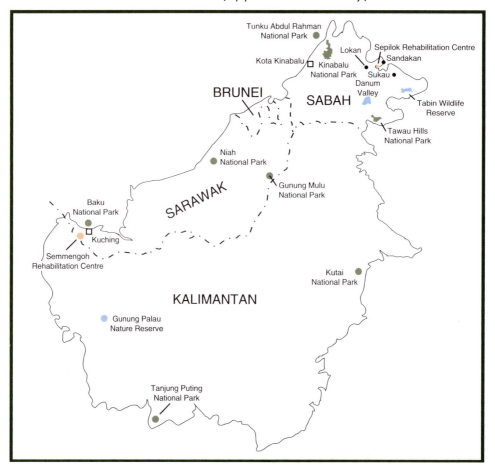

pretending that the intervention is one of only limited communication. If a wild orang-utan infant has just lost its mother, been injured or neglected and undergoes a sudden change of environment into cement cages and bars without some signs of reassurance, we assume that this could be a frightening experience which, precisely because carers try to maintain their distance, could leave scars for life (cf. Turner *et al.* 1969).

A third rehabilitation model has taken on the functions of re-training and health care. In order to maintain them, however, governments have decided to open up these centres to tourists. Tourism was a marginal industry in these regions even 10 years ago, or in some areas even just five years ago. Nevertheless, once the areas were opened up, they gained momentum by themselves. Eco-tourism is now big business. By the early 1990s, it appeared as if half of all travel companies in Europe and Japan, and some in the USA, had made a concerted effort to get tourists to watch orang-utans. The crowds would be the envy of any zoo, replicating as they now do, 42nd Street pedestrian traffic in New York rather than a quiet jungle outpost. At first, at least in Sepilok, there were no charges to the public, but this has now changed. In the majority of rehabilitation centres orang-utans have begun to earn their keep — at a cost (more of this in Chapter 5).

There is, we believe, a fourth model of rehabilitation centres which could and partly does work at some sites. This can only be done by limiting visitors and ensuring that there is sufficient direct hinterland into which orang-utans can be *safely* rehabilitated. An alternative, as has been practised by Rijksen and collaborators, is to rehabilitate groups into areas that no longer have orang-utans, ie where there is no competition, minimising the risks of bringing rehabilitants together with existing wild populations and thus avoiding potential problems of diseases or overcrowding. By 'safely' rehabilitating we refer to viability in the widest sense: that orang-utans will be known to have a large enough foraging area, can reproduce *and* move to other areas as fruiting seasons and other seasonal variations may require. Ground plans for such action have involved and need to involve ecologists, ethologists, scientists and anthropologists (cf. Lardeux-Gilloux 1994).

Sepilok

Our own observational work was largely confined to Sepilok near Sandakan in Sabah and to Semengoh near Kuching in Sarawak.

Sepilok Rehabilitation Centre lies 24 kilometres outside of Sandakan. Sandakan was once the capital city of Sabah or rather of British North Borneo but it lost that position when the city was almost completely destroyed by the Japanese in World War II. As a result Kota Kinabalu (then called Jesselton) became the new capital city. It takes less than an hour by plane to reach Sandakan from Kota Kinabalu and about half an hour by car to get from the city to the rehabilitation centre east of Sandakan. The Sandakan/Sepilok area is defined by the sea, Sandakan Bay being a beautiful, large and sheltered natural harbour. From here, logs were once shipped to Hong Kong and

China and now mainly to Japan and Korea. Sepilok abuts onto another bay that is mainly defined by mangrove swamps and hence forms a natural barrier and border for orang-utans. Unlike proboscis monkeys, orang-utans cannot digest the toxic fruit of the mangrove.

Sepilok Rehabilitation Centre was established in 1964 and upgraded in steps, both to help care for more and more orang-utans and to accommodate tourist demands. Its total size is 4 300 hectares. It is advertised as 'virgin forest' but it used to be an old forest reserve in which logging took place regularly. Logging was finally banned in 1957 and its saving feature was that logging procedures then were based on the old hand methods rather than on powerful chainsaws, hence limiting the damage to some extent and enabling regrowth of some species. As we explained before, 30 or 40 years mean little in terms of tree growth in the tropical rainforest. The Sepilok Rehabilitation Centre is run by the Sabah Wildlife Department, which comes under the auspices of the Minister of Tourism and Environmental Development of Sabah.

Discussions in the last five to 10 years have focused on a manageable interaction between human activity, mainly selective logging, and biodiversity. Some species are more tolerant of logging than others (Johns 1983) but it appears from the evidence collected so far that the orang-utan is one of the less tolerant species. There is relatively little material on how much primary forest is needed to sustain a population and, particularly, in selectively logged areas. Orang-utan density seems to vary with habitat and fruiting seasons.

Sepilok has taken a large number of orang-utans, initially only those confiscated locally but more recently it was asked to take orang-utans from logging areas elsewhere if the orang-utans had been orphaned, injured or isolated. Sepilok was already deemed too small an area to sustain the then existing orang-utan population in 1986 but the Centre continued to take in orang-utans (Davies 1986). To our knowledge, there is no natural corridor to the remaining and relatively close areas which still had healthy orang-utan populations some time ago. These areas include some of the hinterland of Sepilok and in the Sukau area across the bay along the Kinabatangan River. Where travel is not barred by the sea or by mangrove swamps, it is barred by human population and agriculture.

We have not seen any publicly available records of survival rates of orang-utans in Sepilok. Many disappear from view and are never seen again. Of all the orang-utans we knew individually we were personally aware of three deaths over two years of relatively young orang-utans aged one and a half, seven and nine years, or of about 10 percent of those known to us. Figures for the estimated total number in the Sepilok Reserve have fluctuated substantially, some of them suggested a population as high as about 200 (personal communication with Sepilok personnel). This would bring population density to about five per square kilometre or even higher. In the absence of an unusual concentration of fruit trees especially figs, as in the Gunung Leuser Reserve in Sumatra, this would hint at serious overcrowding.

The solutions to overcrowding are problematic. As we mentioned before, Rijsken has tried to rehabilitate groups and take them to areas where orang-utans were no longer present. There are several reasons for having taken this step. One is that the introduction of orang-utans from rehabilitation centres to areas with wild populations can cause the region with wild populations to become overstocked. Another is that ex-captive or rehabilitating orang-utans may have difficulty in social rehabilitation with wild orang-utans, and this has been shown to happen. A third reason is that rehabilitated orang-utans may introduce diseases carried as a result of human contact. Whatever the relocation site, it is difficult, too, to find suitable habitat that is not about to be logged within the next five years.

Sepilok has full medical facilities and holding cages, as well as two provisioning sites supplied and maintained by Sepilok staff. One such site is located near the tourist centre and another, placed further into the reserve, has restricted tourist access. The Sepilok staff also run a Wildlife Education Centre for visitors. This has been a very useful facility in terms of educating the public, be this local or international, about Sabah's wildlife. The area now has one resident adult male orang-utan and a number of sexually mature but not fully developed subadult males. There are several adult females who have successfully reproduced and this natural increase has added to the number of orang-utans brought to the Centre.

3

Debates surrounding the orang-utan

Anatomic and genetic debates

From the seventeenth century to the turn of the nineteenth century, much confusion existed as to the various taxa of primate species. In the older literature gorillas and chimpanzees were named as one species with various sub-names, usually calling the African apes by the name of 'orang-outan' or *pongo* (Schwartz 1987). One needs to be cautious with seventeenth and eighteenth century descriptions as they might indeed pertain to chimpanzees or gorillas rather than to orang-utans (Hill 1966; Harrisson 1987). The assumption that within Borneo there existed at least two species of orang-utans persisted for over 100 years. It is now known that these differences in size and appearance were due to differences in age and sex. As late as 1890, the official *Handbook of British North Borneo* still contained the following entry:

> *There are two species, one large and one small; the largest one sometimes attains a height of four feet six inches, and has large black collops on each side of its face, which, added to the way it blows its throat out when excited, gives it a most ferocious, almost demoniacal, appearance, which stuffed specimen quite fail to convey … Anything like a full-grown specimen of the large kind is hardly ever seen in captivity. The smaller species is easily tamed and is mild and pleasant, domesticated even.*

> (*Handbook* 1890, pp.112–113)

The 'collops' on the side of the face refer to the cheek pads that only fully grown mature males develop. The confusion persisted for as long as it did presumably because of the great variability of appearance even within adult populations. Hence, in 1862, Owen commented in detail on the orang-utan's structural variations and noted that these were greater than in any other quadrumanous species ever observed (cf. Yerkes & Yerkes 1945).

Research conducted by anthropologists, biologists, zoologists and psychologists and also in the medical and veterinary fields, has established a number of important baseline facts about the orang-utan. There have been many articles and papers over the last 100 years debating the differences and similarities in anatomy between orang-utans and humans. However, at the level of *interpretation,* it is often not clear what the anatomical similarities mean. Such debates, apart from scientific curiosity, were often far from value-free.

Most of the earlier studies in some way or another sprang from the same source of conviction about the uniqueness and even perfection of the human body. Whether inadvertently or intentionally, any other species had to be shown to be *less* than human, be this in the context of 'creationism' or evolutionary theory. Having thus established or reconfirmed human superiority it followed naturally that all else was *inferior.* These comparative exercises have dogged both impartial and compassionate enquiry. It is a very recent phenomenon to suggest that difference need not imply inferiority.

To give an example, much has been made of the difference between the existence and function of the ligament of the thigh bone in orang-utans and humans. J.F. Palmer noted in 1837 that 'in the orang, the lower limbs are feebly developed as organs of support, but have a great extent of motion, the hip joint being, like the shoulder joint, without a round ligament' (Palmer 1837). As late as 1988, J.T. Stern reiterated this view, attributing the orang-utan's great hip mobility to a 'lack' of a *ligamentum teres* 'enabling the assumption of bizarre postures in trees' (Stern 1988). Crelin has since disproved this hypothesis by showing that the ligament is indeed extremely important in the orang-utan precisely because of the wide-ranging movement that the hip joint permits (Crelin 1988). It remains for us to judge the emotive language which speaks of the orang-utan's lower limbs as 'feeble' or of their postures adopted in a tree as 'bizarre'.

Some of the inquiries have a more sinister side to them than mere curiosity about evolution. Clearly, the closer the orang-utan's chemico-physical makeup was to that of humans, the more likely it was that the orang-utan would be used for experimentation concerned with human health and medical problems. It seems that the orang-utan has remained a less likely candidate for being experimented on and 'sacrificed' in the interest of science than have the chimpanzee, the rhesus and the vervet monkey. This may be changing as captive breeding programs improve and availability increases. The orang-utans' one protection against laboratory abuse is that they are awkward to keep. They grow too large for small cages. Their strength is several-fold that of humans and they are difficult to contain, having acquired some notoriety as efficient 'gaol breakers'.

In behaviour there are still many gaps in our knowledge, some of which we hope this book will fill, but in terms of the orang-utan's biology, especially anatomically and genetically, there are only a few if any remaining mysteries in the basic facts (Napier & Napier 1967). Our own human genetic makeup is said to differ by a mere two percent from this great ape and by only one percent from the chimpanzee. The orang-utan's genetic endowment is 98 percent identical to ours.

We cannot go into all the complexities of evolutionary arguments, be these derived from genetic examinations or those conducted in physical anthropology (see p.55). Suffice it to say in this section that some of the debates centre around the problem whether identical or similar forms and characteristics (phylogeny and morphology) between humans and orang-utans can be regarded as proof of evolutionary relatedness, as Schwartz has argued (Schwartz 1984, 1987), or whether these are rather just expressions of analogous relationships, ie similar functional developments in parallel (Andrews 1987; Groves 1987). There are some proponents of the view that evidence of several shared characteristics between humans and orang-utans is evidence of greater evolutionary closeness than has been suggested in the past. In Schwartz's schemata, for instance, the orang-utan moves from third closest relative to first closest relative of humans (see p.58). Although convincingly challenged by Andrews and Groves, new anatomical evidence raises these theoretical issues at every level anew. For instance, the study by Thiranagama *et al.* (1991) on superficial venous systems in the primate forelimb shows that only orang-utans and humans possess the characteristic of certain veins (polymorphic lateral vein and medial vein) in the forearm. In all other great apes the medial vein is absent. Although they argue that these findings by themselves cannot resolve the question of phylogeny in humans and great apes, arguments on relationships between orang-utans and humans need to take account of similarities in conjunction with observations concerning the retention of neotenous forms in both species (Thiranagama *et al.* 1991). We shall come back to this in Chapter 4.

Of all the similarities between humans and orang-utans we must mention illnesses and diseases and other medical problems, for these have a direct bearing on their survival. Orang-utans can suffer the same diseases and illnesses as we do. Among them are many life-threatening ones, such as tuberculosis, intestinal diseases, malaria and pneumonia. Tuberculosis tends to occur more often in captivity than in the wild. It is indeed quite common in captivity (Francis 1958; Fiennes 1979). Where rehabilitation centres are established, tuberculosis is now kept in check by regular inoculation and testing (Kehoe *et al.* 1984). Intestinal problems are less easily controlled because infestation of gastrointestinal parasites often occurs through soil eating (Munson & Montali 1990; cf. also Collet *et al.* 1986). There have also been reports on gastroenteritis and the occasionally fatal eosinophilic enterocolitis and their respective treatment (Citino *et al.* 1985). The common cold, headaches, toothaches, as well as gingivitis and periodontitis which have been shown to occur frequently in captivity (Braswell 1994), can also plague orang-utans just as much as humans. Perinatal bacterial infections, diarrhoea and cardiac fibrosis also rank high amongst orang-utan illnesses (Munson & Montali 1990). Among the many reasons why they need to receive medical help are accidents, particularly bone fractures. In Sepilok alone, 21 orang-utans were treated for bone fractures in a six-year period. Almost all of them were under five years old and 70 percent of them had incurred the injury as a result of falling from a tree (Kehoe & Chan 1986). This has implications which we will raise again in Chapter 4.

Estimates of life expectancy vary rather widely but this has to do with the life circumstances of orang-utans and with our ability to observe them. It is harder today than in the past to ascertain how long a normal lifespan may be because so few, if any (and of these we may never know), are privileged enough to live an undisturbed life and die of old age. MacKinnon thought that orang-utans lived at least 30 years. The local Dayak population thought that orang-utans had a longer lifespan than they had themselves. It is thought that the normal lifespan is at least about 40 years, although amongst the subspecies in northern Sumatra, one of the older resident males is known to be around 45 years old (Western 1994) and several zoo orang-utans are older than that. Life expectancy in zoos was once at an appallingly low level of one or two years of caged existence, independent of the age upon arrival (Harrisson 1955b). Galdikas estimates life expectancy of orang-utans in the wild to be even 60 years of age (cited in Woods 1989). Overall then, it may be said that life expectancy is generally thought to be roughly similar to human life expectancy before the onset of modern medicine and subject to the same fluctuations due to diseases and other variables, in a range of 30 to 60 years.

For our purposes it is more important to note that similarities between humans and orang-utans in anatomy, function and development (ontogeny) are interwoven with behavioural similarities and psychological attributes. To give just one example. This interrelationship between behaviour and anatomy is cogently demonstrated in a study by Röhrer-Ertl (1989) relying on three sites: Deli and Atjeh in Sumatra and Skalau in West Borneo. He shows that the increasing growth of the mastication apparatus in orang-utans in the wild, especially in males, is attributable to increased activities which might have required increased use of the jaw. He theorises that this activity is 'considered to reflect a broadening of behavioural repertory' (Röhrer-Ertl 1989). The crucial point is that his study results are in direct contrast to similar studies carried out in zoos. Röhrer-Ertl concludes therefore two things with which we find ourselves in total agreement: zoo orang-utans exhibit atypical behaviour and therefore more studies in the wild are needed to obtain a more accurate assessment of the species even at the level of phenotype and morphology. These findings may also make some of us aware of the necessity to continually distinguish between studies carried out in zoos and those carried out in the wild, especially when findings imply relevance beyond a particular zoo environment (see Chapter 5). The morphology of orang-utans appears to be as dependent on ethological background (ie *use* of structure) as does that of humans. Röhrer-Ertl (1989) has dismissed the comparison of purely morphological features in humans and orang-utans as insufficient and insufficient grounds on which to base evolutionary hypotheses. We are dealing, then, with a host of subtle processes and interactions between environment, biology and behaviour. These include considerations of such complex issues as learning and even concepts such as culture. We will develop these themes in Chapters 4 and 6.

We should reiterate that phenotypical variability in orang-utans is comparable to that of humans and well above the average of other great apes (Röhrer-Ertl 1989), a point that Owen made in 1862 without any noticeable effect on the thinking of the time. This cautions us against assuming that, by having measured or observed a select or small group of orang-utans, we have said something at the population level, let alone at the species level. To recognise the diversity of appearance and diversity of behaviour in the orang-utan is to appreciate our relative paucity of knowledge about a complex thinking and feeling being.

Genes and evolution

Apes are our closest relatives, but exactly how close are they to us genetically? The genetic proximity of various species to humans can be determined using DNA hybridisation techniques. The genetic material (the DNA) from one species is mixed with that of another species to see how much matching (hybridisation) there is between the two types of DNA. The DNA molecule is made up of a string of sub-units called nucleic acids, each of which is like a word in a sentence. Strung together these 'words' spell out the genetic information that is passed on from generation to generation. The more these messages match up between two species, the closer they are genetically. This can then be translated into evolutionary distance or proximity. The further apart in time two species are in terms of their evolution the greater the difference in their DNA because over time the DNA accumulates mutations, changes in the 'word' (nucleic acid) sequences. Thus, genetic difference indicates separation in evolutionary time (see Jones *et al.* 1992 for a more detailed explanation).

Using the hybridisation approach, chimpanzees are found to be closest to us, the pygmy chimpanzee, or bonobo, being closer than the common chimpanzee. These methods have revealed that we share 99 percent of our genetic material with chimpanzees (King & Wilson 1975; and see Gribbin & Gribbin 1988); next comes the gorilla and then, as we said before, the orang-utan, with about 98 percent of its genetic material the same as ours; the orang-utan is followed by the lesser apes, the gibbons and siamang (genus *Hylobates*).

Evolutionary trees can be constructed from DNA hybridisation or other molecular studies and, of course, also from fossil records. From the study of fossils, it has been determined that primates evolved within the mammalian line about 63 million years ago in the Paleocene when forms very similar to the present-day lemurs of Madagascar first appeared. These are known as the lower primates or prosimians. In the Oligocene, about 40 million years ago, the primates split into two main lineages, the New World platyrrhine monkeys of South America, the living forms of which include marmosets, tamarins, howler monkeys, etc, and the Old World catarrhine monkeys of Africa, today including the cercopithecoids (baboons, macaques, etc) and the hominoids (apes and humans; see Figure 8).

The anthropoids (monkeys and apes) may have evolved from the prosimians when there was a demand for diurnal (daytime) activity and colour vision for detecting food, such as fruit (Pickford 1986). Most of the prosimians are 'creatures of the night'. Colour vision is not greatly required for their nocturnal lifestyle. Thus, the New and Old World monkeys may have evolved with improved colour vision to go with their diurnal activity patterns. As many non-primate mammals have well-developed colour vision, this was probably a 're-discovery' of colour vision that had evolved prior to the primates and was lost with the nocturnal existence of lower primates. In addition, one form of vision used in depth perception, known as stereopsis, evolved, or at least re-appeared, with the monkeys. Its evolution was accompanied by the formation of a bony division (called the postorbital septum) behind the eye that serves to hold the eyes in alignment during chewing. Stereopsis is not possible without very precise alignment of the eyes. The postorbital septum separates the eyes from the temporal muscles and thus prevents mechanical disturbance of eye alignment and stereopsis during feeding. Without this bony partition, depth perception by stereopsis would be lost during feeding. Thus, colour vision and stereopsis appeared with the evolution of monkeys from prosimians.

The first member of the hominoid lineage (apes to humans) was *Proconsul*, appearing in the Miocene epoch, 17 to 23 million years ago. *Proconsul* possessed many of the structural characteristics of modern apes (Lewin 1989). There is some suggestion that this genus moved by hanging from branches or by palm-walking, not knuckle-walking (Klein 1989). *Proconsul* evolved in the East African rainforests of that time and from this beginning the hominoids are thought to have spread through Europe to Asia. As we have already mentioned, the apes surviving today are the lesser apes of Asia (the gibbons and siamang) and the great apes of Africa (the common chimpanzee, the pygmy chimpanzee or bonobo, and the gorilla) and Asia (the orang-utan).

There is a gap in the fossil records from around 18 million years ago to 12 million years ago but, from the DNA hybridisation data, the gibbons are thought to

Figure 8: Evolutionary tree of primates

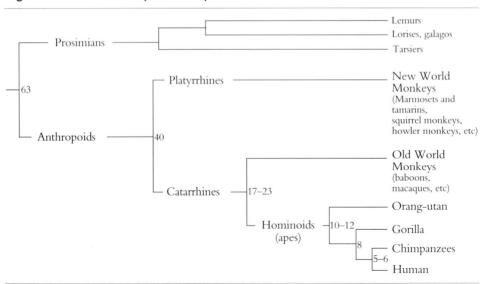

The evolutionary tree for the primates. The right hand column lists some of the presently existing primates. The numbers indicate approximate times, in millions of years, at which each of the lines of evolution diverged. The times given for the apes are according to the most popular hypothesis, placing the chimpanzees closest to humans, but see Figure 9 for a possible alternative.

have evolved around 17 million years ago (Harrison *et al.* 1988; Lewin 1989). A large arboreal and fruit-eating hominoid, known as *Sivapithecus* (a category that now subsumes *Ramapithecus*), evolved at around 12 million years ago or somewhat earlier, and it may well have been the ancestor of the orang-utan. Placing the ancestor of the orang-utan at this date is said to match the information obtained by DNA hybridisation. Also, the jaws and teeth of *Sivapithecus* are very similar to those of the orang-utan.

Sivapithecus was fruit-eating and sexually dimorphic (males and females differing in size and structure), much like the orang-utans of the present. Male orang-utans have a number of larger cranial dimensions compared to females. These sexually dimorphic characteristics of the skull appear by mid-juvenile age (Leutenegger & Masterson 1989; Winkler 1987).

The gorilla and the chimpanzee are believed to have evolved more recently than the orang-utan, the gorilla at around eight million years ago and the chimpanzees (*Pan paniscus* and *Pan troglodytes*) around six million years ago. A new form of DNA hybridisation using DNA from the mitochondria, rather than the nucleus, of cells has largely confirmed this date for the evolution of the chimpanzees (Ruvolo *et al.* 1991), but this is not conclusive (see later).

It is commonly believed that all of the apes, including the hominids (early humans), evolved in the warm forests of north-eastern Africa and spread out to reach Asia at a later period. *Homo* (the genus to which humans belong) first appeared as little as 2.5 million years ago, although some calculations place the origin of humans back at five million years ago (Sibley 1992). Some argue that *Homo* rose to the challenge of the ice ages, but others consider this suggestion to be too simplistic (Harrison *et al.* 1988). However, it would seem that *Homo* became more bipedal as increasingly arid conditions led to the dwindling of the rainforests and two-footed locomotion became advantageous for roaming and hunting on the open savannahs (see Gribbin & Gribbin 1988). Meanwhile, the ancestral forms of the orang-utan presumably had made their way to the rainforests of Asia, where they stayed. At least, this is the most commonly accepted hypothesis, based on both fossil and DNA hybridisation evidence.

Some consider that, in view of our substantial genetic proximity to chimpanzees, it may be possible for successful interbreeding to occur (Lovejoy 1981). Indeed, the results of modern molecular genetic techniques have led some to suggest that humans are not the sole example of the family Hominidea as distinct from Pongidea, which contains the great apes (chimpanzees, gorillas and orang-utans), but rather that humans, chimpanzees and gorillas should all be grouped under Hominidea, leaving only the orang-utan in Pongidea (Lewin 1988). Interbreeding with apes has been one of the deepest taboos in modern human culture (not necessarily in indigenous cultures, as we have shown in Chapter 1) and there are countless stories portraying male apes raping young women. The thought of a possible reproductive success has spawned horror stories of women giving birth to monsters and hence to the devil himself who, incidentally, is either described as a goat or as an ape with red hair (cf. for instance, the novel *The Inheritors* by Golding).

When Schwartz (1984, 1987) argued that orang-utans are closer to humans than the other apes, he touched one of the very raw nerves of white western cultures. Obviously Schwartz had not understood that the idea of the orang-utan as a contender for the position of our closest relative opens up a Pandora's box. Public opinion is against him, for the orang-utans are too close to the image of the 'red devil', too close in their sexuality to humans (see Chapter 4) and too similar morphologically to give comfort. According to his view, *Sivapithecus*, the orang-utan and *Homo* should share one grouping, with the chimpanzee and gorilla in a separate grouping (Schwartz 1984).

While the rough outlines of the evolutionary tree are agreed upon by science, there are still substantial and important disagreements within the finer points of great ape and human evolution. Indeed, on reading the literature on this particular issue one remains surprised how many alternative views still exist. The story is far from complete and the various speculations provide a different finishing touch each time. We mentioned some of the physiological and structural similarities between orang-utans and humans but it is generally accepted that the DNA hybridisation studies would tend to eliminate the possibility of a closer genetic and evolutionary proximity to humans than the chimpanzees. Nevertheless, according to Weiss (1987) there are two possible evolutionary trees that fit the DNA hybridisation data. One as just discussed and shown in Figure 8 and the other with *Homo* on a branch before the chimpanzees and the gorilla and, therefore, closer to the orang-utan (see Figure 9). The latter is more in line with the suggestion of Schwartz. It would also solve the problem of knuckle-walking. Only gorillas and chimpanzees knuckle walk, whereas *Homo* shows no evidence of knuckle-walking ancestory. This means that either knuckle-walking evolved separately in chimpanzees and gorillas or that they had a common knuckle-walking ancestor not shared by *Homo* (see Appendix 2).

Figure 9: Alternative family trees for the apes

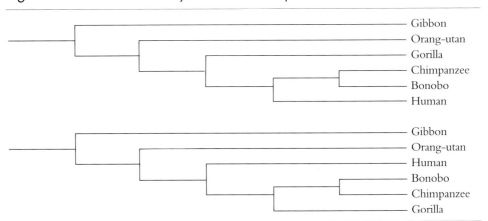

Two alternative, as well as the most likely, family trees for the apes (after Weiss 1987). Bonobo refers to *Pan paniscus*, the pygmy chimpanzee.

Each age produces theories and postulates hypotheses only to the extent to which it can cope with these conceptually. Molecular analysis is a rather recent technique and there is a tendency to take as read whatever results are acquired by technology. The problem is that technological determinism overlooks that technological tools are made by humans, programmed by humans and directed to and focused on specific tasks. Technology itself is not value-free. We propose that one should not be over-confident, for instance, of the results of molecular hybridisation experiments. The amount of matching between the DNA from two species needs to be translated into evolutionary time and that introduces inaccuracies. The 'molecular clock' used to determine when evolutionary divergences occurred is based on the accumulation of mutations in the DNA (nuclear or mitochondrial DNA, the latter being in the cytoplasm of the cell) and this clock must be calibrated according to independent anthropological evidence for species divergence and known rates of mutation. There is no full agreement on these values. Also, inaccuracies can arise from gene 'leakage' of paternal mitochondrial DNA into the maternal mitochondrial DNA line (see Avise 1991) and possible regional variations in mutation rate (Lewin 1984; Wolpoff 1989).

Added to this, the sequence in which the genes are read out during development may be just as important in determining physical similarities as the actual amount of DNA hybridisation (King & Wilson 1975). In fact, it has been argued that 'the genetic distance between humans and the chimpanzee is probably too small to account for their substantial organismal differences' (King & Wilson 1975). Therefore, these authors reason, the organismal (physical and physiological) differences might be determined by the sequence in which the genes are expressed or by the particular genes which are expressed. Not all genes are expressed at any one time and they are expressed according to a particular sequence during development. Thus, despite the fact that humans and chimpanzees have 99 percent of their genes in common, differences in phenotype may emerge because different sets of genes are expressed at different times. Of course, this may simply be an argument to keep humans at a great distance from chimpanzees, but we might well extrapolate this reasoning to the issue of humans versus orang-utans. Since we share so many 'organismal' characteristics with orang-utans (Schwartz 1984), maybe very similar sets of genes are expressed in both humans and orang-utans. That is, despite the fact that humans share only 98 percent of our DNA material with orang-utans, compared to the 99 percent with chimpanzees, we may be more similar to the orang-utan because we actually make use of a very similar subset of genes. Presently available techniques in molecular genetics cannot give an answer to this possibility. There is still room for debate.

Locomotion

Having briefly outlined some of the debates on evolutionary aspects of similarities between orang-utans and humans, one needs to recall some characteristics that are typical and specific to orang-utans and are distinctly different from humans. Some of the differences between orang-utans and humans are immediately apparent even to the most casual observer. These mainly concern body proportions (see Tuttle's review 1974), leaving aside obvious differences in the appearance of the face and the shape of the head. The orang-utan arms are longer than those of humans while orang-utan legs are proportionately a good deal shorter than those of humans. Of all animals to live in trees the orang-utan is by far the largest (Napier & Napier 1967). Adult males tend to weigh around 80 kg but may weigh as much as 97 kg or more, adult females are considerably lighter, weighing around 40 kg, the largest weighing about half of the weight of the largest males (Rodman 1984). Their height, even when erect, is rarely above 1.2 metres. No one knows exactly how tall the largest orang-utan might have been in the past but to our knowledge, reports have never exceeded 1.4 m, although travellers' logbooks and local stories keep suggesting sizes of up to 1.8 m (Sureng 1960). In present times, no orang-utans of this height have been known either in captivity or in the wild. By comparison with their body size, their arm span of up to 2.4 m is impressive. The latter is just one of the many features useful for arboreal living.

The orang-utan's arboreal existence relative to its size has excited the imagination of adventurers and scientists alike. From the nineteenth century onwards theoretical interest among anthropologists and scientists has focused on a number of issues related to living in the canopies of the tropical forests of South East Asia. We cannot here go into all the details of locomotion theories and arboreal life in evolutionary terms other than to suggest that the orang-utan, as the only one of the great apes to live relatively permanently in trees, has raised intriguing questions.

Among the evolutionary questions is not only why orang-utans have stayed in trees but whether they have always lived in trees as teBoekhorst speculates (1989). Whether or not they were once larger than today and possibly more ground dwelling is also part of an ongoing theoretical debate. How is the anatomy explicable in evolutionary terms? What, for instance, is the correlation of body weight with choice of arboreal behaviour? Is hanging (suspensory behaviour) an adaptation to weight? Are the morphological features of orang-utans adaptations to climbing or swinging (brachiation) from branch to branch? Body weight in itself is an important factor in terms of mobility in trees, specifically in canopies. This in turn may determine choices of diet and ability to travel or vice versa; body weight may have developed as a consequence of dietary choices. The size of branches (often referred to as 'weight bearing structures' or WBS) relative to the body weight has given rise to the classic suspensory ape paradigm. What are the advantages and disadvantages in evolutionary terms? At which level of the canopy do orang-utans travel? Is there a pattern or is it all random? Is there an age, sex or dominance difference, particularly important for foraging and food searching?

There was no dearth of qualitative studies describing locomotion and the various movements of orang-utans. We still needed to know, however, how often particular forms of behaviour occur, where they occur in relation to each other and what is to be derived from such information. One of the first to provide quantitative information on locomotion was the study by Sugardjito (1982), followed by Cant's research (Cant 1985, 1986, 1987).

In their ecological study Sugardjito and van Hooff (1986) investigated in detail which part of the forest stratum orang-utans used for travelling. They found that females and younger orang-utans, ie all orang-utans of lighter weight, used the middle and upper stratum of the canopy, typically between 20 and 30 m above ground, while heavier males travelled more readily in the lower section of the forest below 20 m. The weight and size difference also results in different forms of transfer from one tree to another. Heavier males tend to use the stronger more stable lower parts of the tree structures in resting and feeding positions but for travelling they tend to choose lighter and more pliable branches or slim trunks to create a strong swaying motion. This facilitates effective bridging from one tree or branch to another. There has been disagreement as to whether the argument can be sustained for a causal relationship between spatial separation, sex differences, food preferences and size (Galdikas 1978; Sugardjito & van Hooff 1986).

There is no disagreement that body size affects foraging and travel capabilities (Peters 1983; Grand 1984; Temerin *et al.* 1984) and ultimately diet (Gaulin & Konner 1986) but the question is: why should this be so? Some writers have suggested that there was a sound survival strategy in younger and more defenceless primates travelling in the higher parts of the canopy (Crompton 1983). First, in the case of orang-utans, the clouded leopard would not easily reach there and second, enemies could be spotted far more readily from a very high vantage point (van Schaik *et al.* 1983). This would certainly make sense if it were not for the observation by Sugardjito and van Hooff that a mother with her young baby travelled at a *lower* part of the canopy than she did before pregnancy and lower than other females of her age and weight. They stipulate that she travelled at a lower level because, with the baby, her weight had increased. Thus, weight alone could be seen as an explanation for this behaviour (Sugardjito & van Hooff 1986).

In a recent study of chimpanzees (*Pan troglodytes*) it has been posited that not just body size but social rank is an important variable in positional behaviour (Hunt 1992). In many ways it confirms the findings of Sugardjito and van Hooff (1986) but Hunt warns that their findings demonstrate 'a complex interrelationship between social rank, body size, nearness of competitors and weight-bearing structure diameter that confounds simple comparison between large and small individuals' (Hunt 1992). In this study, the highest ranking males always secured the most stable sites (biggest branches/thickest tangles) suggesting that this stability allowed for two-handed feeding and less energy expenditure. To our knowledge, similar studies of the orang-utan taking account of possible rank do not exist, and of course such studies would be far more ambivalent and difficult to pursue in a species with a reputation for solitariness and elusiveness in treetops.

Köhler (1921) was one of the first to comment on a lack of leaping motions in the orang-utan compared to the chimpanzee. That information is borne out by other observations of orang-utans in their natural environment. In his extensive field studies,

MacKinnon saw only one example of a leaping orang-utan and this occurred when the animal was fleeing from the researcher (MacKinnon 1971). Unlike Köhler, who saw lack of leaping as a deficiency, we interpret it as another adaptation to a highly arboreal life by a large animal. The orang-utan moves from tree to tree by swinging or scrambling and always grasping a branch or creeper with at least one hand or foot, and usually more (Sugardjito & van Hooff 1986). Leaping is never used, although contrary to Köhler's claim, 'temporary energy derived from the motion of the body-mass' is in fact used, particularly in swaying. In a sense, this is assisted 'leaping', the only safe way for a large animal to move in the trees. The fact that neither the hands nor the feet are designed for landing on the ground but for gripping cylinder-shaped objects, such as branches (Napier 1960), is another consequence of adaptation to arboreal life rather than being an explanation for the absence of leaping, as Köhler claims (Rogers & Kaplan 1993). Thus, many of the behaviour patterns of orang-utans become more explicable when they are observed in their natural environment.

We want to say just a few more words on feet and posture in terms of locomotion. The feet of the orang-utan are designed more as a second pair of hands than as feet. When orang-utans walk, they tend to roll their feet on the outside, keeping the toes curled and they tend to avoid touching the ground with the whole sole of the foot. Orang-utans can stand upright and can also walk upright. One can occasionally observe them standing erect in a tree, but walking upright on the ground in the wild is rare and generally only observed in orang-utans who have been in human company for a long time (see photographs next page). Harrisson noted that young orang-utans attempted to stand erect from the age of 18 months onwards (B. Harrisson 1960) but this does not disprove our observations as these infant orang-utans were under Harrisson's charge and hence constantly exposed to humans.

There are numerous examples of erect posture in standing and walking in zoo environments. In the few cases of erect walking we have observed in semi-wild juvenile and subadult orang-utans at Sepilok, the individuals concerned supported themselves on a fixed structure, such as a bridge railing, horizontal branches or by leaning one hand against a house wall. Furthermore, these individuals had once been held as pets by locals, who presumably forced them to walk bipedally before they were released back into the forest. Even with practice and imitation, such a walk will never look easy to us, let alone elegant, precisely because their feet and even legs are not designed for landing on the ground and generally not for bipedal use. Again, the earlier literature on orang-utans tended to see these traits as deficiencies (cf. Yerkes & Yerkes {1945} re discussion of body posture from earlier observations).

To aid locomotion when walking on the ground orang-utans prefer to support themselves with their hands, using their knuckles together with other parts of the hand to touch the ground, although orang-utans do not perform 'true' knuckle-walking characteristic of chimpanzees and gorillas (Schwartz 1987). While their knuckles touch the ground their palm does so as well, as distinct from placing the entire weight of the body solely on the knuckles. It is not true, as has sometimes been claimed (Schlegel & Müller 1844, cited in Yerkes & Yerkes 1945), that orang-utans are awkward and slow,

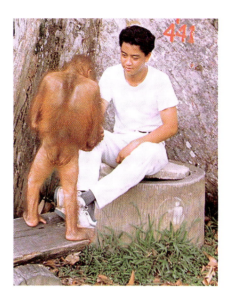

Bipedal posture

An upright stance when on the ground is more common amongst well-habituated orang-utans, such as BJ (above left) and Julie (above right) who managed to stand freely or walk with support. Amongst semi-wild orang-utans with less habituation but still some exposure to humans, we have seen this posture only once: standing upright in a tree (below). Here is the 'person of the forest' (orang-utan).

even helpless (Hornaday 1885) on the ground. They are indeed very fast when they desire to move quickly, and decidedly too fast for us. Of course a species without any noteworthy natural enemies, except for the now near-extinct clouded leopard and the python (and humans), without deadlines to meet and buses to catch, without the urgency of a hunter or being hunted, is usually not in a hurry. Moreover, the orang-utan throughout its long history of existence has been used to an abundance of food, unshared, as it is in its relatively solitary existence in a large terrain teeming with the most diverse plant life and fruit on earth.

Ground versus arboreal living

Every book on orang-utans repeats the statement that orang-utans are an arboreal species and the only one of the great apes to live almost exclusively in trees. In the process of attempting to understand locomotion in the canopies, it has remained almost a forgotten issue that orang-utans also may spend substantial periods of time on the ground. Human presence by itself may inhibit ground dwelling, walking, travelling or foraging. According to Harrisson, orang-utans did not just forage for fruit, nuts and other plant foods in the trees but searched for roots and vegetables on the ground.

Throughout the literature, from the eighteenth century onwards until very recently, there have been reports of very large ground-walking male orang-utans. For example, in 1971 John MacKinnon very nearly 'ran into' such a ground-walking, super-sized orang-utan in central Borneo (MacKinnon 1971). Biruté Galdikas spoke of such an encounter, too, when she first went to Tanjung Puting:

> I was rounding a turn in a ladang path when a huge orang-utan appeared, heading straight toward me. He was just ambling along, head down, oblivious to my presence. Then he stopped dead in his tracks less than twelve feet away. For long seconds he stared and stared. Abruptly, he whirled around and was gone.

> (cited in Freeman 1979)

Such meetings are not all that uncommon. We had a similar encounter with a large adult female called Clementine and her baby who seemed to appear from nowhere on the forest floor a mere half metre in front of us. There was nothing dramatic at all in this meeting. She looked at us and we looked at her. Gisela's camera was dangling around her chest and ready for use. So brief was the encounter that there was barely time to take a photograph (without flash). Clementine went off into the scrub and only seconds later we had lost sight of her. We saw her again later, high up in the canopy, quietly feeding while her infant was at liberty to climb nearby branches. Orang-utans move very quietly. The only noises one learns to distinguish in association with their travel is the rustling of branches or the occasional snapping sound of a twig. Ground-walking orang-utans may not break any twigs and even with good ears and an ever alert eye, it is very easy to miss their presence.

In the instances of ground walking we have cited so far, a relationship can be made between ground walking and weight. Clearly, for orang-utans of about 100 kg, locomotion in trees is affected by weight. The only adult male we ever saw on the ground at close enough range for extended observation presented himself on three different occasions over several years. On each of these occasions, he came down from the lower section of the canopy, sought a sheltered spot in thick scrub, sat on the forest floor and began feeding on whatever he had collected in one of his hands and mouth. This example may not refer so much to a need for locomotion on the ground because of weight but because he felt more comfortable feeding on the ground than in a tree. Of course, although a fully rehabilitated orang-utan, this behaviour may have been a consequence of exposure to human company.

But what of those average sized orang-utans who weigh a good deal less? Our own observations are inconclusive and anecdotal and, as just mentioned, they too were of rehabilitating orang-utans. We can report that from observations of 50 orang-utans, some individuals (one adolescent female and three young female orang-utans) spent as much as 50 percent of their time on the ground. Some subadult males stayed about a third of daily activity hours on the ground. Galdikas reported on one male who regularly travelled and foraged for as much as six hours per day on the ground (Freeman 1979). Galdikas even saw ground nests made by orang-utans for sleeping at night and resting during the day. In her field work she once followed a large male orang-utan for days, and in time he came down from the trees. It was her interpretation that eventually he lost his fear (or suspicion or just discomfort of having her follow him) that ultimately made him descend (Galdikas 1981b).

Various writers have given different explanations for these seemingly inconsistent observations. Van Hooff (1994) declared that in evolutionary terms, the orang-utan was 'the odd man out'. Harrisson concluded that it was 'fear of man' which drove orang-utans back into the trees (B. Harrisson 1960). teBoekhorst argued that orang-utans, just like other great apes, had not initially stayed in trees but had been driven back into an arboreal lifestyle by circumstances (teBoekhorst 1989). MacKinnon similarly pondered over the question of whether the orang-utans actually 'belonged' in the trees. Evidence from the Niah caves, such as teeth, had shown that generations ago the Bornean orang-utan was much larger than today and also showed more pronounced sexual dimorphism than even today (Harrisson 1957; Hooijer 1960). Like most other researchers, MacKinnon remained doubtful as to what might have caused a return to the trees, assuming that orang-utans had indeed once shifted to being ground-dwelling primates (MacKinnon 1971). His explanation involved a combination of factors. For one, he too cited the presence of human beings as the only ground-dwelling serious menace to orang-utans and interestingly he speculated that ground-dwelling parasites might have aided the return to the trees as well but he was not completely satisfied with this idea (MacKinnon 1971). There are leeches, mosquitoes, and other irritating or even dangerous parasites which can make life on the forest floor rather unpleasant. We hypothesise later that the orang-utan may well have been equipped with natural defences against most of these. Hence, we agree with MacKinnon that this latter explanation too remains unsatisfactory.

Ground dwelling, observed on so many occasions, is pitted against claims of near-exclusive arboreality in orang-utans. If a less arboreal past were systematically substantiated, it could lend some weight to teBoekhorst's evolutionary thesis but this requires at least one further qualification. The Sumatran orang-utan tends to be more arboreal than orang-utans in Borneo and the Sumatran subspecies is usually also smaller and lighter. The latter might explain their greater arboreality but the main reason given for their near exclusive arboreal existence has been that in Sumatra there still exists a formidable ground predator, the Sumatran tiger (Western 1994, Rijksen 1978). If this is the explanation it would suggest that orang-utans can easily adapt from one territory ground or trees to another, depending upon the absence or presence of risk. These questions, however, remain unanswered, as do many other issues about the evolution of the orang-utan.

Dietary habits of the orang-utan

The issue of locomotion and the theoretical questions associated with this and with arboreality cannot be solved by observing just their behaviour. We also need to consider their food sources. In the last chapter we described some of the features of the rainforest. One of the questions raised in the section on locomotion was: who travels at which level of the canopy and why? Various answers have been given. Studies on chimpanzees also revealed that positioning and type of locomotion is not just determined by weight or by issues of security but also by rank. The latter is more difficult to ascertain for orang-utans because they do not form close-knit family groups or troops and not all observations of rare orang-utan interactions can lead to unambiguous findings.

However, asking an entirely different question may shed new light on the matter. The question is: *where do trees bear fruit?* The variety of fruits of relevance to the orang-utan come from so-called 'primitive' trees, thus called by botanists for their place in the evolutionary story of plants (Corner 1949). They are said to be primitive because of their flowering and fruiting characteristics. Figs, durian, *langsat* and jackfruit belong to this category. They all bear fruit, not at the end of twigs and slender branches, but rather on the trunk itself or on the lower, thicker stems. The flowering and fruiting on the trunks, described first by Beccari (1904), is referred to as 'cauliflory' and that on the thicker lower branches as 'ramiflory'. Cauliflory (meaning growing on stalks/stems) in some species also involves fruiting right at the foot of the plant or even below ground, on the roots.

The theory that botanists put forward to explain these fruiting characteristics is that 'the fruit is thus placed within easy reach of the larger animals who will eat it and disperse the seed' (Veevers-Carter 1991). As we said before, several studies have already established that male orang-utans tend to travel and forage at *lower* levels of the canopy and females and juveniles at a higher level. It was also argued that females with infants or older offspring move to the lower part of the canopy (Mitani 1989). We suggest that similar to the study by Hunt (1992), it could be that the choice of height for foraging is not so much related to weight as to an expectation for finding the best fruit. Thus, dietary needs, as well as social ones, may determine the niche chosen by an orang-utan. It is of interest in this context that Galdikas after 10 years of study of the orang-utan in Tanjung Puting never once observed a female feeding in a tree in which a male was already foraging (Galdikas 1984). Rodman and Mitani have expressed reservations about a causal relationship between niche divergence and sexual dimorphism (Rodman & Mitani 1987) but, although the evidence is circumstantial, sexual differences in foraging would at least suggest a causal interrelationship explicable in terms of the position of fruiting on trees.

Studies on chimpanzees have also found substantial sex differences in dietary choices. In one study females were seen consistently to be engaged in termite fishing three times as often as their male counterparts and they consistently consumed less meat (McGrew 1992). Likewise in chimpanzees, the strong seasonality of some food items were noted that were not in themselves dependent on the seasons. Reports on carnivorous behaviour of females, and even on variety of mammalian species consumed, increased in certain months of the year (McGrew 1992).

We simply do not have the same detailed data analysis for the dietary habits of orang-utans as are available for chimpanzees and several other primate species (see Appendix 1). However, we do know from countless travel and scientific accounts that the fig and the durian belong to the staple diet of orang-utans and form some of their favourite foods (Wallace 1890; Hornaday 1885; MacKinnon 1974a). Locomotion and energy studies suggest that travel time decreases when a rich food source has been found (Galdikas 1988). MacKinnon noted that feeding time increased on fruit, particularly on durian (MacKinnon 1974a), while others have claimed that more time is spent feeding on leaves and bark because these take longer to process (Hladik 1977; Rodman 1984). These conflicting reports have not been resolved to date. Another source of food for the orang-utan and other primates is provided by the family of *Artocarpus* to which the breadfruit and the jackfruit belong. Clearly, orang-utans have an extremely high sugar intake. They will also brave bees' nests to get at honeycomb and have been observed to be successful in this (Western 1994).

To come back to the durian, it is by no means a food source just for orang-utans. Leaving aside the many insects which pollinate and feed on durian, quite a number of species, including elephants for instance, congregate at these trees at the time of ripening, attracted by the pungent smell. Orang-utans have succeeded in creating their own competitive niche for getting more than their share of durian. Clearly, if orang-utans had to compete with elephants for fruit, they would be forced to retreat. Instead, orang-utans are the only species who have learned to crack open the prickly hard shell before it opens of its own accord. They can therefore feed on the durian before it is ripe (Veevers-Carter 1991). This may give them a head-start of several days, enough to gorge themselves on the rich sugary (and intensely smelly) fruit. For the durian itself the orang-utan invasion is of little assistance. Most seeds are consumed and, as they are dropped in an unripe state before the shell bursts they are not able to germinate.

Most field researchers have noticed that at the time of the fruiting of the durian, orang-utans assemble in the durian tree in large numbers. It is certainly an indication of it being a favourite for the orang-utan palate. The fruiting season for the durian is actually rather long, from August through to December and peaking in the month of October.

Davenport's remark on the distribution of the durian is of some interest in terms of travelling time spent by orang-utans. He noted that uncultivated varieties occur at about one per 1.5 square kilometres (Davenport 1967). This observation suggests several things. It indicates that a predilection for the durian would still require a good deal of travel. While orang-utans (like most locals) gorge themselves on the fruit and may stay until they have exhausted the supply on a specific tree, thereby reducing their travel time, their interest in this food is such that they will eventually have to seek out another supply further afield, which could be as far as a few kilometres away.

The fact that all field researchers have noted a concentration of orang-utans in one tree during the fruiting months to some extent contradicts the notion of a stable foraging territory and the idea of 'resident' orang-utans in one terrain. Yet this is precisely what Rodman (1973), Horr (1975), Galdikas (1979) and Mitani (1985a, 1985b) found. Similar observations were made in Sumatra, more recently by Schürmann and Van Hooff (1986), Sugardjito *et al.* (1987) and teBoekhorst *et al.* (1990). Mitani *et al.* summarised their findings in this way:

> *All of these populations consisted of a stable set of resident adult females with dependent and older immature offspring. These females occupied overlapping but non-identical ranges. There were adult and subadult males in each population that lived within a fixed area; the home ranges of males overlapped those of one or more females. In addition to these resident animals, all populations included a set of non-resident individuals, which appeared to wander over larger regions. These patterns were consistent between studies and revealed that associations outside the maternal family were ephemeral.*

(Mitani *et al.* 1991)

The consistency in the reporting of these facts raises some questions. We recall the low density of orang-utans of one or two individuals per two square kilometres in most areas. This implies that every individual's territory (whether lone male or female and offspring group) might contain one durian tree and that the territory was chosen perhaps because of its presence. This tree could conceivably then become the exclusive 'property' of that resident orang-utan. Further, if any other orang-utan(s) entered the terrain and wanted to claim that tree, the 'resident' one would defend his/her 'property' and ward off the intruder. We know, of course, that nothing like this happens. Orang-utans usually do not engage in what is termed 'contest competition' (van Hooff 1994) and do not monopolise resources (see Chapter 6). The presence of a large number of orang-utans feeding peacefully together in one tree is ample evidence of this.

But where do the other orang-utans come from? Some must have left their own 'fixed' area in order to get to the durian tree. It is not always easy to decide between the push-and-pull phenomenon of species mobility. Did they leave their area because their own range at that time was unable to sustain them (pushed) or did they move because they were lured by the durian as a favourite food (pulled)? One argument that could be sustained is that, for such an assembly of orang-utans to occur, it would require the visiting orang-utans to know in advance of their travel that a durian tree existed further afield from their own home range. Why else would they leave their territory especially if that territory is sufficiently large to feed them?

Another reasonable explanation suggests far less premeditation and foreknowledge. We could then argue that they moved because their own territory could not provide enough food at certain times, forcing them further afield to search for new food sources. Although we have ample evidence that orang-utans know *what* they can eat, this does not necessarily imply that they also know *where* it can be found. The rainforest is diverse enough to permit a fairly haphazard trial-and-error wandering and stumbling in and out of various ranges without leading to starvation. It does not mean either that roaming provides them with the mental map of the area enabling them in the next season to remember the location and to find the same tree again. We suspect that they, in fact, do have a sound knowledge and sense of geography and know precisely where to find items of great interest to them. However, this question remains unsettled. They may possibly detect the fruit by smell at some distance.

In our view there is as much merit in the reports that argue for a seasonally determined semi-nomadic lifestyle of orang-utans. The observations of orang-utans gathered at durian trees do not need to contradict this at all. Semi-nomadic existence is defined as movement that follows a stable route of repeatedly visited areas according to seasons and usually has at least one anchor point or base camp. Even semi-nomadic groups can be regarded as having a home range encompassing the entire route of their travel. This definition is commonly used for human nomads and can be applied to orang-utans as well. Hence, Hornaday devised a locality timetable for orang-utans which clearly described seasonal movements. According to his observations, between January and May orang-utans were largely in the hills where fruiting occurred, then they moved to the depth of the forest between May and July and began to appear at the rivers in August, remaining there until about November/December (Hornaday 1885; cf. Reynolds 1967).

Such seasonal shifts would also help explain why we obtain such vastly different observational results on the percentage of time spent on ingesting certain food items. Davenport, for instance, noted that orang-utans fed on leaves and shoots for nearly 90 percent of the time (Davenport 1967). Rodman, on the other hand, established that orang-utans spend 64 percent of their feeding time on fruit, 21 percent on leaves, nine percent on bark, four percent on insects and two percent on 'other' food matters (Rodman 1988). The latter would presumably also include soil eating. These different observations may relate to seasonality and availability of food items. Orang-utans indeed use a large variety of leaves, particularly in non-fruiting times, and eat nuts and seeds of several trees, such as those of several oak species. They may also feed rather heavily on bark from some dipterocarp species (see Appendix 1). Here an important morphological difference from the other great apes becomes important, as Rodman and Mitani write:

> *The anterior dentition differs sharply from that of the African apes in the large size of the central upper incisors and the small size of the lateral upper incisors. Their molar*

teeth have thickened enamel like human molars, unlike those of chimpanzees and gorillas. These conditions resemble closely the dentition of Miocene hominoids of Africa and Asia classified as Sivapithecus and Ramapithecus (Pilbeam 1984).

(Rodman & Mitani 1987)

With the incisors they can gnaw away the inner cambium of the bark, discarding the fibrous parts. Yet, like chimpanzees and gorillas, orang-utans are largely frugivorous (fruit-eating).

Whatever arguments may be put forward for claiming a preponderance of one food over another at a given time, the overall and consistently observed pattern, reported by all field researchers, is that orang-utans eat a large variety of different things. Beccari was one of the first with a keen interest in orang-utan food sources. He commented on interesting fruit, such as the *Garcinia*, a mangosteen variant with an edible fruit, soursops (*Anona miricata*), the pawpaw (*Carica papaya*) and a fruit called *bua ruppi* of the *Euphorbia* tree (Beccari 1904). Schaller compiled a food list in 1961 on his first explorations. MacKinnon has provided an inventory of all foods eaten by orang-utans he found in his study area of Ulu Segama (see Appendix 1) and Biruté Galdikas has collected an impressive record of over 400 different food items (Galdikas 1994, personal communication). Furthermore, there have been studies of captive orang-utans, adding interesting information to and extending the food repertoire (Markham 1986). More of this later.

Over and above the frugivorous and herbivorous diets, there are now also extensive records to show that animal proteins are frequently and deliberately ingested (Tutin & Fernandez 1992) and are nutritionally important. There is a wide range of studies of the use of resources, both of plant and animal protein consumption, in chimpanzees. The internationally published information on orang-utans is, by contrast, relatively scanty. There are reports that suggest that orang-utans have similar habits and possibly similar requirements to chimpanzees. Harrisson noted the consumption of insects from bark and rotten timber and also mentioned bird and turtle eggs (B. Harrisson 1960). Similar observations, involving consumption of birds' eggs, especially those of seagulls, were recorded in Sumatra (Rijksen 1978). By far the most overwhelming evidence of ingestion of meat proteins is provided in the many reports of orang-utans feeding on ants, termites and a large variety of other insect species (B. Harrisson 1960; MacKinnon 1974a; Rijksen 1978; Galdikas 1978). Interestingly, before parturition two orang-utans increased their consumption of ants and termites dramatically (Galdikas 1982a). In addition, snails, slugs, worms and maggots were also regularly eaten.

More uncommonly, there is some evidence that orang-utans will very occasionally eat birds, lizards, mice and squirrels (see Markham 1986). Sugardjito and Nurhuda observed a rare and remarkable case of carnivorous behaviour in an adult female orang-utan who consumed an infant gibbon (Sugardjito & Nurhuda 1981). There are no examples of carnivorous bouts for the gorilla, whereas certain chimpanzee populations have developed extensive hunting skills, be this in Tai National Park in the Ivory Coast, West Africa (Boesch 1990) or at Gombe and Mahale National Parks, Tanzania. All of these different groups will regularly consume meat, usually from freshly caught monkeys.

The Tai chimpanzees however had developed better organisational skills as hunting teams than those at Gombe. Nevertheless, in Gombe National Park, an unbroken record of 10 years (1982–1991) clearly revealed that 400 colobus monkeys were killed and consumed by chimpanzees in that period (Stanford *et al.* 1993).

An interesting result with respect to African primates has been achieved in a study by Cheney and Wrangham, who were able to show an interrelationship between predation, body weight and arboreal/terrestrial lifestyle. In their study, arboreal primates had a consistently and considerably lower rate of successful predation than terrestrial ones and heavier arboreal primates above a certain weight were shown to score zero on the annual predation rate (Cheney & Wrangham 1987). Clearly, weight is an advantage on the ground if the strategy is to overpower an opponent but a distinct disadvantage in the trees, particularly when the prey is lighter and faster. Orang-utans would probably never succeed in capturing a live gibbon in a tree because of its fast locomotion and leaping capacity. The unusual sighting by Sugardjito and Nurhuda referred to a gibbon that was already dead. There have been several observations that some orang-utan females will eat the whole placenta or part thereof after birth (see Chapter 4 and Table 4), providing a nutritional requirement specifically for post-parturition females possibly related to lactation. There has been a recent report by Utami (1994) of orang-utans killing and eating slow loris (*Nicticebus coucang*). The observations were made at Ketambe, and there were six cases, five of the same individual. Both individuals performing this behaviour were females with babies. They appeared to stumble on the slow loris, then stared at it for up to 15 minutes before slapping it so that it fell to the ground. The orang-utan pursued the slow loris, grabbing it by the scruff of the neck and killing it by biting the cranium. The prey was then eaten. This may represent opportunistic carnivory, and it is not common.

It has also been shown that primates use certain plant foods, such as *Vernonia amygdalina,* for their medicinal value against a number of parasites, intestinal problems and even malaria (Huffman & Seifu 1989). Such regular use of leaf or stem eating for preventative or curative purposes has been recorded for baboons (Hamilton *et al.* 1978; Phillips-Conroy 1986) and for wild chimpanzees (Takasaki & Hunt 1987). Further analysis of leaves and stems of specific plants eaten by primates, such as *Aspilia mossambicensis* and *A. pluriseta*, revealed that these contained thiarubrine A, a potent (photoactive) antibiotic with possible medicinal value in secondary infections of certain immune diseases, such as AIDS. These plants are ingested in areas where corresponding diseases or infections are known to occur in relatively high incidence (Dossaji *et al.* 1989). Such detail has not yet been recorded for orang-utans.

As an aside, it may also be noted that one of the early studies reported soil-eating and smearing of soil on the body. Köhler judged these habits as 'unclean' (Köhler 1921). Sometimes clay is smeared over the face and arms, as Barbara Harrisson (1960) reported, and we also observed it at Semengoh. Soil-eating is common in orang-utans living in their natural environment, and has also been reported for gorillas (Mahaney 1993). Presumably ingestions may help alleviate dietary deficiencies in, for example, certain minerals. Alternatively, certain substances could play a role in curing intestinal ailments or simply assist in digestion. We observed soil-eating on several occasions at Sepilok, confirming Harrisson's observations (1963) and those by other field workers. Three orang-utans under Harrisson's charge ate soil regularly from an early age, one preferring clay and the other a variety of soils (B. Harrisson 1960).

This female orang-utan in Semengoh, Sarawak, had smeared her entire body with mud. We have not seen similar behaviour in Sabah, although we noticed traces of mud on one or two orang-utan juveniles on one occasion.

4

Sexual behaviour and reproduction

Sociality and gender difference

Before moving on to discuss forms of sexual behaviour in the orang-utan, it is essential to refer first to their social organisation and interactions. The single most important observation to be made in this context is that orang-utans differ substantially from other primates and especially from the other great apes in their social organisation. Orang-utans are less well described by referring to troops, dominance hierarchies or communities. As we have already pointed out in previous chapters, orang-utans tend to move solitarily or in small 'natal' groups, ie mother with offspring. It is less easy to impose upon the orang-utan the kind of vocabulary with which we tend to describe human society, as a basically gregarious, group-living organisation. Words like 'competition' or 'status', for instance, can do relatively little to confer knowledge and meaning on orang-utan behaviour. Another example might be to refer to play behaviour, to which we tend to ascribe important social and survival functions. Much of play behaviour is dependent on group interaction. This is true of non-human primates and humans. In play, infants are said to develop the skills that they will later need for survival (Baldwin 1986). In the orang-utan, there is relatively little evidence of play with other individuals in the natural environment and its occurrence is rudimentary compared to chimpanzees and gorillas (Horr 1977). Free-ranging infants in their natural habitat often have just one companion, their mother, who will play only rarely (Maple & Zucker 1978). In captivity or in situations of overcrowding, as at rehabilitation centres, orang-utan juveniles may play extensively with each other but it would be difficult to maintain that their survival depends on play learning. It would be equally absurd to propose that they are deprived in the natural habitat, a 'problem' only overcome by overcrowding or captivity. It is possible that increased playing in captivity helps the orang-utans to adjust to the greater need to be more

73

sociable. We cannot enter here into the complex debates on play theories other than to suggest that, again conceptually, it is difficult to adapt a whole body of theories to descriptions of orang-utan behaviour.

In field studies it is often difficult to say what the biological relationships between orang-utans are and whether mother and daughter or siblings meet again later in life and retain loose ties with each other. Until about 10 years ago, we had little information other than anecdotal accounts of the social interaction (sociality) of orang-utans. Such systematic studies began with Rijksen in Sumatra and with Galdikas in Kalimantan Tengah. By far the largest and most consistent study of orang-utan sociality comes from Galdikas, based on continuous observation of free-ranging orang-utans in the Tanjung Puting National Park. Over the many years of her observations, a much clearer picture has emerged, at least for the population in the Tanjung Puting region. According to these observations, there is a strong sex and age difference in sociality among orang-utans (based on Galdikas 1985). Her observations are valuable precisely because of the distinctions made according to age and sex. We summarise this material here in order to highlight some important aspects of social interaction which have a bearing on sexual behaviour.

According to Galdikas, and reconfirmed in many other studies preceding and post-dating her work, mature adult males show a marked aversion to each other. They live solitary lives for 91 percent of the time. The remaining nine percent is composed of three types of contact involving physical proximity; the most important one consisting of sexual consortships with one female. Such a consort relationship may last for a few weeks at a time. In the Galdikas study, contacts exclusively with other males accounted for a total of only 1.1 percent of social contacts, one percent of which was with subadult males. The remaining small fraction of 0.1 percent describes all the contact ever observed which a mature adult male in the Tanjung Puting area has had with another mature adult male (Galdikas 1985a). There are countless reports from the nineteenth century onwards to verify that, when these rare encounters occur, they are generally hostile, ranging from threat gestures to confrontation and even brief but fierce fights causing at times severe injuries (Hornaday 1885; Galdikas 1994).

From Galdikas' observations it can be ascertained that *social* life is almost entirely female-centred. Although adult females do not spend any more time with other orang-utans than do males (about 10 to 13 percent), there is an important difference; the 87 to 90 percent counted as 'solitary' may not necessarily imply that adult females are alone because they often have their own offspring with them. This could mean one or two offspring of different ages spread over a period of five to seven years at any one time after giving birth to the first offspring. This is a substantial period of time. In general, this period of time of rearing an offspring is oddly considered part of 'solitary' life. From the perspective of human society, the contact with an offspring may not be regarded as 'satisfying'. Obviously, human prejudice regards any contact with a conspecific (member of the same species) as a social interaction only if the other is considered of 'peer-group' status, ie of similar age and an adult. Contact of mother and child is considered 'solitary', both from the point of view of the offspring and from the point of view of the mother. Hence data for solitary time and time spent with mother or mother with offspring are usually counted together as one.

Whatever the definition may be, the adult female in fact spends very little time *alone*. If adult females do spend time with others outside the mother–offspring dyad or tryad, it is largely with a consorting adult male (75 percent of all social encounters) and the remainder of the time subdivided amongst subadults or other adult females (Galdikas 1984). Adolescent females are the most gregarious. They spend half their time in either their 'natal' group (family of origin, including mother and possibly another sibling) or alone, and the other half of their time with others, either with other adolescent females or with subadult males. Subadult males will usually choose females for company rather than a male (Galdikas 1984, 1985c).

When orang-utans are seen together, there can be a number of groupings and arrangements. Some of these may be quite fleeting and accidental and dictated by a specific and preferred food source. Two adult females with their offspring may stay together for a few hours or even days. Adolescent females may travel together and subadult males may hang about where adult females and adolescent females are found. We observed an adult female with her six-month old infant and a subadult male staying together for the best part of four days. The subadult male had in fact adopted, or been adopted by, an 18-month old orphaned infant male but during his encounter with the adult female his charge was not with him. Galdikas has observed 67 different combinations of groupings and of those 27 were seen only once. But whatever the groupings were at the time, whether consorting couples, natal groups, casual 'friendships' or brief associations, none of these could aptly be described as constituting a community structure (Galdikas 1984).

Hornaday, and later Zuckerman implied a community structure by suggesting that the social life 'of the orang has its basis in the harem, which is maintained by the dominance of its overlord' (Zuckerman 1981). This is a drastically different interpretation to our claim that the social life of the orang-utan is female-centred. The deduction was made initially by Hornaday after evidence of witnessing severe fighting amongst adult males which resulted, as mentioned before, in mutilation and severe injuries (Hornaday 1885).

There are several reasons why their (Hornaday's and Zuckerman's) suggestion of a social structure based on harems needs to be treated with caution. When Hornaday visited Borneo, one of his main purposes for the expedition was to take back specimens of orang-utans for use in the museums of Europe. About two hundred orang-utans were exported to Europe in a very brief period around the time of Hornaday's Borneo experience. All the orang-utans were taken from Sarawak. To gain live samples, the mothers were shot. It is possible that the carnage brought about by massive exports caused a severe shortage of females and that the remaining orang-utans fled from the onslaught. A combination of lowering the number of females and herding the males into several areas would have been an unnatural and atypical occurrence and might have resulted in high stress and high levels of aggressive behaviour. MacKinnon noted that the presence of several adult males in one region produced bouts of ill-temper, increased the number of long calls and reduced the reproductive rates of females (MacKinnon 1984).

Further, the common assumption of territorial claims by male orang-utans, ie defending territory and females, has only rarely been observed. This is an assumption taken from chimpanzee research where territorial behaviour of males has been shown (Kawanaka 1989). Rather, there is evidence, as Galdikas suggests, that adult males defend their own *personal* space rather than a large area that may be defined as a territory and will be irritated if this is encroached upon (Galdikas 1985a, 1985b). In general, male orang-utans seem to be increasingly intolerant of each other with growing age. Bashing of leaves and snagging can be seen when one adult male hears another adult male call.

Individual development and sexual behaviour

The individual development of the orang-utan, particularly of the reproductive and sexual characteristics of the female, is one of the most intriguing aspects in terms of evolutionary debates. We have raised some evolutionary arguments in the last chapter. The sexual and reproductive behaviour of orang-utans raises these again, even more forcefully. The question was posed in the previous chapter whether similarity of characteristics was evidence of common ancestry or an expression of analogous relationships. Schwartz posits that particularly in the area of reproduction, uniquely shared morphologies between humans and orang-utans point to evolutionary relatedness, and one that is closer than has been hitherto assumed. In a review article (Schwartz 1984) he assembled a table of shared morphologies for all great apes and humans, listing nine morphological features that humans and all the great apes have in common. He found only one feature that chimpanzees and gorillas share (concerning knuckle-walking), but 17 morphological features that occur only in humans and orang-utans. If we add to the 17 morphologies the later discovery made by Thiranagama *et al.* (1991) of the presence of a medial vein in the forearm exclusively found in humans and orang-utans, we obtain a total of 18 morphological features shared by humans and orang-utans but not the other apes. Significantly, six of these shared features in Schwartz's schemata concern reproduction and sexual behaviour (see Appendix 2).

As Table 4 below shows, there are substantial similarities between the reproductive cycles in human and orang-utan females. For the onset of menstrual cycles (menarche) we have few reliable data. The age of five, listed here as premature menarche onset, was observed in a zoo environment and similar data come from other captive environments. Prematurity may be a function of stress. We do not have sufficient data for onset of menarche from free-ranging orang-utans to reliably establish the range. Judging by the first successful pregnancies of females in the wild one would be led to believe that it may occur between the ages of nine and 11, just slightly earlier than in human females. The data for menopause are equally scanty. One captive orang-utan female was reported to have normal menstrual cycles still at the age of 47 (Master &

Table 4: Reproductive cycle of the orang-utan

Event/Process	Period/Age	Symptoms	Papers on subject
Menarche onset	5 years (premature) 11 years (late) average of 7–8		
Menopause	48 years		Masters & Markham 1991
Menstrual cycle	22 days (shortest) 30 days (longest) (the number of cycles may vary from 5 to 51 cycles per annum)		Collins *et al.* 1975 Graham 1981 Nadler *et al.* 1984 Markham 1990 Masters & Markham 1991
Pregnancy detection	16–22 days after conception and possibly earlier	labial swelling (abrupt appearance of oedema of the labia majora)	Galdikas 1981 van der Werfften-Bosch 1982 Schürmann 1982 Sodaro 1988
Gestation period	227–301 days average of 8 months or more	behaviour variations sometimes very marked and developing progressively	Napier & Napier 1967 Schultz 1969 Brandt & Mitchell 1971 Martin 1981 Galdikas 1982a
Labour/birth	1–4 hours		Graham-Jones & Hill 1962 Asano 1967 Brandt & Mitchell 1971 De Silva 1972 Maple 1980
Lactation	2–4 years	suppression of cyclic ovation activity reported (amenorrhoea)	Markham 1990 Masters & Markham 1991
Postpartum care	immediate	licking infant, breathing into mouth, biting off umbilical cord, eating of placenta observed at times, also blowing air into nostrils of infant	De Silva 1972, Horr 1977, Galdikas 1981a

Source: Voight 1984

Markham 1991). Again, this age would be very similar to menopause experienced in human females. Considerable variability occurs both in humans and in orang-utans.

The menstrual cycle itself is identical to the human menstrual cycle, but more importantly, both orang-utan and human females show the highest oestriol levels of any primates or great apes during the menstrual cycle. Also, the gestation period of humans and orang-utans are very atypical of primates and very distinct from the other great apes. In both, the gestation period is about nine months, although in orang-utans it is on average two weeks shorter than in humans but much longer than in other great apes. Both human babies and orang-utan infants are helpless at birth. Development of an offspring in primates takes longest in humans and orang-utans and then produces the least viable offspring for independent survival. There are some differences in development rates of motor coordination, the human baby needing longer than the orang-utan infant in some ways, but beyond basic motor coordination (clinging in the orang-utan), both need years of support and care before independence.

Pregnancy in orang-utans generally follows the same pattern as in humans. Progressively, the abdomen and the mammae become enlarged, noticeably so in the third trimester. Behavioural changes have also been noted as for most other primates (Coe 1990). These may involve vomiting, postural changes and unusual postures. Just a few hours prior to giving birth, as Galdikas noted, a wild female orang-utan was agitated, often changed position and hugged the trunk of a tree (1981a). Unusual postures have been regarded as a way of attempting to ease the strain of pregnancy on the lower back and/or to decrease fluid accumulation in the lower extremities, 'as occurs in humans' (Shively & Mitchell 1986).

Several births have been described but almost all of them concerned births in captive environments and one has been described in the context of the Sepilok Rehabilitation Centre (De Silva 1972). It is difficult to observe a birth in the wild because it rarely occurs. Females often have few offspring with long inter-birth intervals (Galdikas & Wood 1990). The adults are dispersed through the forest and, when the time comes for giving birth, females build nests, obstructing the view of observers. Birth (parturition) takes place in the nest high above in a tree and it usually occurs at night. The female may not leave the nest for a day following parturition (Galdikas 1981a). The period of labour appears to be shorter than in human females but the intensity and sequencing of contractions is similar. From the data we have, Shively and Mitchell (1986) conclude that there is a great deal of variability in behaviour at the time of giving birth. Differences occurred between orang-utan females who had given birth before (multipara) and those females who gave birth for the first time (primipara). Multipara labours tended to be shorter and easier labours and females also appeared more 'confident' before and after birth (Shively & Mitchell 1986). The similarity with human behaviour is evident. There are, however, instances where orang-utan females have been observed consuming part or all of the placenta (placentophagia) also observed in a diverse number of primate species (Coe 1990). This does not always occur, however, and was not noted in the observed birth in the wild. Here the cord and placenta were still attached the day after birth and the cord fell off on the third day after birth (Galdikas 1981a).

There is far less material available on the development of secondary sexual characteristics in male orang-utans and on age of maturation. Great variability also marks the sexual developmental stages in the male. Sub-adulthood in males is often defined as the period between the ages of eight and 15 years, after which time they may rapidly grow the pronounced cheek pads so distinctive in the Bornean orang-utan (*Pongo pygmaeus pygmaeus*) as well as the full laryngeal sac, which enables the male orang-utan to make calls that are audible for miles. The age range of sub-adulthood has been described differently by different observers: either age eight to 13 or 15 (Rijksen 1978) or 10–15 (MacKinnon 1971). However, the onset of the full development of sexual maturity and of secondary sex characteristics is context dependent. In captive orang-utans, fertile matings have occurred as early as at the age of six, although it has also been noted that subadult sexual behaviour had the least reproductive success. On the other hand, full cheek pad development has been delayed until the age of 19, depending on the presence of another male (Winkler 1989). The presence of another adult male is said to suppress or at least retard the development of cheek pads. One dramatic example has been given in a zoo environment where the adult was removed and the subadult left behind. The cheek pads developed immediately (Maple 1980). This is puzzling in so far as cheek pad development does not coincide with sexual maturity. Both the cheek pad compartment and the laryngeal sacs are present in all ages and both sexes but they develop fully only in males (Winkler 1989).

We know that birth intervals in other great apes are relatively long. For mountain gorillas these are about four to five years and for chimpanzees, six years (cf. Galdikas 1982a). It has recently been established that birth intervals in orang-utans are 92.6 months ± 2.4, giving an average birth-spacing for the orang-utan of about eight years (Galdikas & Wood 1990). This extremely low reproductive rate hints at two important and inter-related variables. It suggests a low infant mortality and an extremely high investment in care to ensure the survival of offspring. From an evolutionary point of view it furthermore suggests an absence of predators. Once a predator appears in large numbers, as humans have, the species as a whole is extremely vulnerable and threatened because its reproductive tempo is not geared for a fast replenishing of individuals. Moreover, as we have shown in the first section of this chapter, the social organisation is such that meeting of other orang-utans is sporadic and by no means assured on a regular basis. This is one substantial difference from humans and one that may well be fatal to the orang-utans.

Sexual interaction

The most profound similarity between humans and orang-utans, however, concerns sexuality in general and the sexual act itself. The latter is different from that of the gorilla and the common chimpanzee. In these great ape species sexual activity follows a well-identified set of rules and serves reproduction. Gorilla and common chimpanzee males mount females from behind. The actual intercourse is a matter of seconds or at least under one minute. Males mount females when they are in oestrus and sexual activity does not occur otherwise. Group living allows the males to regularly inspect whether a female has come into oestrus and he can time his sexual activity accordingly. Female genitalia swell and often change colour as well, giving a clear signal to the male about the receptivity of the female.

None of this efficient system of reproduction is repeated in the orang-utans or in humans. There are a number of findings worth reiterating here in order to exemplify that in orang-utans, as in humans, sexuality is not sufficiently explained by understanding and describing reproduction. Indeed, orang-utans display sexual activity outside the context of reproduction. Sexual interest may be intense from an early age. Captive orang-utan males have been observed to have erections at 13 months of age and of showing interest in the anogenital region of others by the age of 16 months (Voigt 1984; see Table 5 below). Amongst semi-wild, free-ranging orang-utans we observed an erection in an 18–24-month old infant. We filmed a half-hour sequence of a mother–infant interaction in poor light. Upon viewing the film, we realised that the entire sequence showed sexually exploratory behaviour by the male infant. The mother rested comfortably on her back in a tree with her legs spread apart. The infant explored her vagina in detail, both by touching, by inserting a finger into her vagina and by pressing his own genitals against hers. He also lip-touched her vagina and licked it tentatively. He repeated these sequences several times, being distracted every time by his erect penis at which he kept looking in short intervals. The mother remained motionless throughout the period of his exploratory behaviour. His penis eventually became flaccid and the infant turned his attention to some leaves and branches next to the mother's legs. Harrisson reported that young males masturbate frequently and she observed erections in free-ranging orang-utan infants at the age of four and a half months. One favourite in Barbara Harrisson's group of infants and juveniles used to rub his penis in between her toes (B. Harrisson 1960). We have seen no reports of female masturbation but there are reports of adolescent females making 'unmistakable advances' to subadult males, either by placing their genitals near a male's face in an inviting gesture or by beginning to manipulate his penis (Kavanagh 1983).

Table 5: Developmental stages of orang-utan infants (male and female) aged 12–18 months in captivity (group of infants without mother)

Behaviour	Age (in months)
First erection	13
Active approach to others in group	14
Object directed behaviour	14
Interest in own genitalia	16
Interest in the anogenital region of others	16
First nest-building motions	16
Using twigs as pillow	16

Source: Voigt 1984

Instances of 'flirts'

An adolescent female approaching a subadult male and touching him (top). A flirt in slow motion (bottom left and right). Subadult male (Raja) has approached adult female (Jessica). He first sat near her, slowly edging his left hand to touch hers. Notice that he finally 'kissed' Jessica's knee. In the entire sequence (half an hour) the two mostly avoided each other's gaze (see Chapter 6).

Subadult males are the most promiscuous. Their sex life is well developed and they will try to obtain a sexual opportunity by just about any means. Befriending an adolescent female is one way; another that subadult males have been known to use is to follow a consorting pair and, when the male is out of auditory range of twig breaking and rustling sounds, he will quickly attempt to reach the female and mate with her (Galdikas 1985c). In nearly a third of all sexual activity, the subadult male attempts to seek gratification through rape. Rape tends to occur not by ambushing a lone female but usually within a group (Galdikas 1985c). Rape attacks have been observed to be almost surprise attacks that follow within minutes of meeting the female. Rape usually occurs by holding the victim down. Females usually scream and struggle and not every rape leads to penis insertion or to ejaculation. Infants of adult females are also known to attack these subadult males by trying to pull them away from their mother (Kavanagh 1983). Reports from captive and free-ranging orang-utans suggest that females do not get pregnant from rape but only from mutually motivated sex (Kavanagh 1983). In other words, sexual behaviours in orang-utans suggest that sexuality occurs, irrespective of reproduction, just as in humans and in bonobos (pygmy chimpanzees).

The sexual act, and the lead-up to it, likewise finds no equivalent in primate behaviour other than that in humans. Amongst the non-human primates the orang-utan is the only one practising sex exclusively in the frontal position as humans do. Amongst the great apes (gorilla, chimpanzee, bonobo, orang-utan) face-to-face sex occurs only amongst bonobos and orang-utans but exclusively so only in orang-utans. In bonobos, up to a quarter of all matings may be face-to-face, with the qualification that more of this behaviour occurs in captivity than in the wild and that a large percentage of face-to-face sexual encounters are between females (Thompson-Handler *et al.* 1984). We recall that male gorillas and common chimpanzees mount females from behind. There is no foreplay involved in male–female mounting amongst gorillas and chimpanzees, including the bonobo, although sexual intercourse may be initiated by females in almost half of all cases of matings observed amongst chimpanzees (Tutin & McGinnis 1981; Graham & Nadler 1990).

The difference in behaviour in the orang-utan is partly explicable by the lack of swelling (tumescence) of the female genitalia at the time of receptivity. Gorilla and chimpanzee males may well walk around inspecting their females from behind but orang-utan males have no such easy task. As in humans, there are no outward signs for males to judge the receptivity of females. We have seen no evidence in the literature that orang-utan males can identify receptiveness by smell. It therefore appears that amongst orang-utans, as in humans, making sexual contact is a guessing game, based on some negotiation and persuasion. Copulation amongst orang-utans is not confined to a specific part of the menstrual cycle (Schwartz 1984), although Masters and Markham (1991) have noted that sexual activities of females were concentrated in days 11 to 17 of the menstrual cycle (75 percent of all sexual activity). We have further evidence that sexual activity is partly at least determined by the female. In a test of captive adult orang-utans, mating behaviour was observed. When the adult male had free access to the female, the number of copulatory bouts increased well beyond that known in the wild and also resulted in rape (Nadler 1977; Nadler & Collins 1991). However, when access was restricted and was determined solely by the adult female, copulations decreased substantially (Nadler 1988; Nadler & Collins 1991). This is in agreement with observations of female orang-utans in the wild who have been seen to move to higher ground and away on hearing the male long call from a distance (Horr 1975) and avoiding male contact when they had infants to care for.

In orang-utans, foreplay may be extensive and unhurried. We have seen part of this behaviour ourselves in Sabah. 'Making advances' can take a variety of forms. This may involve sitting next to each other and casually touching the body of the other. Subadult males have been observed to put their arms around the female (Kavanagh 1983, and own observation) and/or touch the face of the other and the region of the ear with their lips. In the instances we have observed, a subadult male with an adult female (Raja and Jessica), the female looked away and gave an air of total lack of interest during the proceedings. We know, however, that in situations when the female is definitely not interested, she will either move away or even threaten the male, be this a subadult or a fully grown mature male (Horr 1975). Unless she actively solicits, which, as we said, does happen, her passive behaviour defines at least a lack of protest. Part of the sexual foreplay includes the male licking the female genitalia and fondling of the anogenital region (Kavanagh 1983).

Intercourse between consorting orang-utan pairs, as said, occurs face-to-face and may be executed in a number of positions. This may take the form of hanging from branches, facing each other and embracing each other with the legs. In the 'missionary position' the female lies on her back and the male is seated between her legs or on top of her, although not touching her body. Alternatively, the male may lie on his back against the branches of a tree and be straddled by the female who performs the thrusting motions (Kavanagh 1983). Copulatory bouts are the longest amongst non-human primates and are equal in length of time only to those of humans. The average copulation time in the Tanjung Puting area was observed to be 10.8 minutes, ranging from 3–28 minutes in the wild and even longer in captivity (Galdikas & Wood 1990). Furthermore, the fact that females may scream towards or at the end of the copulatory bout suggests that the female has a sexual experience which may be described as orgasmic. She may also emit a specific vocalisation during rape. These particular screams do not occur at any other time and are hence strongly associated with intercourse (MacKinnon 1971; cf. also Kavanagh 1983 for different vocalisation in rape). Rodman and Mitani (1987) noted that the marked sexual dimorphism of orang-utans may have evolved because it confers a mating advantage of older males over younger male rivals. Indeed, large males have been known to disrupt mating by other males and adult males may supplant smaller ones (Rodman & Mitani 1987). Such a change of partner during intercourse would hardly be possible if the mating bout lasted only a few seconds. Thus, mating in the orang-utan is vulnerable to interruption because it takes so long to complete the act of copulation, compared to the gorilla and the chimpanzee.

Sexual activity by a consorting couple may continue on a daily basis for a number of weeks. Thereafter, both go their separate way. The duration of oestrus is five to six days in female orang-utans, two to three in gorillas and 10–14 days in chimpanzees (Graham & Nadler 1990). Following the consorting period, pregnancy may be detected two to three weeks after conception. The outer labia begin to swell and the swelling becomes very pronounced (Schürmann 1982; Sodaro 1988). This is one time when sniffing by subadult males seems to occur. On sniffing the region of the swelling, they will let go of the female and not make any sexual advances. The pregnant female tends to go off on her own and except for the presence of another offspring, she usually gives birth on her own. Males do not take part in any parenting, nor have they been seen to function as protectors of females, except when warding off males from a receptive female. Early reports from observation of wild orang-utans in Borneo suggested that males did come to the defence of females but the social context of these observations was not made clear (Beccari 1904). Bornean female orang-utans derive no benefit from their males other than sexual contact and the offspring itself.

Mother–infant interaction

It is now obvious that the neonatal orang-utan is not born into a group, has no aunts, uncles, cousins or nursemaids. It may have a sibling, who may behave in ways that would suggest extreme jealousy, but otherwise there are few contacts apart from the mother in early life. Unlike any other primate species, the orang-utan mother provides the sum total of life experience for the infant. She is its only means of transport, of support, food, comfort, safety, often the only source of information and of providing essential learning experiences. She is the sole caregiver and the infant is dependent on her abilities and attentions to an extent rarely found in other species.

Moreover, apart from humans, orang-utans have the slowest rate of development of any primate. Contact behaviour in the first 12 months of life is extremely high and, with some fluctuations, is maintained well beyond the first year of life (Horwich 1989). Mother–infant interaction, while not demonstrative in most cases, is nevertheless intense. Harrisson observed that the infant communicates affection to the mother in a number of distinct ways. It may expose its gums or teeth (ie smile), open the mouth widely, 'bite' the mother's face gently and lick the mother's lips and mouth occasionally. Another affectionate behaviour seen has been a 'combing' of the hair and limbs with the mouth and with the fingertips (B. Harrisson 1960). We have wondered whether the gestures by Abbie towards Gisela, tracing the lines of Gisela's hands with her fingertips (see Chapter 5), has its origin in the affectionate repertoire observed in orang-utan infants.

The mother, in turn, will respond in several ways. She will provide the transport, the security and the food that is needed. MacKinnon has described some play behaviour of mothers towards their infants, such as tickling, biting, poking and gently knocking with closed fists (MacKinnon 1971). The orang-utan mother will occasionally respond to the infant's movements and signs of affection by hugging and cradling (especially when the infant is very young). We have observed a primiparous mother with a six-day old infant. She fondled and touched the infant repeatedly over a two-hour

Jessica cradling her baby (top). This is observed only in the very first stages of development after birth although clinging behaviour is apparent even for the neonate. Later on, the infant will cling to the mother independently. Note Jessica's smile. Jessica about to place a kiss on the tiny hand of the neonate which she has slipped around her middle finger (bottom left). The mother places her mouth very gently over the entire face of the neonate (bottom right). We have not seen this behaviour before or since and could not find an explanation for it.

observation period, investigating the infant's arms, legs, taking the small hands gently into hers and inspecting the fingers. She also took the infant's head and placed the face as far into her mouth as she could. She cradled and held it closely seeming entirely absorbed in her baby and, judging by her facial expression, she was smiling (see photograph on p.85).

Orang-utan mothers will not seek contact with other males and may ward them off, even mature adult males. In its early infancy, she will ensure that the infant is constantly attached to her body (see Table 6) and, when the infant is allowed brief periods of independent investigation, swinging, playing or climbing, she ensures that it remains close to her. From early on she restricts the infant from moving away and may emit a deep belching sound to recall it. In most cases the infant will instantly return to her (Davenport 1967). Between the first and second year of the infant's development there is evidence of some independent feeding (MacKinnon 1971). With these foraging or playful excursions the proximal interaction diminishes slightly. The offspring has learned to respond instantly on the minutest signal of its mother and will rush back to her. By the age of two years, the young orang-utan moves and feeds independently of its mother. There may be situations when the infant needs help in climbing or in getting to another tree. In these cases, the mother will give assistance (Davenport 1967; MacKinnon 1971). Even the juvenile will follow the mother for a long time, sometimes holding on to her hair on the rump (Davenport 1967). Hence also the distal behaviours, ie behaviours that require no touching but some form of communication (Lewis 1978), suggest a mutual reliance on appropriate signals between mother and offspring.

The infant, as a complex and sophisticated organism, is a discovery of the twentieth century. William James (*The Principles of Psychology,* 1890) still thought that infants were 'insensate' and their sensory perception was scrambled and confused. We know now that this is not the case. Infants are capable of processing very complex information (Lewis 1978) and further studies on primate infants and those of the great apes have confirmed this view. Indeed, studies on neonatal chimpanzees revealed sustained attention to visual and auditory stimuli (Bard *et al.* 1992). In the response to the external world, it has been found that social stimuli result in higher attention rates than non-social stimuli, ie the face of the mother or her sounds and gestures. This, Bard *et al.* argued, showed that humans were not unique among primates in the ability to engage in face-to-face contact (Bard *et al.* 1992).

Coe distinguishes three phases of maternal behaviour: developmentally the first phase is one of support and solicitousness. At the time of the infant's ability to stray from the mother's body, her behaviours are described as being ambivalent towards infant autonomy (phase two), and finally there is a period of weaning and of active rejection (see Table 6). These stages in maternal care are fitted into a period of three to six months for prosimians, six to 12 months for monkeys and four to six *years* for apes (Coe 1990). As the development of orang-utans is the slowest amongst the great apes, the primary (and only) caregiving by the mother is the longest and most intense period of any primate except humans. Hence also the period of proximal behaviour is the

Table 6: Infant Development

Age	Feeding	Relation to Mother	Reports
Birth (weight average 1.5kg)			Walker 1964
Birth	suckling induced	• cradled, held, resting on ventrum	Galdikas 1982a
First day	suckling	• possibly still held or resting on ventrum, female may stay in nest	Horr 1977
Days 2–5	suckling	• clinging to mother has been observed	Brandes 1939
1–6 months	suckling occasional manipulation of solid food items, mother masticates food and presents it to infant's mouth	• does not leave mother's body but crawls over the body and may hang from it • transported exclusively on mother • mothers may readjust infants prior to locomotion • Horr suggests that mothers sometimes withhold the breast from infants of about 4–5 months as part of a long weaning process	Horr 1977 Horr 1977
8–12 months	suckling, plucks and mouths food objects might ingest some solids	• occasional departure from mother's body when mother rests or feeds, hanging from nearby branch, increase of this activity by 11 months • substantial amount of manipulation of objects • mimicking of mother's threat behaviour • mimicking feeding behaviour in mirror image • also first attempts to construct nest contact with a sibling usually prevented by mother (stops infant from crawling to older sibling)	Horr 1977 Horr 1977 Kaplan & Roger (in this book)
Juvenile (aged 2 years)	weaned	• increased distancing of mother from sibling, juvenile may feed several trees away from mother but will travel at a distance of a maximum of 18–27 m behind mother and closely behind her in difficult terrain	MacKinnon 1971 Horr 1977
$3\frac{1}{2}$ years		• mother may give assistance when needed to bridge trees, mimicking locomotion of mother, juvenile anxious when distance increased	
$4\frac{1}{2}$+ years		• mother begins to reject juvenile by warding-off grunts and back of hand push; • 'spectacular' tantrum by juvenile when mother prevents juvenile entering nest	
4–6 years		• nursed in captivity for up to six years of age	Walker 1964

most intense and longest of any primate species, again with the exception of humans. One needs to add that chimpanzees, gorillas and humans raise their young typically in groups or families and infants may therefore not have such intimate mothering as orang-utan infants are given.

There are several consequences of this degree of dependency and emotional closeness between mother and infant. When the mother dies or is separated from the infant, the entire world and all its resources go with it for the orang-utan infant. An interesting study by Codner and Nadler tested the hypothesis that, amongst the great apes, emotional dependency occurred between infants and mothers. They found that,

Jessica with her six-day old neonate: intense involvement with her baby. Jessica has formed a comfortable 'nest' for the neonate by crossing arms and legs.

once the mother and infant were separated, interaction between infants and juveniles increased initially but then decreased sharply, while depressive behaviour was initially low and then increased significantly (Codner & Nadler 1984). Other studies have argued that the mother offers a secure base for exploration and if this base is taken away, the infant or juvenile becomes anxious and avoids contact with anything new and unfamiliar (Vochteloo et al. 1993). Finally, the slow and gradual process of skill development is interrupted and may even be terminated at whatever point the separation occurs. This may include appropriate foraging behaviour, climbing and adequate locomotion in trees. For instance, we mentioned before that between 1978 and 1984 the Sepilok Rehabilitation Centre treated 21 cases of fractures in orang-utans. Of those 76 percent or 16 individuals were below the age of puberty. Six were less than two years of age and ten ranged from three to five years of age. All of these cases were the result of falling off a tree and, at times, from a great height, as much as 50 metres (Kehoe & Chan 1986). Knowledge of locomotion, climbing and appropriate foraging behaviour are all part of the most important skills for survival.

As Coe said, the induction of maternal behaviour in primates in general is largely not mediated by hormones but by experiential and cognitive factors (Coe 1990). The mother learns as the offspring learns. Primate literature has long since established that primiparous mothers (mothers with one firstborn offspring) show less mothering skill and are more anxious than multiparous mothers (mothers who have reared several young) (Baldwin 1986). Studies of infant abuse amongst primates have indicated that early social deprivation and poor treatment lead to abusive or neglectful parenting, just as in humans (Nadler 1983). However, maternal care tends to improve with subsequent offspring (Shively & Mitchell 1986). The effect of learning is unmistakable. In response to these findings, zoos run programs to teach primates appropriate maternal care (Maple & Hoff 1982; Shively & Mitchell 1986).

The mode of travel on the mother varies according to age and according to specific circumstances. We will come back to this in Chapter 6. Suffice it to say here that the infant is largely transported ventrally when very young and then clinging to the side of the trunk or on the hip. When the mother descends a tree backwards, the infant rides in the lower part of her back and climbing upwards on a trunk the infant may move up high on her back (Davenport 1967). Apart from the first week of life, the infant is not supported by the mother and has to cling on to her hair. Whenever the mother is about to move on, she may scoop up her infant and place it in a position that is comfortable to her. We have observed this scooping motion on a number of different occasions and by three different females with infants under 18 months of age. The only cradling of an infant that we saw occurred in its first week of life.

We do not know precisely how learning in the orang-utan infant occurs. We have observed imitative behaviour in feeding (see Chapter 6). Davenport has described instances of imitation by a juvenile who was being weaned. The juvenile followed the mother in an almost comical manner, stopping when she did, proceeding when she did and negotiating the same branches as she had done (Davenport 1967). However, beyond this imitative behaviour, learning must take place in other ways as well, such as by observation and deduction. When the juvenile finally leaves the mother, it needs to be equipped with a complex knowledge of edible items and of ways of obtaining food. Solitary learning by trial and error also occurs. We have observed orang-utans trial food items both by smell and by inspection, by placing a berry or leaf on the lower lip, pushing the lip forward and inspecting it. Sniffing new objects has been observed by Harrisson (B. Harrisson 1960). First and foremost it needs to be stressed that the power of observation in orang-utans is unparalleled. Walker described an incident in 1964 when a young male orang-utan, still in a travelling cage, had watched workmen nearby. When they left he took the screwdriver and proceeded to unscrew the bars of his cage. He would have succeeded had his action not been discovered (Walker 1964). The orang-utan was unlikely to have had any exposure to screwdrivers before and this kind of tool use is certainly not known in the wild. Reports over the last decades have confirmed the orang-utan's unusual capacity for quickly adopting (imitating) *and* adapting behaviours and actions that they have observed, both in captivity and the wild. We will come back to this and discuss the issue more fully under 'problem solving' in Chapter 6.

Maternal care is also learned by observing the mother interact with her next offspring. Primate literature on mother–infant interaction continues to stress that maternal care is learned behaviour and that mothers with firstborns are poorer mothers than those with several offspring. Although the literature admits that primipara *may* provide adequate care, the implication for the orang-utan is that most ought to be poor mothers. This theory clearly does not work in the case of orang-utans. For every adult female with offspring there would normally be only one offspring to have watched the rearing of an infant, namely the firstborn, because orang-utans often-raise only about two offspring. The watching orang-utan offspring may not always be a female but may be a male and that learning experience is wasted. Hence at least half of the growing orang-utan females have never had the opportunity to observe maternal behaviour except for brief encounters with other orang-utan females with offspring. Learning of mothering for these females then must depend on the few chance encounters they have with other adult females and their offspring. There is no evidence that orang-utans make poor mothers or poorer mothers than other primate species with ample opportunity to learn, but there is substantial evidence that a female infant removed from its mother before its learning period is complete may have severe psychological damage and be unable to mother effectively as an adult.

5

Introducing 'our' orang-utans

How does one get to know an orang-utan?

In general, one does not get to know an orang-utan. Either we see orang-utans caged in zoo enclosures or, if we have the rare opportunity, we may see them in the wild and be unable to get near them. The only other venue for meeting orang-utans is in rehabilitation centres and wildlife reserves, but even here access is restricted. Usually one is not permitted to touch and have close communication with rehabilitative orang-utans (see below). One might well ask whether close communication is at all relevant and whether it would change or improve our relationship with this species. Our aim was to observe the behaviour of orang-utans as undisturbed by us as possible and learn as much about them as we could from observation. In most cases we succeeded in doing so. We kept our distance and generally the orang-utans kept theirs. This objectified distance was maintained for most of the time even though there were no bars or cages for the orang-utans and no walk-rails or barriers for the human visitor. This was at a time when hardly any general rules and regulations were in force or needed to be strictly enforced for the rare visitor. Hence we were able to move freely amongst them and to encounter rehabilitating free-ranging orang-utans leisurely and at times personally. Unavoidably, without defining barriers or supervision, our paths crossed quite often and naturally. Most of the time an orang-utan would pass us without as much as giving us a glance. They largely ignored us when we were standing next to the tree in which they had taken up temporary residence. Yet some young and very curious ones persisted in investigating us more closely, drawn to our tripod, the camera equipment and our pockets. There were instances when we had to fight for our note and scoring pads and for every page of recording. We had to try and convince some juvenile and sometimes rather difficult adolescent orang-utans that tripods were not another tree and that pencils were not just branches on which one could chew at will. Even these were brief encounters and ultimately had little significance.

First meeting with Abbie

(This page)
Abbie has approached Gisela (above on the left) to be held and carried. Korashi is more content to chew Lesley's pencil. Abbie is settling in (left).

Second meeting with Abbie ▶

(Opposite page) Abbie makes contact. Notice the closeness but eye aversion (top left and right). Throughout, Abbie was holding on to Gisela's hand. Top right, she also held on to Gisela's arm, but still averted her head (see Chapter 6). Later (bottom), eye-to-eye contact is made.

Getting to know someone usually means a little more than silently walking past them or having a little scuffle. One may get to know orang-utans to a point by merely observing them but we begin to relate to an 'other' only when we interact. There is no comparison between the silent impersonal chance encounter and even the briefest two-way communication and interaction. Across species, particularly between humans and free-ranging animals, such moments of interaction become truly memorable. Novels have been written and films been made about such moments. The brief scene in which a mountain gorilla touched the hand of Dian Fossey became the lynch-pin for the entire film of *Gorillas in the Mist*. The point was not that there was a romantic moment of hand holding but that a wild mountain gorilla had chosen to interact with and communicate something to the human observer: a simple gesture of good will and (cautious) trust. Ultimately, it is these moments that speak more eloquently and convince more lastingly than any other that every living thing on this planet has a right to be, has intrinsic value and deserves empathy and good manners.

For the sake of intellectual honesty, it is important to admit here that we had such an encounter ourselves which we regarded as unusual, significant and which retrospectively proved of greater value and importance than all the textbooks we had read. We actually got to know one orang-utan personally. More importantly, it was the orang-utan's choice, not ours, that we did. Her name was Abbie, a juvenile female. We shall continue to be grateful that she chose to infringe our detached observer space. This started a long love affair, particularly with Gisela, which is certainly one valid explanation why she has felt compelled to return to the same spot of the Bornean forest again and again.

Abbie was no more than three years old when we first met her, having just recently lost her mother. As said in the previous chapter, orang-utan infants under the age of five are not in a position to fend for themselves or to know enough about their world to survive on their own. Indeed, they stay with or near their mothers quite often until the age of seven before they begin wandering off by themselves (see previous chapter). Apart from the learning they need to do in the first four to five years of their lives, we believe that they need love and attention just like human infants and juveniles. Abbie's behaviour certainly gave the impression of someone who simply wanted to be close. She had no particular curiosity for any item that Gisela possessed, not even the tripod. Instead, after a few hesitant advances, she clambered up from behind, eventually settling on Gisela's hips not, as it turned out, for a brief cuddle but seemingly permanently. Close up, one's perceptions about the 'other' change dramatically. Here was not just a representative of a 'species'. Even the word 'animal' seemed inappropriate for the type of loving (clinging) contact that was established. It was in this proximity that we first felt we were learning something about the orang-utan, or rather, we felt we had come a step closer to some emotive, intuitive understanding of orang-utans by having met her.

We continued to return to Sabah in the years following this encounter, especially thinking of Abbie and hoping that we would find her again. We always did and not just that. On every encounter we felt proud that she looked healthier, bigger and with every step had obviously become more independent. Her appearances at the feeding station or even just near the terrain of the feeding station had decreased to no more than once or twice in a four-week period. And yet, even in these short encounters with the provisioning area, we bore witness to her communication with us.

Two years later, we were searching for her every day after our return to the forest, finally spotting her after three weeks. The tourists had just left and we were alone. Once we saw her, we called out to her and then just stood and waited. She responded by remaining totally still for some time but we saw that she eyed us from a distance before she began to slowly and deliberately amble across. Gisela had decided to sit down on the forest floor. There was every evidence that Abbie's behaviour was goal-directed and that she headed straight for us. When Abbie reached Gisela, she simply sat down opposite her. A few greeting silences passed, usually with eyes averted, but Abbie remained seated close. Inexplicably, she eventually took Gisela's hand, turned its palm upwards and ran her index finger over the lines on the hand (see Chapter 4 for comments). Rollins (1993) describes a similar moving event when he made contact with an orang-utan at the zoo: the orang-utan seized his arm and traced her finger along a scar on his forearm.

After this contact with Abbie, we sat still for a good while, literally just holding hands and listening to the deafening sound of the cicadas. Eventually she got up and disappeared only to return a little while later with another female juvenile her age. We felt a little like parents whose primary school child had brought home her first school friend. As far as one can speak of friendships among orang-utans, Alice was certainly a friend or a least a good playmate. The two of them capered about in front of us, barely half a metre away and showed us all manner of tricks. Then Abbie got up again and gravely took Gisela's hands again, just holding them. When she let go finally, she slowly turned around and walked away (see p.93).

On another visit, several years later, she also meandered towards us and sat down near us but no longer sought to touch us. This time she had another companion. Almost old enough to be a mother herself by now, she had instead adopted a three-year old male juvenile (or been adopted by him), who had lost his mother in similar circumstances to Abbie's. Tom could not be left. Whenever she turned only ever so slightly away, he anxiously clung to her, grabbed her and if she wanted a few minutes to herself, he shrieked in absolute terror. Tom was not the kind of charge that would have allowed Abbie a quiet, contemplative meeting with us on the jungle floor, but she stayed close, about half a metre away, looking intently at Gisela. Similarly as before she then proceeded to show us, in an impressive range of mischievousness, what she could do. She swayed hard from a liana, made somersaults over and over again, played with all sorts of branches and leaves, hopped, jumped, sat, pulled a playing face, all in rather rapid sequence. When we sat there watching her bravado, her spirited performance and her incredible repertoire of activities and clowning skills, we could not help but think sadly of orang-utans in zoos who never seem to have occasion for such exuberance. She had grown into an exceptionally strong and large subadult.

Interactions of this kind are an excellent way of giving meaning to behaviour. Some of the rather unorthodox and personal observations we made fell far outside our expectations. At our first meeting, Abbie accommodated herself on Gisela's torso, engulfed her hip with her strong legs clamping these tightly together, feet touching at the back (see p.92). In this secure posture she was unable to fall, no matter whether Gisela bent over or not. There was no doubt that Abbie was safe and would have been able to hold her position even if Gisela had started climbing a tree or swayed and scrambled from tree to tree. Although she was rather heavy, like a two- or three-year old child, she successfully maintained that position for hours. Abbie eventually settled in. Once she realised she was not being pushed away, Abbie's whole posture relaxed and she began purring, a soft gutteral purr, not unlike that of a cat. Vocalisation has been described in detail in a variety of research and field reports but we have seen no reference to this soft purring sound which was audible only at close range (see Chapter 6). We were inclined to interpret this vocalisation as an expression of satisfaction (see also Appendix 3).

Third meeting with Abbie

An independent 'young woman' with her 'adopted' juvenile charge called Tom, who anxiously avoided the briefest separation from his foster mother.

Another observation concerning scent was also directly the result of the intimacy with Abbie. Usually one does not describe the odour or scent of a species. This is a consequence of the relatively under-developed nature of olfaction in the human species, which continues to receive explicit attention rarely beyond cultural definitions of fragrance. Among animals, a sense of smell is often highly developed and essential to survival, for community life and recognition of offspring. We do not know and have not seen any detailed reference to olfaction in orang-utans and therefore cannot judge what function, if any, olfaction has in their survival or generally for their communication. Harrisson noted in her extensive work with orang-utans, particularly with infants, that 'her' orang-utans tended to investigate any new object (alive or inanimate) by first looking at it, then touching or teasing it. Only if it seemed safe, she noted, would they then proceed to smell it (B. Harrisson 1960). If this were true generally, then a sense of smell would not function as a discriminator between dangerous and non-dangerous items but as a memory for things pleasant or at least un-dangerous. Subadults will occasionally sniff female genitalia when swollen due to pregnancy (Crawford & Galdikas 1986).

Hence it was not an un-orang-utan thing to do to investigate by smelling. Gisela wanted to know what an orang-utan smelled like. We thus reversed species expectations when we turned to sniff this orang-utan, burying our noses into Abbie's coat near the neck, on the chest and arm. When we 'sampled' our experience in this way it was during the pre-fruiting season. The orang-utans at that time would have little or no access to fruit except bananas from the provisioning at the rehabilitation feeding station. The only way to describe the smell was to compare it to the scent of orange peel or the fragrance of citrus fruit, or even of lemon flowers. Although little droplets of sweat were visible on her skin, not surprisingly given the heat and an engulfing humidity of 98 percent, there was no single detectible odour of sweat equivalent to that of humans or any smell we tend to associate with unpleasant things.

The scent might have been a consequence of the foods consumed. Since orang-utans eat a large variety of leaves and berries, it may be surmised that the scent is partly an excretion resulting from the ingested food. It is common to infer that any feature of a species other than our own needs to be explicable in terms of a specific function. It is of course entirely possible that this scent has no function whatsoever, but if one were to speculate, such an odour may perhaps act as an insect repellent. In the tropics there are a number of substantial risks involved in receiving mosquito bites. For instance, scratching such bites and creating tiny skin breaks can turn the minutest open sore septic and can be even life-threatening (see O'Hanlon's description 1984). Moreover, as was mentioned in Chapter 2, in the area of Sabah mosquitoes are carriers of different types of malaria, one lethal (*Plasmodium falciparum*) and the others causing chronic ailment (*Plasmodium ovale* and *malarie*), also of Denghe fever and of elephantiasis. Mosquitoes are plentiful and insects fill the air throughout most of the year. We had noticed that mosquitoes surrounded orang-utans but rarely settled on their skin.

Another reason for mosquitoes not managing to obtain entry was clearly the orang-utan's hair. Orang-utan hair tends to look thick only from a distance. That coarse look of their hair is often deceptive for their hair is very fine and, despite enormous differences between individuals, tends not to grow in great density on the skin. Instead, it stands up from the skin by about two to five millimetres before curving to the side. When a mosquito settles on the hair it is too far from the skin to pierce it. Hence, in the combination of hair and smell, orang-utans might have developed the best possible protection from annoying insects such as mosquitoes and flies which tend to plague many other mammals.

The other observation that we found surprising and strangely moving was to discover how soft, delicate and even vulnerable their skin is and how unmistakably human it looks and feels. Orang-utan skin, at least of young orang-utans and usually of all females, is very soft and delicate, not like that of a baby but of an aged person. Those initial experiences of physical contact alone made it difficult for us in future to ignore the closeness between the orang-utan (*Pongo pygmaeus*) and *Homo sapiens*.

Orang-utans and human contact

Orang-utans now depend on humans for their survival. They are kept in many environments in close contact with humans and their habitat shrinks at a very high rate each year. For the preservation and safeguarding of the species in the wild, the questions are what kind of human contact is harmful and how much of it can be sustained or should be prevented. These questions are of course especially pertinent in a rehabilitative framework.

Eco-tourism

Some of the rules restricting contact have come about largely because of the rise of eco-tourism. The matter of eco-tourism, just as the rehabilitative process itself, is a thorny issue. It is easy to see that hordes of tourists patting orang-utans would neither be a learning experience for the orang-utan nor aid their successful return to the wild. After sampling tourist behaviour at several sites we are less convinced of this kind of eco-tourism as a viable form for ensuring the maintenance of orang-utans in the wild. We saw noticeably frightened orang-utans being hotly pursued by some tourists who insisted on getting their money's worth by at least taking the appropriate photographs home — still exercising the trophy mentality, not unlike the hunters of the past. We have seen groups of people crowding out young and frightened orang-utans, literally overpowering them. We cringed at the senseless shouting of well-dressed tourists as if oblivious to the fact that they were walking into primeval rainforest. We saw wildlife photographers who came in for quick shots of orang-utans before catching the next plane to New York or Nepal, not hesitating to use suitcase-sized flashes directed at the eyes of orang-utans. Continued and frequent flashes of this strength can blind an orang-utan. No doubt, we will have seen the results: some super-perfect well-lit photographs in glossy wildlife magazines. Such magazines have learned to exploit conservationist and naturalist concerns and make wildlife issues big business. How else could these magazines justify accepting photographs that are likely to have been harmful to the species they portray? It has been shown for some time, that certain actions by humans will cause psychological stress in non-human primates (J. Kaplan 1986), others may even cause physical damage. Touching and getting too close to orang-utans now need to be prohibited.

Apart from the senseless noise and rather aggressive intrusion on the life of a solitary species, there is a good deal of measurable damage being done by the presence of a large number of people. The rainforest gets trampled down, an endless stream of cars and tourist buses pollute the locality, wider roads get built for easier access and more splendid trees need to be felled, ironically, in order to better display the forest. Other species may move further into the jungle or totally disappear from the area as a result of this human onslaught. Most Bornean wildlife species, including birds, are extremely shy.

Tourists have different reasons for wanting to see orang-utans. The problem is that not all of them are based on an interest in the species. Eco-tourism, in our experience, has encouraged a new creed of people to invade the forest; they do this 'off the beaten track' travel as a jetsetting hobby and for snob value. As long as they have been there and have photographs to prove it, the visit fulfils its dubious functions when back home. It is needless to add that eco-tourism is not centrally concerned with any species of flora and fauna. It is a market niche that has been successfully developed for a spoiled and wealthy western clientele who 'consume' environmentalism as a leisure activity. There are some areas in the world where the balance between public demand and species needs are a little bit more in favour of the survival of the species than in others. For instance, on some uninhabited islands of the Galapagos the number of visitors is restricted in movement, in number, in area and in transport. On the narrowest possible path, one can walk across the island. People are asked not to speak and only small groups in single file can be at one place at a time, limiting island visits for all small vessels to one small time slot per day. The money obtained from these visitors is used to pay for wildlife officers and staff employed to maintain and care for the area (and to deal with the many introduced species which have become pests since the last century). Perhaps it is all a matter of degree. A minimalist approach seems the best so far in the difficult balance between money making and species conservation. In our view, mass-tourism is detrimental to the locality, both for the species and for the natural environment, wherever it occurs.

Our ambivalence about eco-tourism has increased over the years. It seems that only the minority of people actually come because they have a genuine interest in the 'wildlife' they are about to see and few have respect for the environment they are visiting. The problem is that those who can afford to travel to such specialised areas of interest are the well-to-do and the western urban populations. Most of them have long since lost any sense of what nature might mean, any sense of the word 'wildlife' and any concept of respect for their surroundings. We suggested this problem in a previous chapter. Wildlife programs are regularly shown on television. While many of these programs are made for educational purposes, they are also entertainment, aesthetically pleasing and usually neither threatening nor confronting. Zoos are now so well planned and designed that one can stroll through parks, occasionally glancing at a species behind bars, without the slightest sense of having had an 'experience'. In most of the western world, life is regular and regulated. No part of the environment is not handled by humans and somehow structured and modelled to fit human whims or needs.

Our own mood when we step into tropical rainforest is that of extreme awe; indeed it is tantamount to a religious experience of entering something sacred. Others need not share our specific reasons for being there. The question rather is: how good or bad are these onslaughts for orang-utans and what effect will those truly meaningless contacts with humans have on the orang-utans? To be sure, if one has a choice between two evils, that is, either seeing the remaining rainforest sacrificed to logging and the orang-utan's habitat completely destroyed, or tolerating the tourist invasion but saving their environment, we would support eco-tourism. Eco-tourism can save some (enough?) acreage of tropical rainforest but can it save the species?

Felling rainforest trees to make room for a widened tourist car park and to accommodate a cafeteria. We used to have lunch with the wildlife employees and partook of simple but satisfying local foods. Times have changed.

Human contact and rehabilitation

Our views on eco-tourism do not imply that all human contact is intrinsically bad. It depends on the nature of the human interaction. Of course, one wishes that pockets of natural habitat will remain unaltered and that there will continue to be rainforests where humans will not intrude upon the lives of orang-utans but this is increasingly rare. Rather, the intrusion has now become so intense and so damaging that rehabilitation centres are a necessity for containing at least some of the damage already caused. Rules that some rehabilitation centres have introduced include the prevention of human and orang-utan interaction and touching. These rules may generally be necessary to prevent orang-utans from contracting any of our diseases. We are less convinced that the strict separation from all direct human contact is necessary or a prerequisite to a successful rehabilitation program. Opinions on this latter subject vary considerably and this question has remained a matter of controversy (Galdikas 1994; Lardeux-Gilloux 1994; Smits & Herlyanto 1994). For instance, the caring role of staff and of individuals may be an important ingredient in the healing process from trauma and injury. This is true particularly for juveniles. In other words, a personal and caring approach may be essential or at least beneficial. We have raised these issues in our discussion on current orang-utan habitat and have spoken of the different models that have so far evolved. Here, we need to expand on the issue of human contact from the point of view of the individual orang-utan.

In all of these issues, one crucial consideration should be the history of the particular orang-utan concerned. This is quite often done now at the rehabilitation sites. It may, of course, not always be possible to establish a full history of an orang-utan who is found injured or brought to a rehabilitation centre but, in general, the new carers may be able to piece together some evidence. Apart from the value for the rehabilitative process, this information is equally important for research purposes. There are still research reports that slide back and forth from captive to free-ranging environments as if these differences did not matter. The assumption is made that biology, heredity and hence innateness of behaviour dominate and species-specific behaviour comes to the fore in any environment. In human society, we employ very fine discriminatory measures such as those of class, race, ethnicity, religion and culture as a matter of course. When we describe behaviours we do so by clearly identifying the parameters to signal difference. We believe that the same care needs to be taken in the study of a specific species, particularly when this species, in free-ranging situations, exists in several subspecies and fragmented populations, and also exists in zoos. In their own way, all different experiences and locations affect development and behaviour in the broadest sense, and may even alter morphological characteristics (see previous chapters). Some of the emerging differences between individuals fall into distinct groups.

Group one

Group number one is made up of captive orang-utans held anywhere in the world in zoo environments, research centres, laboratories and relatively confined wildlife enclosures constructed for human observation, or even in circuses. There are important gradations and differences within these enclosed environments. They are worth debating but not in this context since our study was conducted outside these parameters. We mention them to indicate that the orang-utan and all other great apes show a high degree of responsiveness to specific environments. Such responsiveness may signal a change in a whole range of behaviours and events (such as illnesses), and even basic life data may occur in one environment and not in another.

Disappointingly little is said about the possible rate and manner of release and rehabilitation of such *captive* populations. There is little discussion even of the genuine possibility of their release. To our knowledge, very little thought has been put into establishing any formalised ways in which living orang-utans or other primates may be properly 'disposed of' once they have served their purpose in medical or other laboratory research, or in entertainment. We know of only a few altruistic ventures by individuals who have taken it upon themselves (and their purse) to care for discarded research laboratory primates (Koebner 1984). We believe it should become an international law of ethics that the post-research phase is satisfactorily planned out, financially covered and accounted for, and that concerted efforts are made to rehabilitate them into more humane conditions and, preferably, back into their natural habitat. Moreover, very few zoos seriously entertain the notion of voluntarily giving up orang-utans after they have served a few years as entertainment for the public. These orang-utans, too, could be considered for rehabilitation into the wild, as has happened for instance with a male orang-utan who was returned to Sabah from a German zoo. The international concern of zoos about genetic diversity of this species in future is ultimately false because such diversity would be well-assured if their habitat was left intact and they were all returned from whence they came! But these matters have hardly been raised.

Group two

Our second group consists of former pets, ie those orang-utans whose contact with humans has been intense and may have occurred at the expense of contact with other orang-utans, especially of maternal or sibling interaction. Into this second group we put those orang-utans who have been taken by locals and raised as pets. The quality of that interaction and experience may differ vastly from one household to the next. Here we find examples of orang-utans being kept in appalling conditions and living in extremely small cages. Such orang-utans are very obviously much worse off than those that are professionally cared for in zoos who may enjoy luxury accommodation. The fact that they have remained in the vicinity of their natural habitat is of no specific benefit to them and we are not suggesting simplistic models of 'ideal-type' environments. Those pet orang-utans have long-standing memories of and possible attachment to human company. These experiences may be bad or good ones, depending on the quality of care and love they have received. In many cases of personal pet ownership, the orang-utan loses out in the end. Orang-utans are generally considered cute and lovable when small but, when they grow in strength, the problems of keeping them outweigh attachment for them. Apparently, orang-utans are difficult to be 'house-trained' and they continue in their habit of dismantling and breaking whatever strikes their fancy (B. Harrisson 1960). It is then that orang-utan pets often get neglected and are presented to the rehabilitation centres in appalling conditions. By law, be this in East Malaysia or Kalimantan, no one is permitted to keep orang-utans as pets. When such pets are discovered they are taken away from their 'owners' or foster parents and put into rehabilitation programs for reintroduction to the wild.

In many ways, out of all categories (a third and a fourth are described below), the former pet is the most difficult to rehabilitate into the wild, if there has been no contact with other orang-utans. They may have missed out altogether on any relevant learning. They may never have climbed a tree. They may not know or have ever seen what they can eat. In other words, every aspect of knowledge for survival, including mothering for females (see last chapter), has been omitted and has to be taught. Young orang-utans without prior or too little foraging experience have to take regular climbing lessons. They will not climb of their own accord if this was not part of their infant experience. Worse, they will not necessarily be good climbers. When to hold on and when to let go can be a decision of life and death in the top of a canopy. Distances from tree to tree and branch to branch need to be judged and negotiated. Even the strength of branches and the manner of supporting oneself is a matter of great acquired skill. They need to learn what they can eat, which part of the plant/nut/fruit and how they can reach the edible part of a particular item. Rehabilitation centres have developed a school curriculum for orang-utans. In one of them, orang-utans are not released until they can distinguish between at least one hundred plants (Smits & Herlyanto 1994).

Then there are the social and communicative aspects between orang-utans and the idiosyncrasies of such relationships. Even more subtle and intangible are such things as local cultures. It has been shown beyond doubt amongst chimpanzee populations that habits and skills may develop in one group but not in another. The nut-cracking habit of some groups of chimpanzees is just one example of culture (see Chapter 6).

Many examples in the past have shown that even former pet orang-utans can be fully rehabilitated. By 'fully rehabilitated' we mean that they could maintain themselves and reproduce. Although those rehabilitation efforts take inordinate amounts of time and resources, it can and has been done. Galdikas argues that ten years are needed for one such successful rehabilitation (Galdikas 1994). 'Fully rehabilitated' does not necessarily imply something that we call by the peculiar name of 'wild'. Orang-utans who have been raised and socialised with humans, even on full rehabilitation will be a very different product to an undisturbed orang-utan who has never seen, let alone interacted with, humans. Galdikas put it well when she argued recently, in her speech on winning an international award, that those orang-utans become 'bi-cultural' (Galdikas 1994). They have learned to live in both environments, ie they have learned to respond to either environment in a manner that appears adapted and appropriate.

Some of them fail the test. We have met and known several failures in this category, failures only in terms of rehabilitation aims, not in terms of individual adaptation. The 'failures' are those who for one reason or another cannot be fully rehabilitated and remain fixated on human contact. In Sepilok, there were two females at one time in this category. Another one was an adolescent male called BJ, who had been raised as a pet under circumstances we could not ascertain. We suspect that he had not been treated well. We actually liked him a good deal. He is dead now and never made it back into the forest or past sub-adulthood. There is evidence that some intestinal infection killed him before his ninth birthday.

For several years before his death we had ample opportunity to observe him and on more than one occasion to interact with him. He seemed to us highly intelligent but he had used his intelligence to become street-wise. He was mischievous, clever in his deceptions, a gang kid from a bad neighbourhood. He had learned all the tricks on how to get at people. We were always glad that many years ago both of us had had some high school teaching experience in bad neighbourhoods. This experience proved useful when coping with someone like BJ and helped us keep control in some rather delicate situations. BJ was just like a difficult 14 year old, carrying his knife in his boots, so to speak, and defiantly believing that the world was his to taunt and tease against any form of authority or interference. In the lingo of modern educators and social workers, BJ would certainly have been considered a behavioural problem and he would no doubt have turned into a substantial problem had he reached adulthood, not because of his bad manners but because of his fixation on humans.

BJ often lay in ambush waiting for people. His favourite game was to suddenly jump out of the bushes, raise his arms and look dangerous. We watched him as people took flight. This act alone always delighted him. He tried the same trick on us when we first encountered him. However, we did not flee. Once he realised that his ploy had failed BJ actually sulked, but not for long. He then launched an outright offensive for Lesley's notebook and managed to get hold of it, running (upright) into the jungle. Gisela followed him and determinedly, as she would have acted in the juvenile class of misfits, she plucked each one of his fingers off the pages of the notebook, telling him that he had to give it back. In the end, he gave up (although he was a good deal stronger than both of us together) and ran mortified into the bush. An odd kind of truce between us reigned almost uninterruptedly from that day on. Meanwhile, some unsuspecting tourists had lost their handbags, one had lost a camera and, on one occasion, Lesley had to call for help when he had grabbed her camera with his feet and proceeded to pull her hand towards him in order to sink his teeth into her flesh. The combined effort of both of us prevented this. After that incident, he never singled us out again but he found plenty of others for his games. What would have happened to him had he reached adulthood? It was a difficult thing to contemplate. We know of another male orang-utan elsewhere who, after all rehabilitation attempts and considerable freedom, ended up in a small steel cage because he had become too dangerous.

Another failure in terms of rehabilitation aims was Judy. Judy was just the opposite. Perhaps she no longer knew that she was an orang-utan. She was entirely fixated on humans but, apart from minor mischievous attacks, she had a very pleasant, even sunny, disposition. Judy was six years old when we first met her. She had also been kept as a pet. Local rehabilitation staff considered her too habituated to humans to be returned to the wild. Her adaptation into human society was complete. She wanted absolutely nothing to do with the forest. She is one of two orang-utans who were shown regularly to tourists. She would walk hand in hand with a keeper and face the crowds to charm them. Outside these display hours she amused herself around the buildings. She, like BJ, and other orang-utans, was free to go anywhere she liked. While we were visiting, a telling incident happened. Judy used to walk to the bus stop where locals boarded the bus to go to the rehabilitation centre and nearby villages. One day Judy waited at that bus stop and when the bus arrived she got in to take a ride. The bus driver and conductor graciously allowed her free passage. She was then dropped off at the stop nearest to the rehabilitation centre. She had not paid her fare but, as locals told us, she had behaved like a lady, sitting in just one designated seat with crossed legs throughout the entire trip! We scored neither Judy's nor BJ's behaviour.

Group three

The third group is the one we generally refer to as semi-wild. There are substantial variations within this group but what they have in common is either fleeting or extended contact with humans. Typically, in this group, all orang-utans are born in the wild. At some stage in their lives they have needed help, perhaps because they have become ill or have sustained a fracture or other injuries. In such cases, the rehabilitation centre's function has been short-term medical assistance, treating the individuals, keeping them until a full recovery was made and then returning them into their familiar surroundings. Such human contact could last for a few weeks or a few months. Simbo was such a case. When we met him he was a 27-year old, fully grown male, who had just spent half a year of his life in human care. To all intents and purposes the life he led was that of a wild orang-utan, the only difference being that he knew where the feeding table was, which also attracted a large stock of young females, and he had some knowledge of human contact. We cannot judge what influence this had on his life.

In this third group there occurs another circumstance, one that is worryingly large. In it we find orang-utans who have gone through very traumatic experiences, usually at human hands. These include infant and juvenile orang-utans who have lost their mothers through poaching. It was, and still is, the practice to kill the mother in order to get the young (and manageable) infant. The age of these young orang-utans at the time of losing their mothers varies but often they are well under or about three years of age. In those age groups, a good deal of learning is still necessary for independent survival. This incomplete training, coupled with the trauma associated with the loss of their mothers and their experience of capture, produces its own challenges for attempts at successful rehabilitation.

The previous chapter has described the intensity of the mother–infant interaction and the substantial disadvantages accumulating from a disruptive infancy and a disturbance of the crucial learning phase up to five years of age. Studies have also revealed that, very similarly to humans, trauma and stress in non-human primates can develop into behavioural problems in the young, adolescent and adult (Dienske & Griffin 1978). The many orang-utans separated from their mothers at an early age are indeed very damaged and there is no telling what effect this will ultimately have on the future of orang-utan populations. Yet for definitional purposes, even this category is 'semi-wild'. They have had a few or several years of life with their mothers and after a few years of training and provisioning they are destined for a return into the forest. 'Our' Abbie is one of the very successful examples of this group. Despite her early deprivation and trauma she grew into a strong and healthy female, capable of taking on an orphaned infant and largely feeding herself and him independently.

Group four

The fourth group is less problematic and a group we have less and less opportunity to watch and study. These are the 'wild' orang-utans. By this we mean individuals who have not interacted with or needed to depend on humans. But even within this group we now need to distinguish two separate kinds of experiences. The first concerns orang-utans that have remained in their native environment of Borneo or Sumatra and the second concerns those 'wild' orang-utans who live in areas that are designated specifically for them and therefore attract researchers from all over the world. Such a place is Danum Valley. Orang-utan research always has unpredictable elements and it may well be possible not to see any individuals for weeks but generally they can be found in this area. Who knows how many different research groups actually studied exactly the same individuals.

Those that have become subjects of study must be regarded as a group that is not entirely untainted by the experience of having been constantly watched and followed. Clearly, while we as wildlife researchers attempt to be non-intrusive, our mere presence is noticed. Such a presence could be disquieting, possibly uncomfortable, unnerving or just a nuisance for the orang-utan (cf. MacKinnon's extensive comments on this, 1971, 1974). The one and only entirely wild male orang-utan we ever observed in the Sukau area seemed very aware of our presence. When he had finished building his nest, he kept bashing the branches and his nest in powerful strokes, checking on us at regular intervals by peering over the edge. Even if orang-utans appear to ignore humans, their presence cannot be entirely without effect. Indeed, several field researchers have reported that their own presence aggravated wild orang-utans into hurling twigs and branches, shaking trees and branches, urinating and defecating on the human observer with a seemingly clear message to go away (Davenport 1967, MacKinnon 1971). Hence, the most well-intentioned, quiet and respectful presence of humans can lead to a change in behaviour and an adaptation to new circumstances.

Provisioning

A final word on human contact and primate research must address the thorny issue of provisioning (regular supplying of food). Provisioning is used in a number of studies of free-ranging apes in order to facilitate habituation to human presence for the sake of the research project. As a methodology, it has been used to allow observers closer proximity to the group or individuals being studied without making the particular group nervous or anxious. In these cases, it is a pay-off device (I will give you something if you stay). McGrew (1992) noted that few studies on chimpanzees have been able to do entirely without such aids. In the rehabilitative situation the provisioning occurs as part of the rehabilitative process preceding any research endeavour and is therefore not part of the methodology as such. Irrespective of the reason for provisioning, it has been established for a long time that provisioning profoundly affects the provisioned individual or group. It changes the feeding and travelling habits as well as the overall activity cycle for the day. There may be variations in the behaviour depending on the kind of food items that are being offered. High-energy foods such as bananas and breadfruit, both of which have been offered in the Sarawak and Sabah rehabilitation centres, may be enticing or not. One theory at Sepilok held that orang-utans are not very fond of bananas, particularly if given every day, and they will therefore not be too keen to return to the provisioning table unless there is a general fruit and food shortage. Whether liked or not, high-energy foods are nutritionally intrusive and invariably result in changed patterns of foraging and probably in changed diets altogether. The matter is different for juveniles who cannot as yet forage on their own. If the latter is the case, a monotonous diet becomes inadequate very quickly and may lead to deficiencies unless otherwise supplemented.

Provisioning affects a number of other variables, such as locality. After a short period, provisioning sites for orang-utans sustain a good deal of damage to the surrounding flora. A large number of visiting orang-utans will break too many branches, strip too many leaves and pick bark off the trees. It takes little time before a substantial patch of the forest appears denuded and littered with debris. Amongst free-ranging orang-utans the damage is held to a minimum because of the overall low density and scattered distribution. Frequently changing sites for provisioning is one way to overcome the problem but this can only occur when the area is large enough and relatively easy to access for the provisioners. Eco-tourism has an added drawback. Those venues that are used for eco-tourist viewing sites have inbuilt in them a degree of inflexibility that makes the constant movement of provisioning sites difficult. For example, it would destroy more bush and cost a good deal more money to build walkways, platforms and bridges for access to several feeding sites, than it would to build just one.

Finally and importantly, provisioning affects inter- and intra-species contact and sociality. As we have already described, orang-utans live relatively solitary lives and if in contact with others, tend to move in small groups. At provisioning sites far larger numbers of orang-utans come together than would normally occur in the wild, excepting the congregation on specially large fruiting trees. Close proximity and even competition may become unavoidable at provisioning sites amongst individuals who would normally avoid each other or only associate briefly with one another. Inter-species proximity and competition are also increased. In Sepilok, we often saw pig-tailed macaques (*Macaca nemistrina*) hovering near the feeding table and taking away what food they could in a 'sneak up from behind and grab' approach. Young juvenile female orang-utans often displayed fear of large adult male macaques. In two instances, two juveniles embraced each other in fear until the large male had disappeared. Adolescent and adult females tended to ignore the macaques and allowed them to remove the food. Only a fully grown mature male showed clear signs of anger when he hurled himself into the company of macaques with swiping arm motions and a blow of the back of the hand. He also shook his head and grunted. The macaques were careful to avoid the powerful arm thrust in their direction and scattered with loud shrieks in an instant. One such performance at the feeding table often stopped the macaques returning for several days.

For the researcher, the advantages of provisioning are obvious. Provisioning of semi-wild orang-utans ensures a constant supply of orang-utans for observation, better viewing access to their activities and longer periods of visibility. At the same time, it is clear that the context has distorting consequences.

The feeding table at the main provisioning site in Sepilok, approximately eight metres above ground.

Introducing 'our' study orang-utans

Throughout this book we have referred to our experiences with orang-utans in the field. Part of these experiences have remained anecdotal in so far as we may have seen a specific behaviour only once or twice or we may have seen the behaviour only in a single individual. We did, however, also observe a sufficiently large number of the same individuals to systematically score their behaviour (Rogers & Kaplan 1995). The target behaviours focused on were for handedness. Our observations were conducted entirely within the 'semi-wild' group (as described above, group 3) and our personal knowledge is derived from it. We have already introduced some orang-utans individually. To introduce the orang-utans used for scoring handedness is partly to suggest again their diversity in appearance and age. We saw and scored over 50 orang-utans and collected sufficient data in all for a total of 20 to 30, depending on the measure. For the remaining ones not enough data could be obtained. They may have come to the feeding table once and were never seen again or they remained only for very brief periods.

The issue of diversity and variation in the species of the orang-utan was mentioned previously in the theoretical discussion. It needs to be repeated here because this is an important criterion in field study. It would be impossible to score behaviour (in any species) unless one knew the individuals and could keep them apart from others. Orang-utans make that requirement of field observation very easy. Not just their features but their personalities differ widely. Age and sex further contribute to the marked differences

These few photos indicate how individually different orang-utans are. They differ both in appearance and in personality. Notice the different skin colouration; Raja (a) being very dark and Judy (b) with a very fair complexion. Simbo (c), the resident fully grown adult male in the Sepilok reserve, 27 years old, rehabilitated, comes only rarely to the provisioning area. Gemacil (d), only 18 months old. He lost his mother and eventually died, unable to survive the trauma at this young age. Alice (e), Abbie's playmate.

between individual orang-utans. Skin colour and the thickness and colour of their coat are further simple markers.

Skin colour of the face and body is an interesting issue. Amongst all the great apes only the orang-utan shows the same skin colour variations as humans do. Judy, mentioned previously, for instance, is very pale and of white and pinkish skin. Raja, by contrast, is evenly black. BJ was tinged olive or 'yellow' and Jessica was rather reddish. Yet others have mottled skin pigmentation, usually black, white and a little red. The colour of the coat does not vary as much as skin colour. Red clearly predominates but there are some with a light hue and others with a very dark to blackish hue.

The thickness of the coat amongst adults was a clear indicator of individual difference. Julie and Judy, for instance, barely had any hair at all. For Julie's infant, as well as for Julie herself, this was quite a sizeable problem. Youngsters hold on to their mother by clutching her hair. Since Julie had none, the little infant had no alternative but to grasp her skin and pinch her as hard as needed not to lose hold during her rocking motions in walking and climbing. Gandipot, on the other hand, was covered in an extremely thick coat. Her infant had no problems whatsoever in getting a good grip. For us, these markers were initially very useful for identification purposes until such time as we had learned to recognise them. We are now not only able to recognise individuals each time that we return to Sepilok but have even recognised them on postcards and calendars sold in Australia and elsewhere. We also scored behaviour of individuals at Semengoh Orang-Utan Rehabilitation Centre in Sarawak, East Malaysia. There we were unable to ascertain the ages of individuals. In most cases, we were able to make a judgment as to their approximate ages, at least within the categories of adult, subadult, juvenile and infant.

Almost all of the orang-utans at the rehabilitation centre have been through some form of social trauma. A few have been born in the reserve and are truly semi-wild, but others have been separated from their mothers and brought to the centre either immediately or after various periods of captivity. Thus all have passed through a period of re-training for life in the rainforest. Many have had to learn to climb and to feed on natural foods. These experiences may well have altered many of their behaviours, including hand preferences, but we can say that all of the orang-utans in the study had ample experience of climbing and forest life before we studied them.

The sample sizes for each data set are stated in the results section. The scoring for this particular aspect of the project occurred over a two-month period in two consecutive years, 1991 and 1992. Observations were made between 0930 and 1630 hours, mostly prior to or after the provisioning of food and after the tourists had left the site. At Sepilok the observations were made at two feeding stations. The one located further into the rainforest was visited only by orang-utans who were generally regarded as rehabilitated.

The data were collected by pen and paper recording in the field, using binoculars for observations and videotaping for later replay and data collection. A total of 250 hours of data recording were made. Before scoring commenced we learned to recognise the individuals. Twelve of the same individuals scored in 1991 were present, recognised and scored in 1992.

Behavioural studies have a number of dimensions which need to be considered over and above the actual behaviour being observed. The reasons for this are well known and concern context dependencies, be these spatial, horizontal (peer groups, networks, etc) or vertical (experiences of the past, upbringing, etc). Since our field work was behavioural, such dimensions become important. One of the most important issues but one far too rarely discussed as a separate debating point is the question of validity of behavioural studies which do not take sufficient account of the variability between individuals. Much variation in orang-utans occurs from one group to another and one individual to another. Therefore, it is not advisable to consider the results of studying one group as being characteristic of the species as a whole.

'Our' orang-utans in Sepilok were aged as follows when we first scored their behaviour:

Table 7: Name and age of individual orang-utans at Sepilok

Life stage and sex	Name	Age	Offspring
Adult male	Simbo	27.0	
Adult females	Gandipot	15.0	one
	Clementine	14.0	one
	Julie	10.0	one
	Jessica	9.0	one
	Masseney	9.0	
	Noreen	8.0	
Subadult males	Raja	12.5	
	King	9.5	
	Boy	9.0	
	Korashi	9.0	
	Edwin	8.5	
Infants and juveniles (males)	CID	6.0	
	Jojo	4.5	
	Gino	4.0	
	Sidon	3.5	
	Ringo	3.0	
	Gemacil	1.6	
(females)	Mosuli	6.0	
	Abbie	6.0	
	Shena	5.5	
	Alice	5.0	
	Bobbie	4.5	
	Ogilyi	4.0	
	Merotai	3.5	
	Boon	3.5	
	Djena	3.0	
	Rafida	3.0	
	Rampit	2.5	

6

A brain like humans?

In Chapters 3 and 4 we discussed issues related to the evolution of orang-utans and the proximity of their relationship to humans. These particular debates were about genetic, anatomical and physiological relatedness. Within their particular framework, they tell us nothing about the evolution of cognitive abilities, the development of communication, problem solving or the formation of complex memories. This information cannot, of course, be obtained from fossil records or genes. We must turn to the living primates to study their differences and similarities in behaviour. Of the apes, the behaviour of the orang-utan is the least well known. There is a pressing need to know more about the behavioural ecology of orang-utans and also their cognitive functioning so that these can be compared to those of other apes, including humans.

Handedness and other left–right differences in the brain

Handedness of non-human primates is of particular interest because it used to be thought that only humans have handedness. A species or population is said to show handedness if the majority of individuals have a preference to use the same hand consistently, as with the predominance of right-handedness in humans. In the simplest case, no handedness is present in the population, or group, if most of the individuals within the population have no preferred hand, but rather use both hands equally. Also, a population of animals is not handed if, for example, half of the individuals prefer to use the left hand and the other half prefer to use the right hand. In such a case, there is no general bias within the population of preferred use of one of the hands.

Handedness is of interest to us because it reflects asymmetrical, or lateralised, use of the brain. Each hand is controlled by its opposite hemisphere (of the brain), and thus dominance of one hemisphere to perform a particular function can be linked to preferred use of the hand on the opposite side of the body. We set out to see whether orang-utans have handedness. That is, whether they preferred to use one hand rather than the other to perform certain tasks.

As far as we know, humans have always been handed, preferring to use the right hand for fine manipulation, such as in writing. Prehistoric art, artefacts and tools indicate that as far back in time as the existence of *Homo habilis* (a hominid, an early ancestor of modern humans), the majority of individuals were right-handed (that is, some 2.5 million years ago). For example, Toth (1985) noted that the flakes removed by early humans from core stones to be used as axes have fracture marks indicating that they were removed by holding the core stone in the left hand and rotating it clockwise while striking it with a hammer stone held in the right hand. Scratch marks on the teeth of Neanderthals and Anteneanderthals also indicate right-handedness. Teeth in skulls collected from sites in France and Spain are marked in a way that suggests that meat was gripped between the teeth while being cut by a stone tool (knife) held in the right hand (Bermúdez de Castro *et al.* 1988). Thus, right-handedness was present early in hominoid evolution (for further discussion see Bradshaw & Rogers 1992).

Not surprisingly, the characteristic of right-handedness has been linked to our acquisition of tool use and ability to use language. Some argue that spoken language evolved from communication gestures performed largely by the right hand (Kendon 1991). If the right hand and left hemisphere were used to make signs that served to communicate between individuals, this may have led to the left hemisphere becoming specialised for language. It is true that both the production of speech and a large proportion of the comprehension of language are functions of the left hemisphere in most humans (see Benson & Geschwind 1985; Kertesz 1985).

There are two main regions in the left hemisphere, known as Broca's area and Wernicke's area, that are involved in speech production and language comprehension respectively. However, this does not mean that the left hemisphere has an exclusive role in language comprehension. The right hemisphere has a role, albeit more limited, in certain types of comprehension, including those used in humour, metaphors and imagery (see Bihrle *et al.* 1988; Gardner *et al.* 1983; McMullen & Bryden 1987).

The association between the left hemisphere's dominant role in speech production and in control of the right hand was first discovered by Dax, over 100 years ago. He recognised that people who had suffered a stroke leaving them paralysed on the right side of the body also tended to suffer aphasia (loss of speech) and a lesion (damage) located in the left hemisphere. Strokes resulting in paralysis of the left side, he found were not accompanied by aphasia and were linked to lesions in the right hemisphere. We now know that each hemisphere of the brain controls a different set of functions and performs different forms of processing of sensory information. The division is not absolute, but the left hemisphere has a greater involvement in analytical thinking, whereas the right hemisphere is more involved in parallel (or 'holistic') mental processes. The right hemisphere is specialised for controlling emotional responses and for processing information about faces (Sergent & Signoret 1992; and see Bradshaw 1989). In fact, the emotions are both expressed and perceived more strongly on the left side of the face, as determined by asking subjects to rate the expressiveness of photographs made up of two left sides (a chimeric image made by putting together the left side with its mirror image on the other side) and two right sides (Sackheim & Gat 1978; Sackheim *et al.* 1978; Christman & Hackworth 1993). As the muscles of each side of the face are largely controlled by the opposite hemisphere, stronger expression of emotions on the left side of the face is consistent with the right hemisphere's dominance for emotional responses.

Figure 10: Areas of the brain involved in speech

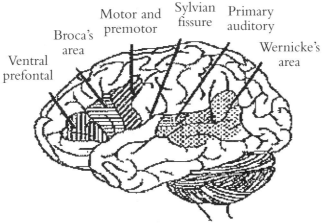

A human brain viewed from its left side. The regions involved in speech production and language comprehension are labelled. Note the Sylvian fissure, which is larger and positioned lower on the left side of the brain.

The left hemisphere's role in the production of speech is reflected in the facial musculature also. When we speak, the right side of the mouth opens more widely and moves at a faster rate than the left (Wolf & Goodale 1987). Thus, the muscle movements of the face reflect the asymmetry of brain functions. In addition, the asymmetry extends to the use of hands in gesturing while speaking. There is a correlation between which side of the mouth moves most while speaking and which hand is used to gesture while speaking (Wolf & Goodale 1987). Individuals who gesture with the left hand also move the left side of the mouth to a greater extent and *vice versa*. The areas of the brain that control the fine, sequential movements involved in both speech and manual dexterity are adjacent to each other in the left hemisphere. It is interesting to note that, even though scientists have only recently developed a strong interest in facial asymmetries, recognition of facial asymmetry has a long history in the world of art. The beautiful face of Venus de Milo is distinctly asymmetrical, a fact that has stimulated debates and has led to monograph publications (see Güntürkün 1991). Perhaps not unexpectedly, the asymmetrical control of the face by the brain may become imprinted on the facial features, such as the angle of holding the mouth or the expression surrounding the eyes.

The functional asymmetries in the human brain also correlate with structural asymmetries within the brain itself. The areas on the left side of the brain which process language and produce speech are larger than their equivalents in the right hemisphere (Geschwind & Levitsky 1968). These areas are the planum temporale and the periSylvian cortex around the Sylvian fissure (see Figure 10). This structural asymmetry varies with handedness in humans, left-handed individuals having on average weaker asymmetry (Hochberg & LeMay 1975). There is also an asymmetry in the front part of the human brain; expressed as a tendency for the frontal lobe to be larger on the right side than on the left side (Kertesz *et al.* 1990). The function of the larger frontal lobes in the right hemisphere is not exactly known, but it could be associated with emotional responses and for processing facial expressions (Sergent & Signoret 1992; and see Bradshaw 1989).

Originally, brain asymmetry was thought to be unique to humans and the explanation for our believed superior 'intelligence' or cognitive capacity. However, examination of the brain structure of primates has revealed that many species do, in fact, have structural asymmetries not unlike those of humans. In baboons, for example, Cain and Wada (1979) found the frontal lobe of the right hemisphere to be larger than the left. If the brain is not available for examination, it is possible to determine the overall brain structure from the skull by taking an endocranial cast. The inside cavity of the skull is filled with a latex rubber and removed after it sets. The cast takes on the superficial form of the brain for that skull. LeMay *et al.* (1982) have measured the endocranial casts of 25 apes and found asymmetries very similar to those of humans in chimpanzees and gorillas. The right frontal lobes and the left occipital poles (further back in the brain) were enlarged, as in the human brain. Similar, although less marked, asymmetries were found in Old World monkeys but not in New World monkeys.

Of most interest to us, they found no asymmetry in the orang-utan. A study by Holloway and de LaCoste-Lareymondie (1982) also found no asymmetry in the orang-utan, compared to clearly evident asymmetry in the gorilla and chimpanzees (both *Pan troglodytes* and *Pan paniscus*). However, it is also possible to look for asymmetry by measuring the length and position of the Sylvian fissure. In humans, this fissure is situated next to one of the areas for speech and is longer and lower in the left hemisphere than in the right (see Figure 10). LeMay and Geschwind (1975) found that the left Sylvian fissure is also longer and lower than the right in orang-utans, as well as in gorillas and chimpanzees. A similar result has been found for several Old World and New World species of monkey (Heilbroner & Holloway 1988).

As for humans, both monkeys and apes have structural asymmetry of the brain hemispheres. What can be said of their function? If there is a unique association between right-handedness, tool use and language ability in humans, we would expect to find no differences in function between the left and right hemispheres of non-human primates despite their anatomical asymmetry. If so, each hemisphere of the latter should control the same functions, and one would not expect non-human primates to have handedness.

At first this seemed to be the case. Although over 100 years ago Ogle noted right hand preferences in some captive monkeys (see Harris 1993), experimental interest in more recent times failed at first to find evidence for handedness in non-human primates.

The early studies found that individuals often had a preference for a particular hand to do a given task but there was no bias for use of the same hand in the majority of individuals in the group (Warren 1980). However, much of this earlier research was performed on small sample sizes and using tasks too simple to reveal the handedness. In 1987 MacNeilage *et al.* reviewed the literature on handedness in non-human primates concluding that there was more than simply suggestive evidence for handedness at a group or population level in a number of species. In many species, there is left handedness for visually guided acts of manual grasping and right-handedness for fine manipulation. A recent volume edited by Ward and Hopkins (1993) has arrived at a similar conclusion. Most of the contributors to this volume agree that there is a great need for more data collection on handedness in primates, using improved methodology and more creative experimental paradigms. There is also a need to increase sample sizes and to use more demanding tasks, as handedness appears to be more obvious in tasks of greater difficulty. In fact, Fragaszy and Adams-Curtis (1993) emphasise the value of using bilateral tasks to assess the relative use of either hand. The latter authors reported hand preferences in crab-eating macaques (*Macaca fascicularis*) tested on a range of unimanual and bimanual tasks and found clearer hand preferences in bimanual tasks, such as puzzle solving requiring two hands to manipulate levers and doors.

However, significant handedness in prosimians (Old World arboreal primates, eg lemurs) has been found in simple reaching for and holding of food. Left-handedness is predominant for several species of prosimians tested so far (Larson *et al.* 1989; Milliken *et al.* 1989, 1991). These species do not usually perform fine manipulation of food objects, but rather visual-motor coordination of the snatch-and-grab type, often used to capture insects. As the right hemisphere performs these visually guided functions better than the left, this may be why left-handedness characterises these species. Other factors influence the strength of handedness. The left hand preference is stronger when the animal is required to stand up on its hind limbs to reach for the food (Sanford *et al.* 1984). In this posture coordinated visual and motor performance is even more essential and, therefore, right hemisphere dominance may be expressed more strongly. The subjects would also be more aroused when they have to stand up and reach, and this may influence the degree to which they express handedness.

MacNeilage *et al.* (1987) hypothesised that brain lateralisation evolved to accommodate postural requirements, the right hand being stronger and used to support the body and the left being used for visually guided reaching, as in gathering food by prosimians. Once bipedalism (ie standing and walking on two feet with the hands not used in supporting the body) evolved there was a shift to using the right hand for manipulation of objects. In other words, once there was no longer a need to hold onto a branch to support the body or to use one hand on the ground as a prop, both hands could be used simultaneously, one holding and the other manipulating an object. According to MacNeilage *et al.* (1987) this explains the right-handedness of humans. The hypothesis would predict that right-handedness occurs in apes that are relatively terrestrial, such as chimpanzees and gorillas, but not in arboreal apes, such as gibbons (lesser apes) and orang-utans.

There is some evidence of right-handedness in chimpanzees and gorillas tested on certain tasks. For example, Olson *et al.* (1990) found a significant right hand preference in 10 out of 12 gorillas tested on tasks requiring retrieval of food, although gibbons showed a left hand preference and orang-utans no group bias (ie no handedness) for the same tasks. Detailed analysis of hand use in 12 chimpanzees reared in a nursery has revealed a right hand bias within the group (Bard *et al.* 1990). Over the first three months of life, the chimpanzees' limb preferences in the following behavioural acts were scored: hand held to mouth, hand-to-hand clasping, defensive grasps after a cloth was placed over the face and the first step taken when the infant was held in a walking position. There was significant right-handedness for putting the hand to the mouth, to a degree equivalent to the right-handedness of humans. The strength of this right hand preference increased with age. A positive relationship was found between this measure and the one for defensive grasping and there was an inverse relationship with hand-to-hand clasping. There was no bias for a preferred foot for setting off to walk. These results were later confirmed for a larger number of subjects (Hopkins & Bard 1993), and extended to two adult chimpanzees trained to use sign language (Morris *et al.* 1993). The latter chimpanzees exhibited right hand preferences for performing fine motor tasks requiring manual dexterity. Captive chimpanzees also use the right hand to throw small objects, usually at unfamiliar humans. Out of 19 chimpanzees, 15 were significantly right-handed (Hopkins *et al.* 1993a). Thus, chimpanzees show hand preferences much like humans. It should be noted, however, that right-handedness for hand-to-mouth behaviours is stronger in nursery-reared chimpanzees (Bard *et al.* 1990; Hopkins & Bard 1993), possibly due to the influence of their right-handed human caregivers (Hopkins & Bard 1993). It therefore appears that handedness is not determined exclusively by the genes but that it is influenced by experience. In fact, a recent field study of hand use in chimpanzees has failed to find any significant handedness (Marchant & McGrew 1994).

Aside from handedness, the hemispheres of primates may be specialised to carry out different *perceptual* functions, much as occurs in humans. The left hemisphere of Japanese macaque monkeys is known to be specialised for processing the vocalisations of this species of macaque (Petersen *et al.* 1984). The right ear sends its input primarily to the left hemisphere and this hemisphere has an advantage in processing the species' own alarm calls. The right hemisphere, by contrast, is specialised for discriminating faces, as shown in rhesus monkeys (Hamilton & Vermeire 1983) and chimpanzees (Morris & Hopkins 1993). The right hemisphere is also specialised for producing facial expressions (Hauser 1993) and for controlling emotional responses (Ifune *et al.* 1984). This is exactly the same as in humans.

The hemispheric specialisations are reflected in different performance abilities of left- and right-handed subjects, even in species that show no evidence of a group preference for using one hand (handedness). For example, rhesus monkeys trained on computer tasks using a joystick to control the program perform better if they are right-handed than if they are left-handed (Hopkins *et al.* 1992). The task involved catching a target stimulus as it moved across the computer screen with a cursor controlled by operation of the joystick. Three chimpanzees tested on this task also displayed better performance with the right hand (Hopkins *et al.* 1989). The results suggest that there is an advantage in using the left hemisphere and its associated right hand on the task requiring fine manipulation of the joystick.

Furthermore, as in humans, monkeys have a preferred eye for viewing certain stimuli through a peep-hole. Rhesus monkeys (*Macaca mulatta*) apparently prefer to use the left eye to look down a tube at a piece of food (Kruper *et al.* 1966). Bushbabies prefer to view food with the left eye, whereas there is a shift away from this left eye preference when individuals view their babies (Rogers *et al.* 1994). Most humans are right eye dominant, but this may vary with the state of arousal and the stimulus being viewed (Rogers *et al.* 1994).

Lateralisations in orang-utans

So far, we have said very little about lateralisation in orang-utans. In fact, before we conducted our study (Rogers & Kaplan 1994a, 1994b, 1995), very little was known of handedness or lateralisation of the brain in this species, apart from the structural asymmetry in the Sylvian fissure, as discussed earlier in this chapter.

Previous studies of handedness and other lateral biases in orang-utans have been confined to captive environments. Heestand (1986) has reported finding a bias for stepping with the right limb during terrestrial locomotion in some zoo orang-utans but this result may have limited relevance since orang-utans are primarily arboreal. Cunningham *et al.* (1989) studied the development of hand preferences in a single, captive orang-utan and found a right hand preference in reaching for food and a left hand preference for touching the face. Brésard and Bresson (1983) conducted a similar detailed study of hand preference in a single orang-utan on a number of tasks, and found consistent use of the right hand, particularly in tasks requiring bimanual coordination. Olson *et al.* (1990) tested eight orang-utans on a task requiring the unfastening of a hasp to obtain a food reward and some other retrieval tasks. The subjects were found to prefer the right or left hand, but there was no group bias (ie handedness). Olson and colleagues attributed this absence of handedness in orang-utans to their inability to perform bipedal locomotion with the consequence that they do not adopt an unstable posture which might lead to handedness. A recent study by Hopkins (1993) examined hand preferences in 40 captive chimpanzees and nine captive orang-utans reaching for food when they were in either a quadrupedal posture or standing upright. There was no group preference indicating handedness when the subjects were in a quadrupedal posture, but in the upright posture significant right-handedness emerged in both chimpanzees and orang-utans. In the upright posture, six orang-utans were right-handed, one left-handed and one showed no preference (one was not tested in the upright position). It should be emphasised, however, that both of these postures are less commonly adopted by orang-utans than chimpanzees.

The orang-utan's left hand preference for face touching found by Cunningham *et al.* (1989) is consistent with an earlier report of the same bias in a sample of eight orang-utans, as well as in monkeys (a mixed group of capuchins and macaques), gorillas, chimpanzees and humans (Dimond & Harries 1984). Face touching was found to be less common in the monkeys, compared to the apes, and their left hand preference was only slight. All of the apes had stronger left hand preferences. However, this result was obtained from a scoring period of only 20 minutes and it has been criticised on a number of other grounds, including sampling methods and statistical analysis (Suarez & Gallop 1986). In a somewhat more comprehensive study of face touching in macaques, the latter researchers found no handedness. However, they did not measure face touching in any of the apes, and other researchers (eg Byrne & Byrne 1991) have substantiated the statistical significance of the left hand preference for these species.

We were keen to assess handedness in orang-utans living in their natural environment with trees to climb and plenty of objects to manipulate. Orang-utans living in captivity have relatively limited access to objects which can be manipulated and they frequently live in isolation or are raised without adequate mother–infant interactions. These factors might well influence the development of hand preferences. The captive orang-utans studied by Olson *et al.* (1990) showed no handedness, but possibly this was due to their lack of opportunities to climb and manipulate objects, if not the posture they adopted during testing in captivity.

There has been only limited investigation of handedness in any of the apes (for a summary of handedness in all apes see Morris *et al.* 1993), and only one conducted in free-living individuals. The latter study was of wild mountain gorillas (*Gorilla gorilla berengei*) and it scored hand use in feeding. The researchers found evidence for individual preferences but no overall bias within the sample of 44 subjects (Byrne & Byrne 1991). There have also been only very few studies on handedness in the orang-utan compared to other apes (Marchant & McGrew 1991).

Orang-utans have well-developed hands that can be used for manipulation of both large and small objects. Despite their smaller thumb and its positioning further down the wrist, compared to gorillas, chimpanzees and humans, orang-utans can oppose the thumb to the fingers for precision gripping and manipulation (Rogers & Kaplan 1993). In addition, their feet are much better adapted for gripping than those of any other ape.

Food holding and manipulation

Most researchers interested in the handedness of primates have scored hand use to reach for or to hold food. After all, feeding is one of the behaviours requiring manipulative use of the hands and it should be relatively easy to score. We therefore decided to score hand use during feeding in the orang-utans, but it was not so easy to score. Orang-utans can use both the feet and hands to hold food and to manipulate it, sometimes by coordinated use of the two hands or a foot and a hand. In addition, while they are feeding, they can adopt a variety of postures when hanging or sitting. We had to take all of these postures into account, as they might influence the hand(s) used.

Thus in our study hand use was scored when the animals were hanging or when they were in a propped, or seated, posture. Bimanual use of the hands could occur more readily in the propped posture but it is not impossible in the hanging posture. The propped posture included being seated, usually on the feeding platform, or standing

Feeding when hanging (LH_3).

Feeding in propped position (LH_2RH_3).

using one hand to support the body. The hand use was ranked from 1 to 3, according to the degree of food manipulation. Category 1 referred to reaching out and taking food (fruit given at the feeding table or leaves eaten away from the table). Category 2 referred to holding the food object in a prehensile grasp together with taking it to the mouth, and Category 3 scores required manipulation of the food object with fine finger movement. Relative use of both hands could be assessed when the food was held simultaneously with both hands. For example, if a piece of food was held in the left hand and peeled by the right hand, it received a score of LH_2RH_3 (=Left Hand, Category 2, Right Hand Category 3). Usually bimanual holding of food involved differential use of either hand, but equivalent use of both hands also occurred (LH_2RH_2 or LH_3RH_3). When the orang-utans were hanging, the use of both hands occurred in only about one-tenth of the observations but when they were seated in the propped position, there was a significantly greater amount of bimanual holding and manipulation (approximately one third of the observations involved use of both hands). This allowed a better assessment of handedness in feeding because the relative use of each hand could be determined.

Use of the feet to hold food was scored as for the hands but it occurred relatively infrequently. When the orang-utans were in the hanging position use of the feet made

Figure 11: Hand use for CID and Mosuli

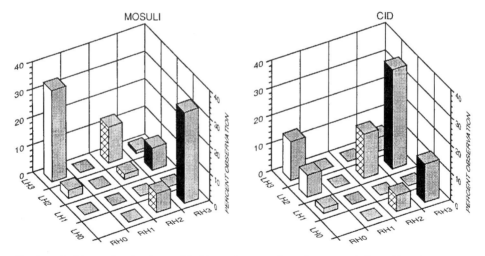

Hand use in bimanual and unimanual holding. These are three dimensional plots of hand use by Mosuli and CID. The scores were collected when these two individuals were seated in the propped position. The hand use has been scored for food holding and manipulation. It has been categorised according to the degree of manipulation (see text) for both unimanual and bimanual holding. For example LH_3RH_0 refers to unimanual holding by the left hand involving manipulation of the food and taking it to the mouth, whereas LH_3RH_2 refers to bimanual holding with use of the right hand to grasp the food and the left hand to manipulate it. The height of each bar gives the mean number of observations of a particular category as a percentage of the total number of observations. Note that both individuals have equal amounts or left- and right-hand use for unimanual holding. For bimanual holding, Mosuli remains ambidextrous but CID is strongly right-handed.

up only five percent of the total observations of food holding. In the propped (or seated) position, use of the feet occurred even less often. In both postures use of the hands is by far the preferred mode of food holding.

First, the results for each individual's hand use were plotted individually as three-dimensional graphs, including both unimanual and bimanual hand use in feeding. Examples of this way of looking at the results for two individuals, CID and Mosuli, are given in Figure 11. Note that when both hands are used together CID shows a clear right hand preference (the LH_2RH_3 column in the figure is greatest), whereas Mosuli is ambidextrous. Both of these individuals show no left or right hand preference in unimanual hand use (the columns of percentage frequency of LH_3RH_0 and LH_0RH_3 are of equal height). Thus, hand preference may be revealed in bimanual, but not unimanual, acts of feeding.

Hand preferences were therefore determined for each individual using only the bimanual scores and looking at the relative use of each hand. Of the 18 individuals for which there was sufficient data, eight had a significant hand preference (three left and five right) and ten had no preference. There were no sex differences in the distribution of handedness. Interestingly, individuals with a significant hand preference were older than those without a preference. A similar relationship between age and strength of handedness has been reported for baboons (Vauclair & Fagot 1987).

In the zero- to five-year age group only one out of the eight individuals had a significant hand preference, whereas of the ten subjects aged more than five years, seven had a significant hand preference. Undifferentiated use of the hands occurred more often in younger individuals, as might be expected. Bimanual use of hands each in a different manner obviously develops with experience. However, Simbo (27 years old), was an exception; he tended to use both hands equally, just like the juveniles. We wonder whether he had ever developed fully differentiated use of his hands or whether he simply ate in this way when he made his rare and rather brief visits to the feeding table, and was eating rapidly, possibly in a state of high arousal.

Let us summarise these results for hand use in feeding. There was no group bias for preferred use of a given hand in unimanual holding in either the hanging or the propped (seated) position. In the propped position, however, bimanual holding increased to approximately 30 percent of the events scored, and therefore it could be used to assess relative use of the hands. As Fragaszy and Adams-Curtis (1993) have emphasised the value of using bilateral tasks to assess handedness, we also considered this to be a more important indicator of handedness in feeding. Nevertheless, although half of the individuals had a significant left or right hand preference, there was still no overall bias for handedness for the group of 18 individuals assessed for relative hand use in bimanual holding.

Our findings for the orang-utans are in line with those obtained for wild gorillas. That is, there is no evidence of a group or population bias for handedness during feeding, although some individuals exhibit a hand preference (Byrne & Byrne 1991). By contrast, a group bias for right-handedness has been found in (captive) bonobos; they apparently hold food in the left hand and eat using the right hand (Hopkins *et al.* 1993b).

Face, head and body touching

We scored touching of the face, head or body by the left or right hand. Our scores were divided into three categories according to the way the hand was used: 1) with the back of the hand or flat palm without finger flexion, 2) front of the hand with finger flexion (usually for scratching), and 3) front of the hand with fine finger movements usually to manipulate the nose, ear, eyes or to pick the teeth. This manipulation usually involved use of the fingers and not the thumb, although sometimes the thumb was opposed to the fingers. Touching the face or head with both hands simultaneously or with the feet was scored but it occurred very rarely.

We obtained a sufficient number of observations (around 30 acts each) for a total of 31 individuals. For touching the face with use of the flat palm of the hand (Category 1), usually to swat insects, there was no preference for use of the left hand more than the right. But use of the hand to touch the face (Categories 2 or 3) was preferentially performed with the left hand. Although the right hand was used sometimes, for almost every individual the left hand was used more often (see Figure 12). This difference was highly significant, particularly for Category 3 movements, involving fine manipulation of parts of the face. In other words, the orang-utans chose the left hand to clean their eyes, ears or teeth. In fact, this was the most common reason why they touched their faces.

Touching the head, as opposed to the face, yielded different results. In this case, the orang-utans showed a significant preference for using the hand with a flat palm to

Figure 12: Hand use for touching face

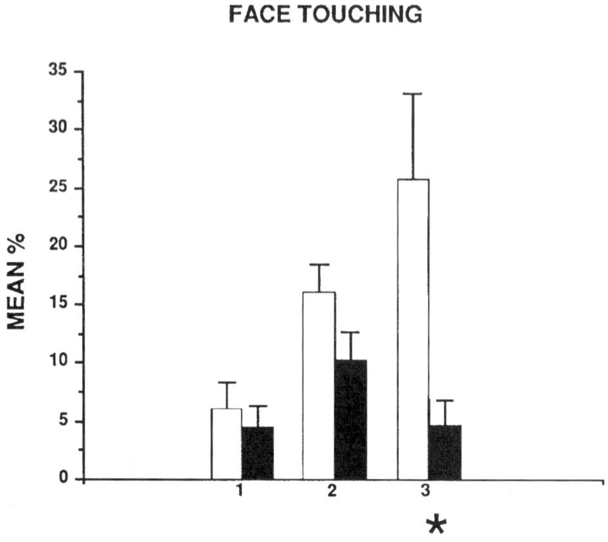

FACE TOUCHING

Hand use for touching the face by orang-utans. The mean occurrence of three categories of hand use is plotted as a percentage of the total amount of face touching. Category 1 refers to touching with the back of the palm or without finger flexion. Category 2 refers to touching with finger flexion (scratching) and Category 3 to manipulation of parts of the face (eg cleaning teeth, eyes or nose). Black bars for right hand, white bars for left hand. The asterisk indicates a significant **left** hand preference for Category 3 face touching.

▲ *Body touching (top). Head touching (Category 2) (bottom left). Face touching, (Category 3) (bottom right).*

swat insects (Category 1), but no preference for either hand for movements of Category 2 or Category 3. As most hand use for touching the head was of the Category 2 type, the left hand preference for Category 1 is a less important form of head touching. Overall, therefore, head touching involves no handedness, whereas face touching is clearly performed with a left hand preference.

Most acts of touching the body, as opposed to the face and head, were of the Category 2 type and there was a tendency to use the left hand in preference to the right. However, this was not a significant preference. Touching the body to manipulate parts of it (Category 3) was performed preferentially by the left hand but the preference was not as marked as for touching the face. Incidentally, most of the Category 3 acts of touching the body involved manipulation of the genitalia.

The strong group bias for left-handedness which we found for touching the face confirms the earlier reports of Dimond and Harries (1984) and Cunningham *et al.* (1989). It appears that apes have a preference for using the left hand to touch the face. However, a recent study of 11 bonobos (*Pan paniscus*) in captivity has failed to find handedness for face touching (Hopkins *et al.* 1993b) and the same is true for a study on chimpanzees (Aruguete *et al.* 1992). There is clearly a need for more measurement of this behaviour, especially in free-ranging subjects. Nevertheless, our study of a large number of orang-utans (31) living in their natural environment provides convincing evidence for handedness of face touching in the orang-utan and hence lateralisation of function in the brain.

There is some evidence that humans show similar left-handedness for touching the face (Dimond & Harries 1984). At least, this has been found for British people but not for Japanese people (Hatta & Dimond 1984). The cultural variation indicates that either the presence of the left hand preference, or its absence, may be learned, and that it does not occur as an obligatory consequence of right-handedness for other tasks requiring fine motor control, such as writing. In orang-utans also the left hand preference for face touching is independent of any group bias for handedness in food holding or manipulation. Therefore, it may be controlled by an independent aspect of difference between the hemispheres. The use of the left hand to touch the face translates to right hemisphere dominance for its control.

In humans, as Dimond and Harries (1984) suggested, the left hand might be used either consciously or unconsciously to heighten the effectiveness of facial expressions of emotion, which are also controlled by the right hemisphere and expressed more strongly on the left side of the face. As we mentioned previously, it is known for both humans and rhesus monkeys that emotions are expressed thus on the left-side of the face (Hauser 1993). As there has been no study of lateralisation of facial expressions in orang-utans, we cannot confirm or reject this as an explanation for our results (but see p.145, bottom). However, much of the face touching which we observed occurred when the orang-utans were in relative isolation, and the left hand preference was most apparent when the face touching involved fine finger movements to manipulate parts of the face for cleaning the teeth, eyes or ears. There was no indication of the left-handed face touching being used to point to the face during communication. The hand was not being used as an enhancer of facial expressions but to perform self-directed manipulation. Moreover, humans primarily touch the chin, whereas apes and monkeys touch the mouth more frequently (Dimond & Harries 1984; Suarez & Gallup 1986). The difference could, of course, reflect cultural taboos in humans, a possibility that cannot be answered until different groups of humans are studied.

Touching conspecifics

We also scored the hand(s) used to touch another orang-utan (a conspecific), although this form of social contact occurred rather rarely. We did not score touching during bouts of play but only brief tactile interactions, for example, when one individual meets another. Touching of conspecifics was not categorised for degree of hand and finger use but it rarely involved fine finger movements to manipulate another individual. Fine finger movements and gripping did occur when the orang-utans were playing but we did not include this in our scoring. Touching with manipulation of a conspecific was, however, observed occasionally in brief encounters, for example, when one orang-utan pinched the chin of another. Thus, Abbie used chin-pinching as a trick to get another orang-utan to give his banana to her.

Over the observation period we scored 22 individuals performing acts of touching a conspecific and the mean number of acts per individual was about ten. Although we could have overlooked some instances of touching a conspecific, as this behaviour was not our main focus, it is clear that this behaviour occurs less commonly in orang-utans than in chimpanzees. There was no group bias for hand preference in touching conspecifics; the mean percent for right-handedness was 50 percent. This means that although orang-utans in Sabah touch their own faces and manipulate parts of their bodies with the left hand, they touch other orang-utans equally with either the left or right hand.

Thumb and finger sucking

Thumb or finger sucking was recorded for 11 individuals and a total of 17 events, mostly prior to the provisioning of food at Semengoh, when the orang-utans exhibited other frustration behaviours such as squealing, or after food had been placed on the platform and the particular individual showed reluctance to approach it. The finger placed in the mouth was either the thumb or the index finger, with no preference for one over the other. Toe sucking was also observed in five of the same individuals that sucked their fingers. The big toe was the one chosen to be sucked. Although our sample size is too small to allow us to draw a conclusion, we found no indication of a group preference for the digits of the left or right hand or foot (17 left to 13 right). It should be noted that finger and toe sucking occurred mainly in infants and juveniles.

Although thumb, finger or toe sucking can be described as self-directed behaviour, it is interesting that unlike face touching there was no hint of handedness. It is not, of course, a behaviour using fine manipulation. Nevertheless, our result may indicate that orang-utans differ from chimpanzees in this behaviour, as Hopkins and Bard (1993)

▲ *Imitation behaviour by infant in feeding with mother Clementine, 'mirror imaging'.*

▼ *Abbie's feeding behaviour is observed closely by Tom.*

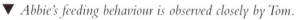

have reported a right hand preference for hand-to-mouth behaviour in infant chimpanzees (see also Bard *et al.* 1990).

Baby carrying

Humans tend to hold babies with their left hand and arm, leaving the right hand free (Lockard *et al.* 1979). A similar tendency has been noted in gorillas (Fischer *et al.* 1982; Lockard 1984) and in a mixed group of captive chimpanzees, gorillas and orang-utans (Manning & Chamberlain 1990; Manning *et al.* 1994). The latter researchers suggested that this positioning of the infant assists the mother's right hemisphere to monitor the infant's emotional responses. Others have noted the placement of the infant's head close to the mother's heart and suggested that it serves to comfort the infant (Salk 1962; Simner 1969). It is not certain, however, whether the position of the infant is determined by the mother or the infant. A preference for the left nipple either by the infant or mother may cause the left-side bias (Nishida 1993). The left-side preference for baby carrying by chimpanzees has, however, not been strongly confirmed in a more recent study of 12 captive subjects, seven of whom exhibited a left-side preference and five a right-side preference (Hopkins *et al.* 1993a). Discrepancies in scoring methods might be the explanation for the different results, and these need to be taken into account in future research.

At Sepilok we observed four mothers with their babies, and the side of the mother to which the baby was clinging, usually when she moved through the canopy, was scored each time a new sighting was made. There was a significant right-side preference in two out of the four mother–infant pairs recorded. Our results do not fit with any of the above mentioned explanations for a side preference in carrying and they are not consistent with those of Manning and Chamberlain (1990). There were four captive orang-utans in their sample, three found to have a left-side preference and one a right-side preference. Whereas these researchers scored holding or cradling of the infant by the mother, in the same manner that humans cradle their babies, all of our observations were for infants clinging to the mother while she used her limbs to brachiate. In fact, only Jessica with a one-week old infant was seen cradling her baby. It is possible that cradling of older infants, as observed by Manning and Chamberlain (1990), occurs more frequently in captivity where brachiation is less possible.

In the mother–infant pairs for which we found a right-side preference, the position of the baby appeared to be determined by the mother, as we frequently observed the mother using a hand to move the baby to her right side. This bias might influence the development of lateralised hand use in the offspring, as found in chimpanzees. Young chimpanzees have hand preferences opposite to their mother's side preference for carrying (Hopkins *et al.* 1993a). The infants of mothers with a left hand preference for cradling reach with their right hand, and vice versa.

The positioning of the baby on the right side might either be determined by the mother's handedness or, alternatively, it might influence the hand used by the mother for feeding. Consistent with the latter hypothesis, Jessica was right-handed when she was scored in 1991 without her baby and had a tendency to be left-handed in 1992 when she was cradling her baby on the right side. Her hand preference for face touching did not change, possibly because this act it was already performed by the left hand.

Some concluding thoughts on handedness

The absence of handedness for feeding in orang-utans might well be explained by their arboreal existence. But why do they exhibit handedness for face touching and not for feeding? Possibly face touching is performed when the orang-utan is more at ease and has time to choose the hand to be used, but one might still expect handedness to emerge when both hands are used in feeding. However, we observed that feeding is often a social event, while face touching is not. This may influence the hand used.

When social interaction occurred during feeding while hanging, it frequently involved two orang-utans hanging by one arm so that they faced each other and adopted the use of opposite hands for holding and hanging. We have called this 'mirror imaging' behaviour (see photograph p.128). It occurred frequently between a mother and her offspring but also in other age groups and social combinations. This pattern of behaviour might be a form of social interaction involving learning (particularly between mother and offspring) or bond confirmation. If such mother–infant learning has a lasting effect on handedness, one might predict that offspring would have hand preferences opposite to their mothers. This would be contrary to some evidence for macaques showing that offspring tend to have the same hand preference as their mother (Brinkman 1984). Perhaps we will have an answer to this as the infants at Sepilok become older.

We mentioned earlier that lower primates use the left hand for visually guided reaching for food and that, once the right hand had been freed for use by the adoption of a more bipedal posture, it could be used for fine manipulation of objects (according to the hypothesis of MacNeilage *et al.* 1987). Our data for orang-utans does not fit neatly into this picture of evolution because they are arboreal and might therefore be expected to have retained the left-handedness of their ancestors, the lower primates. Of course, they might be seen as being part way to the evolution of the right-handedness present in chimpanzees and humans, but there is insufficient data for chimpanzees to be certain of their handedness. Also, being more terrestrial, gorillas should be right-handed, but there is no evidence for this. As mentioned previously, wild mountain gorillas show no handedness (Byrne & Byrne 1991). There has been one study of four captive lowland gorillas reporting right hand preferences for grasping (Fischer *et al.* 1982) and another of 31 subjects reporting no handedness (Annett & Annett 1991). Other contradictory results exist for gorillas. In simple reaching tasks they have been found to have symmetrical hand preferences and in complex problem solving tasks they have exhibited left hand preferences (Vauclair & Fagot 1993). Apparently, handedness may be influenced by task, stress or attention and past experience. This is likely to be the situation for hand use in all primates, including orang-utans.

In our study, age was found to be an important factor contributing to handedness during feeding with both hands. Older individuals were handed, whereas those under five years of age were not. A similar increase in handedness with age has been reported for food reaching and holding in the black lemur, *Lemur macaco* (Forsythe & Ward 1988) whereas Heestand (1986) found no correlation between age and lateralisation of leading limb preference in orang-utans. We found no effect of sex on any of the measures of handedness in the orang-utans, although Ward and her colleagues have reported effects of sex in lower primate species (Milliken *et al.* 1989; Ward *et al.* 1993).

Consistent use of a preferred hand for fine manipulation of food held in the other hand was characteristic of older juvenile or adult orang-utans, irrespective of their sex. Younger orang-utans were less likely to have a hand preference for food holding and manipulation, although they had a left hand preference for touching the face, and they were more likely to feed by using both hands equally, in an undifferentiated manner. This apparently reflects a lesser degree of manipulative ability in young individuals.

There is little doubt that some orang-utans have hand preferences for feeding, even though the group may not display handedness in a consistent direction. Considered together with handedness for face touching, the hand use reflects hemispheric specialisation. This specialisation of the hemispheres occurred early in evolution, probably for processing perceptual information (see Bradshaw & Rogers 1992), and not more recently in response to the postural changes, as suggested by MacNeilage *et al.* (1987). In other words, lateralised use of the hands reflects lateralised cognitive processing in the hemispheres. Handedness, be it for feeding or face touching, is a way of telling us that, contrary to earlier held beliefs, humans share with other primates this particular mode of cognitive processing.

Some researchers have suggested that handedness in feeding may be secondary to lateralised control of the mouth. Thus, right-handedness for feeding in bonobos may occur as a consequence of the left hemisphere's control of the jaw and mouth, later in evolution to become a characteristic of speaking in humans. Similarly, the right hemisphere's control of emotions on the left side of the face may be manifested as left-handedness for touching the face. Furthermore, exactly how the hands are used, even when hand preferences are absent, may depend on the hemisphere in control. For example, capuchin monkeys (*Cebus apella*) use the opposable thumb in a prehensile grip when they use the right hand but not usually when they use the left hand. More detailed information like this for orang-utans and other apes would be of much interest.

Tool using and cognition

Humans have been characterised by right-handedness, tool use, upright bipedal locomotion and language, but it now seems that these traits are not unique to our species. Tool use in primates is an important topic because the use of tools is considered to be one of the main aspects of the development of hominid intelligence.

A tool can be defined strictly as something detached from the user's own body (and therefore not a beak or a claw) and not attached to a substrate which is used to change the state (position or form) of another object (Beck 1980). There are many examples of tool use in wild chimpanzees (Boesch & Boesch 1990). They break off stalks of grass or twigs to an appropriate length and then insert them into termite nests. The termites cling onto the stalk and can be 'fished' out to be eaten from the stalk by the chimpanzees (Goodall 1968; McGrew & Marchant 1992; Nishida & Uehara 1980). This form of tool using occurs in several different groups of chimpanzees in different regions (McGrew & Collins 1985; Yamagiwa *et al.* 1988; Gonzalez-Kirchner & de la Maza 1992) and it occurs frequently (McGrew 1974). At one site nearly 300 termite-fishing tools were found over five months (McGrew & Collins 1985). There has even been a report of a chimpanzee using a stick to 'fish' a squirrel out of its hole, followed by capturing and eating it (Huffman & Kalunde 1993).

Chimpanzees also use stones as hammers to crack open nuts (Boesch 1991; Sakura & Matsuzawa 1991). The nut is placed on a piece of root or another rock, serving as an anvil, and then is hit using the stone 'hammer'. It seems that the chimpanzees may understand the function of these tools because they select ones that make effective hammers or anvils and they place the nut on the hardest spot of the anvil (Sakura & Matsuzawa 1991). They also vary the method of hammering according to quality of the nuts (Hannah & McGrew 1987). The nut-cracking skill is learnt by observation and practice. It is passed on from generation to generation. A mother has been seen teaching her offspring by reorienting the position of a nut on the anvil so that her infant could crack it more easily (Boesch 1991). In another instance, the mother reoriented the hammer in her infant's hand so that it would operate more effectively. Such active teaching indicates an ability to attribute a mental state to another, to be aware of the pupil's state of knowledge. It is therefore an indication of higher cognitive thought.

Nut cracking takes chimpanzees a long time to learn and it seems to require close mother–infant interaction (Boesch 1993). The mother may play a role in the infant's learning simply by stimulating or facilitating the behaviour by placing nuts on an anvil or placing a hammer on the anvil, or she may actively teach as described above.

Chimpanzees also use leaves as sponges to soak up water for drinking from inaccessible crannies (Goodall 1968). Fashioning a tool for use goes one step further, and chimpanzees fashion to an appropriate length the stalks that they use for termite fishing. A captive chimpanzee has been observed to fashion a cutting tool by striking sharp flakes off a cobblestone using a hammer stone to hit it, the cobblestone being held in one hand and the hammer in the other hand. The sharp flakes were used to cut string around a box containing food (Charles *et al.* 1991). This is clearly sophisticated tool use and manufacture, but nothing equivalent to it has yet been observed in wild chimpanzees. Similarly, a captive orang-utan learnt to strike a flake from a flint stone and use the tool produced to open a box containing food by cutting through a cord (Wright 1972).

Wild chimpanzees have been seen to use a series of tools, like a *toolkit,* to get access to a source of honey (Brewer & McGrew 1990). First, a large sharp-ended branch was used to chisel a hole in the wax coating of the nest. Next a smaller and thinner stick was used for more accurate work, and then a green branch fashioned to be about 30 cm in length was inserted into the hole to puncture the seal. Finally, the honey was extracted by dipping a green vine into the hole. Wild orang-utans also like honey. Following an orang-utan's raid on a bees' nest and after being attacked by the bees, the orang-utan went away and returned wearing a hat of small branches, which protected his face while he raided the hive again, this time successfully (Western 1994).

As far as information is available at present, wild orang-utans appear to use tools less frequently than wild chimpanzees, but this could be because orang-utans are more difficult to observe in the rainforest canopy. They have been observed wiping the face with crumpled leaves and breaking off and throwing branches in aggressive displays (Schaller 1961). The latter has been observed frequently in wild orang-utans at Tanjung Puting (Galdikas 1982b). The act is usually accompanied by vocalisations (kiss squeak). Most often this form of aggressive display is directed at or occurs in the vicinity of humans, when they are first encountered; with subsequent encounters the frequency of this display declines. We have also noticed breaking and throwing of branches by the ex-captive orang-utans at Sepilok. According to Beck's strict definition of tool using (see previously), these acts may not be considered as such because they do not involve use of tools to effect change in another object, but a more liberal definition would include it as tool using because the 'tool' is used to effect change in another organism. The throwing of a branch is presumably aimed at changing the behaviour of the human observer (ie asking that person to leave) and so may be considered as use of a tool. Similarly, the breaking of and use of branches to fan away insects, or simply to circulate the humid air, may be considered as tool using. Orang-utans frequently perform this act. They also place large leaves on the head as protection when it is raining, which might also loosely be called tool using. To clean the teeth or ears using a stick falls into the same category. Wild orang-utans have been sighted using leaves to wipe their infants' faeces from their coats (MacKinnon 1974a).

Orang-utans make tree nests for resting and sleeping. These are made by breaking branches and carefully arranging them to make a secure platform. Most researchers do not consider nest building to be an example of tool using, but the broken branches are used to facilitate a change in behaviour. Of, course, a vast number of animal species build nests and this behaviour of orang-utans is not exceptional. Nevertheless, one cannot fail to be impressed by the construction of a large nest high up in the canopy to support a heavy mammal. This engineering feat must surely demand both higher cognitive processes and considerable learning experience. There is, as yet, no information on direct teaching of offspring about nest building by mothers but, as infants are together with the mother when she builds nests, they may begin to learn by observation. Ex-captive orang-utans have to learn how to build nests, and older ones often have great difficulty in doing so (Galdikas 1982b).

Nest building practice commences often at the age of 14 months and by the time of juvenile development, nest building is perfected, enabling the juveniles to make a 'bed' for themselves independent of the mother's quarters, just when their own weight would be an undue stress on the leafy construction of the one nest. The nest functions as a resting place at night, but is also constructed when an orang-utan feels ill or a female is in the later stages of pregnancy and wishes to rest (Galdikas 1982a). Moreover, nests are not only used as structures for giving support and comfort for the resting body but similar structures are built by orang-utans to provide shelter from heavy rain (Davenport 1967). Orang-utans do not seem to mind light rain but when the torrential rains come down in the rainy season, they have been observed to seek shelter and, if this was not available or unsatisfactory, the orang-utans built such shelters themselves.

At Sepilok, infants frequently build nests even for taking a siesta during the hottest part of the day. Once we filmed Bobbie absolutely absorbed in choosing appropriately sized branches and inserting them, almost weaving them, into the nest as she sat on it. A particular branch was inserted several times before she was satisfied that it had been inserted in the right place. Self-learning appeared to be occurring. Incorrect placements of a branch occasionally caused Bobbie to slip out of the nest. Much practice of this kind is likely to have occurred before the orang-utan reaches a size large enough to require the building of particularly strong nests.

There may be a form of 'social tool use' in primates (Bard 1990). This refers to the use of gestures to obtain something or to direct the behaviour of another. For example, an infant may take hold of its mother's hand and pull in order to obtain food being held by its mother. In this case the mother's hand is being used as a tool to obtain the food. Orang-utans as young as seven to ten months of age use this method of sampling the food that the mother is eating. Often the mother ignores or rejects her infant's request, only allowing access to the food on some 20 percent of the occasions (Bard 1990). At Sepilok one of us experienced a memorable attempt by BJ (then five years old, see Chapter 5) to use one of us as a 'social tool' to leave the reserve and enter the area of the field station. While the keeper was busy talking to visitors, BJ came up to Lesley and took hold of her hand. He tugged on her hand and gestured with his head in the direction of the exit path from the reserve. This was repeated surreptitiously each time the keeper looked away. The aim was clearly to solicit help to go to the exit. Orang-utans are known to use gestures to help in locomotion. It can be argued that they apply their cognitive abilities to use gestures as tools. They may well have specialised development of this ability rather than conventional tool using.

Object related, or conventional, tool using is more common in ex-captive orang-utans than in wild orang-utans (Galdikas 1982b) or even in captive orang-utans, provided the latter are given sufficient objects to manipulate. Their greater use of tools compared to wild orang-utans puzzles psychologists. Given that they have such a large capacity to use tools, why is tool using rather uncommon in wild orang-utans? Perhaps the wild orang-utans have used their 'tool using capacity' in social contexts, as Bard (1990) suggests. Alternatively, this capacity may be used in the wild to negotiate gaps and branches during locomotion, as suggested by Galdikas (1982b). Orang-utans require considerable skills to use branches and flexible saplings to cross gaps in the canopy. They often bridge these gaps by swinging back and forth on a flexible straight tree with increasing excursions until they manage to reach across the gap to the next tree. This behaviour is not used for independent locomotion by infants until they are over four years old (Bard 1993). The tree on which they swing is used as a tool for locomotion. Being more terrestrial, chimpanzees do not have to make these negotiated movements. Like orang-utans, capuchin monkeys are primarily arboreal and also in captivity they use a much wider range of tools than they do in the wild (Visalberghi 1987). This finding reinforces the idea that it is being arboreal that reduces conventional tool use, not being an orang-utan or a capuchin. Interestingly, the tool using capabilities of capuchins, together with their relatively large brain, has led some to think of them as being the New World's equivalent to apes (Visalberghi 1993).

Free-ranging (ie ex-captive and rehabilitative) orang-utans make use of a wide variety of tools. In addition to the tool using of wild orang-utans, they use sticks or planks to dig holes in the ground or break open objects, to hit other orang-utans, to pry off loose objects, to break open fruit, to reach for the branch of an adjacent tree when locomoting, to climb onto and balance on when playing or to use as a ladder to reach a window, to stir liquids, to remove biting insects from the hair and to scratch themselves (Rijksen 1978; Galdikas 1982b). They have even been seen using a stick as a paddle or a pole to propel a canoe and dragging logs to the river, then positioning them to form a bridge for crossing the stream (Galdikas 1982b). One orang-utan at Tanjung Puting even learnt to untie the rope attached to the bow of a boat, and then hold it in his mouth as he crossed the stream in the boat. Once on the other bank, he kept the rope in his hand or foot as he fed, to prevent the boat from drifting away, which would make the return trip impossible.

These ex-captive orang-utans probably learn at least some of their tool using skills from humans. Many of the tool using behaviours may be learnt by imitation. For example, at Tanjung Puting the orang-utans had seen workmen bridging the river with logs before they adopted the behaviour themselves (Galdikas 1982b; Russon & Galdikas 1993). Other examples of imitation have been noted in orang-utans in close contact with humans at Camp Leakey, Tanjung Puting. These include siphoning of fuel from drums into cans, imitating the cook's use of fire by fanning embers with a lid and placing a cup of liquid on the fire, imitating the gardener weeding and imitating painting of the floor and buildings (Russon & Galdikas 1993). In every case the imitation learning was rapid. Although chimpanzees take a long time to learn how to use a hammer and anvil to crack nuts, they can learn other forms of tool use rapidly, and so can the orang-utans (Beck 1974). In these behaviours, chimpanzees and orang-utans do not differ. Earlier claims (Köhler 1926) that apes imitate only rarely because they are unable to understand the solution to the problem are clearly incorrect.

Even though imitation has been demonstrated to play a major role in tool use by apes, much of their tool using is acquired by individual experimentation (Tomasello 1993). Most examples of individual discovery of tool using have come from captive primates presented with tools that the experimenter chooses. For example, capuchins given wooden blocks and nuts can discover how to crack the nuts using a block as a hammer (Visalberghi 1987). They will even manufacture tools of the appropriate size and shape to insert into holes for a sweet syrup reward (Westergaard & Fragaszy 1987). Then, once a particular form of tool using has been acquired, it may be passed on from one generation to the next as a form of 'cultural tradition', although it seems that the cultural transmission of nut cracking by chimpanzees is not achieved with ease because it is a difficult skill to acquire and because it occurs in some regions and not neighbouring ones (Sumita *et al.* 1985; Kortlandt & Holzhaus 1987).

The ability of orang-utans to acquire such a wealth of tool-using behaviours indicates their advanced cognitive abilities. While chimpanzees in the wild may have been observed to use tools more frequently than orang-utans, ex-captive orang-utans definitely use as many tools and as frequently as chimpanzees, and captive orang-utans score even better than chimpanzees at complex tool making, such as using a tool to make another tool (Lethmate 1982). Perhaps there is less demand for wild orang-utans to use tools to obtain food in their prolific rainforest habitat, whereas chimpanzees living in open forests bordering on savannah may need to exploit insects and hard nuts to survive (Galdikas 1982b). The use of tools must also depend on their availability in a given area, and this may explain the regional differences in tool use noted for chimpanzees (Boesch & Boesch 1990). Also, it would be more difficult to carry and use tools when climbing in the canopy. Under such circumstances it may be necessary to invent different means of obtaining food, and orang-utans appear to have done this. For example, they crack hard nuts by using their powerful jaws and ensure that the nut does not pop out of the mouth by holding the cheek against a tree trunk or pressing both hands against the cheek (Galdikas 1982b). In fact, this might be a reason why orang-utans retained the large, powerful jaw. Considered to be a more primitive feature, the large jaw might even have been positively selected (evolved) to suit the arboreal existence of orang-utans.

Indeed, we have suggested that the large, protuding lower jaw and lips might have been developed for yet another aspect of feeding (Rogers & Kaplan 1993). We have noticed that orang-utans frequently protrude the lower lip with a berry or some other food substance placed on it and they can look down and examine the food before continuing to eat it. Food is often carried and examined in this way. It is as if the mouth is used as a vessel, one not requiring the use of hands that are otherwise occupied in climbing or hanging.

During our time at Sepilok, we observed several different examples of tool use. These included use of small sticks to clean the teeth or ears (incidentally, using the left hand), use of a large piece of wood to break open a mound of earth, use of a branch with leaves to fan away insects or create a draft for cooling, and use of leaves as a vessel from which to feed. The latter form of tool using had not been reported previously. The orang-utans were seen to select carefully leaves of an appropriate size and strength and then to arrange them into a vessel able to hold semi-fluid material. Into this vessel they spat out masticated food and proceeded to eat from the vessel (Rogers & Kaplan 1994a).

We observed this form of tool using on three occasions, around the time of food provisioning with bananas, other fruits and milk, at the feeding table. In these food provisioning conditions it is not uncommon for the orang-utans to visit the table for a very brief period, grab a bunch of bananas and take it away to feed in isolation or to take a large mouthful of banana flesh and then retreat to a more isolated part of the canopy to eat without interruption. The tool use occurred as part of the latter behaviour. It was observed in three females aged six, nine and 15 years. The 15-year old was

Gandipot and she had a one-year old baby at the time. We were fortunate enough to film her when she was high up in the canopy performing this act of tool using. In fact, it was not until we watched the videotape in detail that we realised what an important sequence of behaviour the camera had captured. From the videotape we were able to make a detailed analysis of the sequence.

The entire behaviour pattern lasted around 20 minutes. Gandipot left the feeding table with her mouth full of banana flesh and milk. With her baby clinging to her side, she quickly climbed to a higher part of the canopy, away from the feeding table, and in a very goal-directed manner picked six to eight large, oblong leaves, probably *Dracontomelon magniferum* of the mango family. Holding these in her right hand, she climbed still higher into another tree, where she seated herself on a horizontal branch, propped in a position that allowed both hands to be free. To the naked eye, she was now just a tiny speck of amber in the canopy but the camera distinguished her features and actions very clearly. At this time her infant moved a short distance away. She then proceeded to arrange the leaves so that the stalks all faced one way. Then the leaves were fashioned into a fan shape. While holding the narrow part of the fan in her right hand and cradling the broad part with her left hand, she spat the masticated food onto it. One minute later her infant approached and began to feed from the vessel but it was allowed access to the food for only three seconds before being pushed away by the mother's left hand. The mother then commenced eating. A second attempt was made by the infant, who reached for the vessel, attempting to use it as a tool also. The gesture was rewarded by the mother moving the vessel towards the baby's mouth for a few seconds. This act was repeated four times during the entire sequence. Each time the baby was allowed only a short period of access to the food, the access being terminated by the mother pushing her infant away or, in one case, by the mother touching the infant's back, followed by the baby withdrawing immediately. Young orang-utans in the wild have been observed to obtain some food items from their mothers (Galdikas & Teleki 1981), but their attempts to acquire food are rather frequently rejected (Bard 1990).

During this tool-using sequence, the mother took all of the food into her mouth, re-arranged the leaves and spat the food out again several times. The hand used to hold the leaves by the narrow section of the fan was exchanged twice; the total time of holding with the right hand was four times that with the left hand. The other two observations of leaves being used as a vessel also involved holding the leaves at the neck of the fan-shape with the right hand. Therefore, there may be perhaps a right hand preference for holding and manipulating the vessel. This contrasts to a left-hand preference by capuchins (*Cebus apella*) and lion-tailed macaques (*Macaca silenus*) for holding and manipulating dipping sticks (Westergaard 1991). This left to right shift from monkeys to apes is consistent with the earlier mentioned hypothesis of MacNeilage *et al.* (1987). Although McGrew and Marchant (1992) found no significant preferred hand in wild chimpanzees fishing for termites, a subsequent communication by the same authors has reported weak but significant left-handedness (McGrew & Marchant 1994). For nut cracking, individual chimpanzees show a hand preference for holding the hammer, particularly as they become older, but there appears to be no strong hand preference within the population (Boesch 1991; Sugiyama *et al.* 1993). Further studies of hand preferences for tool using will be needed before it will be possible to draw a conclusion.

As mentioned already, Galdikas (1982b) has reported that ex-captive orang-utans make more use of tools than do wild orang-utans, and that tool use in wild orang-utans is limited to agonistic displays and nesting behaviour. It is possible that use of leaves as a vessel has developed in the context of food provisioning and may not occur in wild orang-utans. Alternatively, provisioning may have enhanced the occurrence of a behaviour which occurs in wild orang-utans, possibly when they congregate at fruiting trees and wish to withdraw from the group to eat on their own. There is a possibility that at least aspects of the behaviour were learnt from humans during the orang-utans' earlier period of rehabilitation but it is unlikely that this learning would have involved fashioning of the leaves into a vessel. Regardless of how it was acquired, the *adaptation* of the behaviour to the natural environment remains important. Also, it is likely to be transmitted to the next generation because the infant was observing the mother while she performed the act of tool using.

Ex-captive orang-utans mostly use sticks as tools and, of particular interest here, Galdikas (1982b) has observed sticks being used as implements to bring food to the mouth. She also reported that a captive orang-utan placed some rice on a piece of bark and handed it to her. The only use of leaves as a tool that she observed was in rubbing the face with a handful of crumpled leaves. These examples do not, apparently, involve fashioning of the tool, as was clearly the case for arranging the leaves into the fan-shaped vessel. In the latter case there is similarity to termite fishing in chimpanzees, in which the twig used for fishing is stripped of leaves and broken to the appropriate length for dipping into the nest (Goodall 1968; McGrew 1974; McGrew & Marchant 1992). Indeed, there have very recently been observations of wild orang-utans fashioning sticks to probe into holes in trees to obtain insects or honey (van Schaik & Fox 1994). This was seen in orang-utans in a swamp forest region of the Gunung Leuser National Park in Sumatra. A chosen stick was stripped of leaves, chewed at one end and split to give a spatula shape at the other end. The spatulate end was held in the mouth and the chewed end used to hammer in the hole. Next the stick was removed and the chewed end inserted into the mouth for feeding, just as with termite fishing in chimpanzees.

Problem solving

The problem solving abilities of captive orang-utans are impressive. An orang-utan has no difficulty in solving the problem of how to reach bananas suspended at a height, doing so by piling boxes on top of each other (Lethmate 1982). We have discussed the ability of orang-utans to use and even manufacture tools. Another example described by Lethmate (1982) involved joining up to five tubes to make a long pole which could be used to knock down a piece of food suspended overhead. Using a combination of these two examples, a young male orang-utan stood on a box and wielded a stick to reach an object placed at a height.

Complex tool making by captive orang-utans may surpass that of chimpanzees (Lethmate 1982) and it certainly is not inferior. All of the examples of tool-using behaviour in ex-captive and wild orang-utans that we have discussed in the previous section testify to either their powers of imitation, trial and error learning or problem solving. Many authors rather too hastily attribute the problem solving abilities of apes merely to imitation learning, claiming that they have no insight into the solution to the problem being tackled. For example, Lethmate (1982) has reported that during thousands of trials he has conducted with three orang-utans, only nine solutions involved insight learning. We suggest that this result may be influenced by the captive situation and the artificial problems that the orang-utans were given to solve in captivity. It may also be influenced by dependent relationships that develop between the orang-utan and the experimenter.

To give an example of insight learning observed by Lethmate (1982), a young male orang-utan had learnt to insert a long tool into a transparent plastic tube to push out a sweet. At first he bit at the tube and tried unsuccessfully to insert the tool. In frustration he moved away from the tube, sat down, began to perform stereotyped behaviours with the tool and a blanket and then glanced back at the tube. At that moment the insight came to him. He got up, walked to the tube carrying the stick, inserted it into the tube and obtained the sweet.

Another task requiring insight problem solving required the orang-utan to use a series of keys to unbolt boxes. There were five boxes, four of which could be opened by using keys and one a choice box containing the keys. One box contained a food reward, another was empty and the other two boxes contained keys, only one of which would allow access to the food box. The orang-utan had to choose the correct key from the initial choice box to open the box containing the key to the food box. An orang-utan was able to solve this problem without difficulty (Lethmate 1982). In fact, orang-utans are particularly persistent in performing such problems. They seem to enjoy manipulating locks and bolts and solving problems that require a series of manipulations to open a box even though there may be no reward inside. Their interest and perseverance exceeds that of other apes (Parker 1969). Orang-utans have also shown superior abilities in using ropes as tools, compared to other apes (Parker 1974).

Of all of the apes, orang-utans are the best manipulators of objects. This is almost certainly an ability that they use constantly in their natural habitat to move about using vines, branches and flexible trunks. In fact, most of the orang-utan's day is spent manipulating branches or trunks, be this for locomotion, feeding or nest building. It is in the problems posed by these objects that orang-utans excel. In their natural domain they must also remember the location of hundreds of food types and when they will be ripe. These clear indications of superior cognitive abilities have lead some researchers to rank orang-utans higher up the 'intelligence scale' than gorillas or chimpanzees (see Lethmate 1982).

Their cognitive capacities must be specialised to meet different environmental needs and so cannot be ranked on the basis of one measurable criterion alone. Nevertheless, these findings do illustrate that it is incorrect to rank orang-utans below chimpanzees and gorillas merely on the grounds of social behaviour. Under certain circumstances, ex-captive orang-utans may display well-developed social behaviours (Rijksen 1978), even though wild orang-utans have not been observed to use them frequently. In their relatively 'solitary' existence (and this is not to say that they have no sociality, see Chapter 4), wild orang-utans have not developed the same kind of social behaviours as chimpanzees and gorillas. Their social interactions are different and possibly more subtle. Their 'intelligence' is expressed in different ways. Indeed, the orang-utan's intelligence is evidence against the hypothesis that social behaviour led to the evolution of intelligence (Jolly 1966).

To summarise, the capacity of orang-utans for tool use and complex social interactions places them within the rubric of the other non-human apes. In no way do their cognitive abilities reflect an earlier evolution than gorillas or chimpanzees. Their relegation to a relatively inferior position in the past has been primarily due to the different personalities of orang-utans (Parker 1993). They are more contemplative and less actively interactive, but this serves them well in problem solving and manipulation of tools.

In the natural habitat, conventional tool use is relatively rare and/or has not been observed as often. The question arises whether tool use is also not overrated as an index of intelligence. Clearly, when confronted with a problem, the ability to solve it may show intelligence. But what if tool use is not needed in order to gain the favourite food, drink or other comforts for everyday life? What if the natural environment provides for the daily needs without having to become resourceful in the sense of needing to use tools in order to obtain a certain goal? We know already that orang-utans are extremely resourceful if the situation *requires* it, but they need very little extra from the natural environment in order to obtain a livelihood.

Communication

It is commonly assumed that higher cognitive capacity in primates is linked to greater complexity in social organisation (Jolly 1966; Cheney *et al.* 1986). This assertion has been problematic both in terms of assessing indigenous human tribal groups and of assessing primates. In the first quarter of the twentieth century, native Americans for instance were considered more 'advanced' than Australian Aborigines on the basis of their relative social complexity. A 1930s anthropological study of Bornean indigenous tribes even went as far as calling the people 'orang-utans' because of their nomadic lifestyle. Until well into the 1960s, the orang-utans were widely held to be inferior because they not only lacked the complexity of social organisation found in chimpanzees and gorillas but they more or less lacked any form of social organisation. Communication with conspecifics and even with other species is determined by socialisation which in turn needs to make sense within the world in which the individual is to move. From Thomas Hobbes onwards, solitary life has been considered to be a negative and an extremely regrettable thing (see Chapter 1).

Studies such as by Lethmate, observations by Galdikas and experiments with sign language (see below) have led to a substantial revision of this view. It is now known that the orang-utan's problem-solving ability clearly rivals that of the more 'social' chimpanzee; in certain problem-solving tasks the orang-utan may even outwit the chimpanzee. A joke of a comparative assessment of the three great apes claims the following: when one gives a screwdriver to a gorilla, the gorilla will scratch itself, give it to a chimpanzee and it will throw it away, but give it to an orang-utan and the orang-utan will wait until the keeper is gone, carefully unscrew the door and leave. The matter is simplified, of course, but the orang-utan's interest in and ability to acquire mechanical and conceptually complex knowledge of tool use has been observed on many occasions (cf. the screwdriver example in Chapter 4). Social *organisation* may not be related to intelligence, as was thought, but social *communication* may be regarded as an index of the potential for learning.

A second problem is that we equate demonstrativeness with intelligence. A semi-solitary species may not acquire the same demonstrativeness as a group-living one, just as only children tend to relate differently to peers than do children with siblings. The relatively more 'solitary' orang-utan may nevertheless have complex social communication when meetings do occur (albeit less demonstrative than that of chimpanzees) and, although the individuals are more widely dispersed, complex patterns of associations between individuals may still occur over long periods of time (Mitani *et al.* 1991). The other problem in all orang-utan observations is that the social organisation may differ in different localities (Mitani *et al.* 1991) and often it varies substantially between captive and free-ranging individuals. Situations which, compared to their natural habitat, can only be described as overcrowded, produce very different behaviour patterns from those found in their natural habitat.

Finally, assessment of sociality may be a matter of the methodology used by the observer. Rijksen's observations were obtained by a different method, ie only following associating individuals, from those used by Galdikas (cf. Galdikas' discussion 1985a; also Chapter 4). Although the importance of observing group interaction cannot be denied, no matter how infrequently it may occur, the orang-utan may be less disturbed by being solitary than other primates, such as the chimpanzee. Not knowing anything of the social organisation of orang-utans, Köhler expressed astonishment at Catalina's enjoyment of play 'even by herself' (see translation of Köhler 1993). Köhler was unaware at the time that orang-utans spend a good deal of their time on their own, although not as juveniles. In fact, the young orang-utans at Sepilok spend at least as much time on their own as they do with each other. That is, even when ample opportunity for interaction is available, individuals will opt for being alone. Of course, social organisation and bonding may also determine social versus individual play, and this has not yet been studied. Certain individual juveniles do form strong bonds, but an interaction with the other is always interspersed with pursuing individual interests (B. Harrisson

1960). The orang-utans that have been studied by Harrisson and by us are semi-wild and relatively used to human contact. In the rehabilitation centres the forest is overpopulated near the provisioning site. These circumstances foster enhanced sociality which, in the wild, tends to occur with much lower frequency or more sporadically.

Our knowledge of the communication systems of orang-utans is very scanty relative to the substantial number of studies we have on other primates. One of the first systematic attempts to describe vocalisation was undertaken by MacKinnon (1971). To date, the study by Niemitz and Kok (1976) has remained the most comprehensive description of orang-utan vocalisation (see also Appendix 3). Very slowly, new vocalisations are being added to the list compiled by MacKinnon. Galdikas and Insley (1988), for instance, have discovered a call which they termed fast call, emitted only by males (see below). In Chapter 5 we mentioned the low intensity purring vocalisation of Abbie when held by Gisela. To our knowledge, this purring vocalisation has not been described previously. The context in which we heard it led us to deduce that it was likely to convey contentment. There may be more vocalisations of orang-utans that could well be dependent on proximity or even intimacy, a form of communication that we want to refer to as 'whisper' communication. For instance, a soft panting noise in chimpanzees is often associated with a play face and has been read as human-like laughter (Redican 1975). Orang-utans may express a range of strong emotions related to danger or intrusion, such as anger, fear or anxiety, by emitting loud vocalisations, although it has been found that alarm calls made by monkeys are far more highly differentiated than those made by great apes (Cheney & Wrangham 1987). Cheney and Wrangham considered that the reason for this may lie in the lesser vulnerability of great apes to predators. Since the personal groupings (natal groups) of orang-utans rarely exceed three individuals (mother and two offspring), 'whisper' communication may be a very useful form of communication for 'everyday' life, particularly at close proximity.

As in many primates, vocalisation in the orang-utan differs between the sexes. Primate males usually have a different range of calls, coupled with different functions. Once the male orang-utan has grown to full maturity, he is able to advertise his presence and whereabouts by means of the so-called 'long call'. It is best described as a high intensity bellow, produced by first filling the cheek pouches with air and then expelling this air over the vocal chords for a prolonged period. The long call can be heard over large distances. Various opinions exist as to the meaning of the long call. Some field researchers perceive the long call as an unambiguous message to keep other males away, thereby spacing them well apart. This function has been observed in other species, such as the siamang (*Hylobates syndactylus*) (Kawabe 1970). The call may serve as a challenge to anyone not to get too close (MacKinnon 1971; Mitani 1985b). In 394 days of field work MacKinnon heard 241 long calls by males but witnessed only one male/male encounter (MacKinnon 1971). Others argue that the long call also acts as a locating signal for sexually receptive females (Galdikas & Insley 1988). As mentioned previously, Galdikas and Insley recently discovered another form of a long call which they termed fast call. It is similar to the long call but shorter in duration and appears to require a specific set of stimuli before it is uttered. In their field work they established that only 6.4 percent of long calls were ever answered but, of those that were, 62.5 percent of the replies were fast calls (Galdikas & Insley 1988). Galdikas and Insley have attributed a post–conflict/post–contact function to the fast call by male orang-utans.

Communication may occur purely by sound but usually it consists of a variety of signals; these may be body signals such as posture, facial expression, gesturing or touching. Eye movement and the movement of eyelids can have a special function. For instance, in a threat display, vervet monkeys will flash their coloured eyelids as part of the display (Struhsaker 1967). Staring at an opponent may be used effectively to ward off an intruder. We already know from a number of descriptions that orang-utans shake branches and throw twigs to indicate intrusion and annoyance. They may also jump up and down and emit a hissing sound to communicate that message (Galdikas, cited in Woods 1989), but we have seen no reports that eye use is central to any threat display. However, in mother–infant interactions eye contact can become quite important. Juveniles may beg for food from the mother by shifting their gaze back and forth between the mother's eyes and the food item, as also occurs in chimpanzees (Bard 1990). Eye movement and contact among orang-utans is as yet poorly understood. It is possible that eye movements may be a more important means of communication in orang-utans than we have hitherto assumed. It is not clear why ex-captive orang-utans rarely look straight at a human for more than a brief period of time. Orang-utans also avert their gaze when being trained on sign language tasks, even though their other responses indicate that they are paying attention (Shapiro & Galdikas 1994; see later).

Facial expression is clearly an important form of communication in orang-utans. One of the most comprehensive studies of facial expressions is the work by Chevalier-Skolnikoff (1982). Orang-utans seem to display many of the same facial expressions as other primates, including humans. For example, they show the relaxed open-mouth display used in play and the bared teeth display of submission (van Hooff 1972; see p.144). There are threat displays (Redican 1975), and a grimace face with bared teeth or wide-open mouth. According to MacKinnon, fear is expressed by drawing back the side of the mouth, exposing the teeth and making a grimace. Mild worry is expressed by pouting of lips and a threat is accompanied by a 'trumpet' mouth (shaping the lips into a trumpet) and deep grunts followed by gulps (MacKinnon 1974a; for general affect expressions see also Rijksen 1978; Maple 1980). A more recent analysis of the facial behaviour of orang-utans was undertaken by Chevalier-Skolnikoff (1982) in the context of sensorimotor development.

We have already referred to mother–infant communication in regard to the way affection is shown and signals are given to remain in contact. Much of that communication occurs by using gestures. Tomasello *et al.* (1989) found that, for chimpanzees, there is a special range of gestures used exclusively by infants and a special range of gestures used exclusively by adults. Orang-utan infants and juveniles show intentional gesturing to the mother to obtain food from an early age (Bard 1993).

◀ Play face

Both Abbie (top) and Alice (bottom) are in great form. Both displays were followed by rapid action, such as somersaulting and swinging.

BJ watching the world ▶

Changes in facial expression in orang-utans are obvious and can occur in rapid sequence. These photographs were taken less than one minute apart between the first and second and only seconds apart between the second and third.

Usually the infant holds a cupped hand, palm facing upwards, underneath the mother's chin. We have observed Abbie pinching the chin of another orang-utan eating bananas, apparently with the aim of getting the recipient to give her the food. Chin pinching might well have developed from the 'cupped hand under the chin' gesture.

Communication between mother and infant also occurs by touching. Typically, when the mother is eating, her infant may be exploring nearby branches. The mother signals for the infant to return to her body before she moves off by extending a limb, usually a leg, to touch the infant. As far as we have observed, the infant returns to cling to her body instantly. It is possible that the gesture is accompanied by low-intensity vocalisations not heard from the distance of the observer.

So much about orang-utan communication is not yet fully understood. Possibly further study might reveal a substantial communicative competence and complexity. Alternatively, in the absence of such discoveries one may argue that orang-utans had no need to develop communication skills to the same extent as group-living species but that they instead developed their cognitive capacities for solving problems in a relatively solitary existence.

Sign language in orang-utans

So far we have discussed the communication signals used by orang-utans to communicate with members of their own species. Since we cannot understand their 'language', another approach has been adopted to communicate with them, that is to teach an orang-utan to use our language.

From the late 1960s on there has been great interest in teaching sign or symbolic language to apes, beginning with the training of the chimpanzee, Washoe, to use American sign language (Gardner & Gardner 1969). Sign language was chosen because the vocal apparatus of apes is not constructed to produce the full range of formant frequencies used by humans when they are speaking (see Bradshaw & Rogers 1992). More recent studies with chimpanzees have used plastic tokens or computer lexigrams (see Greenfield & Savage-Rumbaugh 1990). The aim is to see what linguistic abilities apes have.

Sign language projects conducted with orang-utans have been far fewer than with chimpanzees, totalling five by 1992 (Furness 1916; Laidler 1978, 1980; Shapiro 1982; Miles 1983, 1990; cf. Bard 1992). Some orang-utans have been taught to use American sign language. These include a 15-month study using four juvenile orang-utans by Shapiro (1982), a recent study of two orang-utans at Camp Leakey by Shapiro and Galdikas (1994) and a comprehensive study of one orang-utan, named Chantek, by Miles (1990). Chantek lived in close contact with his trainer, Lyn White Miles, and other human carers. He learnt 140 signs. Furthermore, he invented extra signs. His vocabulary increased over the period of the study and each day he used on average from one third to two thirds of his existing vocabulary. The rate at which he acquired new signs was marginally better than that found previously in the language-trained chimpanzees.

Very early in his training program, Chantek learnt the sign for UP and used it to ask to be picked up. He was well motivated to learn this sign as he always wanted to be picked up. On the other hand, he took a long time to learn the sign for DOWN, consistent with his lack of motivation to be put down. He was also quick to learn the signs for different types of food and drink, as well as MORE and HURRY. Shapiro (1982) also found that his orang-utans acquired the signs for food items with great ease.

The direction of the orang-utans' eye-gazing is of interest because they largely averted their gaze during questioning and when the trainer was moulding their hands into the sign (Shapiro & Galdikas 1994). Even during the response phase, when the orang-utans responded to the question by signing either correctly or incorrectly, gaze was averted much of the time, although they did look at the trainer during the remainder of the time. Only during the (food) reward phase in Shapiro's training paradigm did the orang-utans fully direct their gaze towards any aspect of the task, and then it was to look at the food reward. This avoidance of eye contact differs greatly from the other apes. Shapiro and Galdikas (1994) found that, when the signing performance improved, the orang-utans made less eye contact. The role of visual attention during training is quite complex and not yet well understood.

Compared to the chimpanzee called Nim, who was also taught sign language (Terrace *et al.* 1979), Chantek performed fewer signs that were simply imitation and performed more spontaneous signing. Almost 40 percent of Chantek's communication was spontaneous and therefore his own decision. As early as the second month of training, Chantek began to combine signs into sequences, such as COME–FOOD–EAT or GIVE–BANANA (Miles 1983, 1994). It should be remembered that sign language does not require the regular/grammatical word order of spoken English, although some critiques have used the absence of regular word order as evidence for their claim that apes are unable to acquire language. The problem with this claim is that two very unequal things are being compared. For the orang-utan, learning sign language is tantamount to learning a second 'language' and one in a different mode, while the human language it is being compared to is spoken English by a native speaker. Hence, comparison between non-human apes and humans should be limited to *signing* humans, not *speaking* humans.

Signing may involve use of signs that have been learned simply by associations with objects. It is much more difficult to understand the meaning of the signs, that is, to acquire representational skills. Development of referential skills may be indicated by the use of signs that are not context dependent or by reference to objects that are not present or at a distance. Chantek demonstrated the ability to do this. To give one example, he signed CAR–RIDE and pulled his carer to the parking lot. We are reminded of BJ at Sepilok when he took hold of Lesley's hand, gestured down the path with his head and pulled at her arm to get her to go with him. At the same time he was making sure not to be seen by the keeper. There was, in fact, an aspect of deception in the act.

Deception is considered to be evidence of higher cognitive ability and Chantek used signing to deceive his carers around three times per week (Miles 1986, 1990). His main act of deception involved signing DIRTY so that he could gain access to the soap, dryer, etc, in the bathroom. In another example of deception, he took his carer's eraser and pretended to swallow it, signing FOOD-EAT. Instead of eating it, he kept it between his cheek and teeth and went to hide it in his bedroom. Miles (1990) describes this as an act of premeditated deception. We are familiar with premeditated acts of deception at Sepilok. BJ had a great desire to gain possession of our tripod and camera. To this end he would lie near Gisela when she was filming and pretend to be looking away at something else or to be absorbed in scratching the ground with a stick until we looked away and then he grabbed the legs of the tripod.

Chantek's cognitive abilities were also tested on the standard Bayley Scale for Infant (mental) Development, which requires building towers of cubes, folding paper and pointing to specific pictures. At 24 months of age his score was equivalent to that of a human aged 13.6 months. At 28 months of age his score was equivalent to a human of 17 months and at 5.5 years his score was equivalent to a human of 20.5 months. Similar results were obtained on two other standard tests. Other indicators of mental development, such as symbolic play and language comprehension and tool using, put Chantek, at five years old, equivalent to a four-year old child (Miles 1990). This impressive result led Miles (1990) to state 'within the lesser-known "red-ape" lies not only a brain but also a mind'.

Epilogue

Interest in a particular species, such as the orang-utan, makes one keenly aware that the natural world has lost its place as a wilderness without boundaries, as an unspoiled environment for all species and the occasional visit of humans. Forty thousand, or even just 20 000 years ago there were no borders. Where groups of humans dwelled they did so in close contact with their environment. The most successful hunter gatherers, such as the Aborigines of Australia, the native Indians of the North and South American subcontinents and the Penans, Ibans and Dayaks of Borneo, were able to maintain some form of equilibrium with their environment. As far as we have records, the human factor in these societies led to less severe degradation of the natural world or to the extinction of fewer species. Where circumstances continued to allow co-existence it was as much a matter of sustainability of small numbers as it was of specific attitudes and beliefs. Concepts of the right of the natural world to exist were often embedded in strong spiritual reverence for animate or inanimate objects. Within many of those belief systems any rape of the natural environment was also considered a rape of the spirits and ultimately the downfall of the human group. These early social forms of human existence have been dismissed as superstitious and 'primitive'.

It has been recognised only recently that many of the views of indigenous people were based on profound insights and a very detailed knowledge of their specific environments. It might even be said that some superstitions served them well in providing compelling ground rules for their habitat conservation. The early Kadazan agriculturalists for instance or the tribes of the hill countries in Papua Niugini practised a form of agriculture which was sustainable. Records of such activities in the highlands go back more than 9 000 years. Yet the supposedly superior forms of agricultural capitalism have resulted in a rapid and devastating degradation and an array of associated problems in less than a few hundred years.

The problems of logging and deforestation are now so well known that we hardly need to reiterate the consequences at the end of this book. We have offered only a few examples of the tragedies that are occurring daily. One, not mentioned so far, is that species of trees, such as the durian, the dipterocarp and the fig (see Chapters 2 and 3), occur on lowlands and are never found above 700 metres. All of them have been described as very major contributors to making tropical rainforests what they are and some of them have been identified as major food sources for the orang-utan, other primates, bears, birds, civets, bats, insects and elephants.

In Borneo, the lowlands are the most vulnerable because they are most suitable for human use, be this for settlement, agriculture or for logging. The selfsame areas are also the most suitable for orang-utans and it is in these regions where the wild orang-utan is most often found. As the lowland forests are cut and disappear, major food sources disappear and with them the orang-utans and other species. For the regions concerned, the disappearance of tree cover sets in motion further destruction, largely because of the poor soil. The function of the various tree families is to sustain the forest balance by water absorption and by generating nutrients above ground for the soil. As a botanist explained: 'the soil conditions [in the tropical rainforest] are only maintained through complex interaction of bacteria, insects, fungi and the function of root systems' (Veevers–Carter 1991).

Selective logging, sometimes claimed as evidence for environmental consciousness, falsely appeases the mind. The World Wide Fund for Nature has established that the felling of just seven grown trees per hectare removes about 34 percent of natural cover. The manner of transportation of timber requires roads and machinery. In many parts of Sabah, as Davis and Henley (1990) point out, 'skidtrails and landings have laid bare over 40 percent of the forest floor' in this process of 'selective logging'. Pearce (1990) called the current policy and view of 'sustainable forestry' a 'policy of wishful thinking', because the forest is anything but sustained. Loss of the canopy leads to exposing the soil to rain and loss of groundcover further exacerbates soil degradation by erosion. The richest tropical rainforest can easily be turned into a wasteland which supports no-one, not even humans.

And the question remains: for what is this devastation wrought? As we indicated in Chapter 1, the majority of people in Sarawak and Sabah reap little, if any, benefit. On the contrary, the local indigenous populations, which had been self-sufficient, are irrevocably turned into paupers. Forests are much more than timber. As Pearce said in 1990 of the Sarawak forests: 'They contain animals to be hunted, fruit and nuts and manioc and rattan and many other products that sustain hundreds of thousands of people'. The World Wide Fund for Nature found that Sarawak's forests alone had provided 20 000 tonnes of bush meat per year (Pearce 1990). Logging by large international companies helps create dysfunctional communities out of highly functional ones by destroying their traditions and cultures for no apparent material advantage to the indigenous peoples. Even the ITTO (the International Timber Trade Organization) concluded that, while fortunes had been made by the concessionaires in Sarawak, village people appeared 'to be on roughly the same standard of living as twenty years ago' (Pearce 1990). Moreover, logging, unlike local agriculture and even the worst form of monocultures, hardly contributes to creating employment. In Sarawak and Sabah, half of the timber goes to Japan. The uncut timbers get shipped to Tokyo and most of the benefit is siphoned off by a few shareholders and the Malaysian (mainland) government. In Japan, the timber 'produced by the oldest and perhaps richest tropical rainforest on earth is used principally for disposable construction forms for pouring concrete and throwaway packing crates' (Davis & Henley 1990).

We leave it to the reader to decide whether the destruction of Borneo's wilderness is due to population pressures, excusable as 'progress', beneficial to locals, now or in future, or can be considered to serve any 'worthwhile cause'. Throwaway packing crates are pitted here against the survival of untold plant and animal species, including the orang-utan, and against human cultures, world climate, ozone layers and more.

Increasingly, even those who are not environmentalists or members of conservation groups have realised the value of co-existence and of the complex interrelationship of all living and growing matter in the ecological system. This time it is not a yearning for a mythical past, a kind of Rousseauean 'back to nature' appeal, and has nothing to do with a hocus-pocus of cravings for harmony and notions of paradise. Diamond aptly entitled one of the chapters in his book *The Third Chimpanzee*, 'The Golden Age that Never Was'. Indeed, he convincingly exemplifies the existence of predatory, exterminating and destructive human activity throughout the ages. He shows that species of plant and animal life became extinct before any population explosion (Diamond 1992), although one needs to add that such destruction, as far as we can ascertain, was typically limited in extent and localised. He verifies what C. Fred Alford and Melanie Klein have referred to as the unalienable rapaciousness of the human species and its bent to destroy and take from nature what it pleases (Alford 1989). This time in human history we have gone too far and need to formulate and practise a set of pragmatic responses.

It is one of the great tragedies of human history that we have understood the meaning of exponential growth of human-induced destruction of the environment at a time when a good deal of that destruction has become irreversible. Just as we have begun to understand the inter-relatedness of all living matter and the importance of biodiversity we (the powerful and rich industrialised countries) watch in despair and see the drama unfold. Today, every wilderness belongs to individual nations and political entities, but in every corner of the world, these nations' 'private' activities in their own backyards are being felt and monitored around the world. Certain wildlife and habitat groups have become international organisations. Politically speaking, these organisations are still in their infancy but eventually they will become as important in settling, deciding and monitoring international events in these areas of concern as the UN is now in matters of war and peace — and hopefully they will be more effective. There are concrete steps that have been undertaken, such as the monitoring and investigative roles of organisations such as CITIES, the Humane Society International (with its regional branches) and the Specialist Primate Group of the IUCN (see Appendix 4 for details). By keeping an eye on the numbers in wild populations and by monitoring and exposing the cruelty involved in transportation of wild primates, they have given a factual basis for the international debate on the plight of primates. Specific organisations, such as the Orangutan Foundation or the World Wide Fund for Nature, have provided money for much needed local studies and maintenance of important research and conservation centres, such as the one run by Professor Biruté Galdikas in Tanjung Puting.

Government legislation can help curb an unending flow of primate exports. For example, the Indonesian government in January 1994 enacted a directive, banning the export of wild-caught long-tailed macaques (*Macaca fascicularis*) and pig-tailed macaques (*Macaca nemestrina*). As mentioned in the Introduction, Indonesia made up 30 percent of the international primate trade, mostly by providing macaques (Telecky 1994). However, it depends on the attitudes of receiving countries whether legislation will help at all. Poaching only stops being of interest if there is no demand for the goods being poached. In our view, it is even more a matter of punishing the buyers than the sellers, and here all nations with valuable primate life must be supported internationally by staunchly refusing to accept tempting but illegal 'merchandise'.

In a contemplative mood.

The debate about the survival of the orang-utan, as for other primates, has drawn very wide circles indeed. Zoos in particular have taken up the challenge of maintaining and providing viable zoo populations of a variety of species. The question is whether zoos can really be suitable alternatives? Zoos themselves now face a crisis in preserving the genetic diversity of orang-utans, since they no longer can rely on replenishment from the wild (Vandevoort *et al.* 1993). In 1982, participating zoos in North America founded 'The Species Survival Plan' program for orang-utans. This program is concerned with international stud books, target 'founder' contribution (TFC) analyses and the maintenance of genetic diversity. 'Founder' refers to wild-caught orang-utans who are not known to be related to any others in the zoo population. Maintaining their alleles across generations is one way to ensure continued diversity (Perkins & Maple 1990). Another way is to step up breeding and improve the reproductive success of captive orang-utans and their health. In an unhealthy lifestyle, as zoo life commonly is, orang-utans develop diabetes and obesity just as do humans.

Zoos have changed in their role dramatically over the years and have begun to play an important part in the overall fate of the orang-utan. Zoo discourse in the 1990s often more closely resembles stud discourse for racehorse breeding than conventional discussions of the great apes. On the one hand, apes in zoos now get treated considerably better than 50 or even just 20 years ago. In the period 1959–1965, the average lifespan of orang-utans in zoos was 10 years (*International Zoo Yearbook* 1959–1965). The data sound better than they are because the figures are highly variable. There may have been seven orang-utans who perished within two years and only three that survived into late adulthood and only one into old age. The figures are improving, as is the manner in which orang-utans are housed, the food they obtain and the medical treatment that orang-utans may be accorded. Now, however, their sexuality is on display and their reproduction a matter of urgency. There are female orang-utans, who normally would bear no more than two to four offspring, being used as birth machines and producing up to 11 offspring. There are those female orang-utans who continue to have miscarriages and are forced to reproduce until they have a viable offspring. Adult males and females are permanently kept together, forcing the female to contend with a far higher rate of intercourse than she would ever have chosen to experience in the wild. Tests have shown female choice for sexual activity to be much lower than that which occurs when the adult male has free access to a female (Nadler & Collins 1991). Confined space, lack of diversion and forced proximity, as well as the fact that they exist in order to be watched, leads to an increase in rape, an unusual occurrence from a fully grown adult male among free-ranging orang-utans (Crawford & Galdikas 1986). In zoos, rape is tolerated and pruriently recorded. That discourse identifies the individuals by International Stud Book Numbers (ISBN), discusses all matters of life and birth in terms of technicalities, and regulates reproduction, sex and every conceivable aspect of sexual and reproductive behaviour as would a business venture.

The methods and discourses are couched in language and practice encapsulating the kind of sexual oppression women have suffered through history. The enactment of the coercion here is unfettered by human social conventions and current insights, because at the very heart of the thinking lies the assumption of a large divide between animals and humans and between orang-utans and humans. We have hopefully shown that this alleged large divide does not really exist, either biologically or psychologically.

Those who consciously or implicitly assume such a divide exists also presuppose somehow that 'animals' have no feelings, no inhibitions, no shame and no understanding of their position, feel less pain and are generally less affected by things that would traumatise us. It used to be thought that black slaves had no feelings of physical or emotional torment either. It took a long time before they were granted these feelings and psychological states and only once they had been declared humans. We may not wish to declare orang-utans as humans, and there is no need to do that. We already know that an orang-utan is an orang-utan. It does not and should not require a change of status in order for orang-utans to be treated humanely. It is our thinking that needs to be changed, and we need to resist the temptation to play God or 'brave new world'. It is simply not sufficient to target our efforts merely towards getting data banks, conserving DNA and preserving genetic material for the future. We are speaking of living, thinking and feeling beings whose lives are normally expressed in a context of skills, culture and knowledge. No DNA can preserve these expressions of life and the technology in itself cannot vouch for any acceptable levels of quality of life.

Preserve the orang-utan for what? Is the future for this species to be just in cages? Balog made an impassioned plea a few years ago by saying:

> Many of the species that survive this wave of extinction will be quasi-domesticated residents of wild-life preserves, where the ecosystem will be controlled by humans rather than by the traditional interaction among animals, plants and earth. Others will be captive, living the artificial twilight zone of zoos. The original wildernesses will be reproduced as tiny enclaves landscaped by foam rocks and bounded by walls of iron. Their 'home range' will be surrounded by human dwellings of fast-food franchises. Their mates will be chosen by computer selection and their reproductive acts will take place in petri dishes.

> (Balog 1990)

Despite recent attempts by some zoos to enrich and improve the environments for their 'display' species and a global zoo reorientation, orang-utans remain caged and deprived. By definition, zoo orang-utans are not at liberty to roam freely and they have few if any choices for their immediate needs, their choice of partners, their food or their sleeping quarters. Indeed, most of the behaviours in which they need to engage in the wild are superfluous in zoos.

Those who have adopted a mentality that rests assured in the knowledge that zoos have taken on the role of guardians, reasoning that it is therefore not all that important whether orang-utans roam freely or not, need to know how inappropriate such complacency is. Having seen free-ranging orang-utans we are convinced that the shadowy existence in zoos is indefensible cruelty. We cannot take away the most basic of rights of all living things: the right to be, grow and feed where they belong by being mollycoddled into thinking that 'survival' is all that matters. Survival cannot happen in a test tube or a cage. No zoo would ever claim to be able to replace the natural environment but in the case of orang-utans there are pertinent questions to be asked and these are: what is being saved, for what and where is it to go?

Zoos are big business and need to think like businesses, at least on one level. Good business is to make zoos attractive enough for large numbers of people to pay entry fees. Modern zoos generally attempt to accommodate special species' needs. Exotic animals are one way to ensure such attractiveness. For instance, Taronga Zoo in Sydney has recently spent $2.6 million to improve the housing for orang-utans, partly with donated funds (Beale 1994). There is no doubt that such efforts are welcome improvements within zoo environments and we have no intention to belittle them. However, some species should perhaps never dwell permanently in zoos. We do not think that the orang-utan is suitable for zoo living. Similar claims might be made for other species but we know too little about these to comment. Our chosen species is the orang-utan. The more we have learned about the orang-utans, the more we have realised that their confinement, often over a lifetime, is a tragedy and that it would be a tragedy for the species if zoo dwellers were all that was left of them *as* a species. Much of the orang-utan's life is based on a complex set of learning tasks and on an untold amount of stimulation which the rainforest environment supplies in its endless variety of sounds, colours, shapes and smells. The orang-utan's survival and wellbeing relies on substantial knowledge of plants and animals, and on cultural transmission. This book was written to make the point about the orang-utan's complexity and psychology.

Appendix 1

Orang-utan menue card: some observed food items

Plants (Sabah and Sarawak)

Anacardiaceae (the mango family)
    Bouea oppestifolia — 1 sp
    Dracontomelum — 2 sp
    Koordersidodendron — 1 sp

Annonaceae (the custard apple family)
    Neouvaria — 2 sp
    Polyalthia — 8 sp
    Xylopia — 1 sp
    A climber (?) — 1 sp

Apocynaceae (the chewing gum family ??) 1 sp

Bombacaceae (the durian family)
    Durio — 3 sp

Burseracea
    Canarium — 2 sp
    Santiria — 1 sp

Combretaceae
    Combretum — 1 sp

Connaraceae
    Connarus villonis Jack — 1 sp
    Rurea minosoide — 1 sp

Cucurbitaceae
    ? — 1 sp

Dilleniaceae (the simpoh family)
    Dillenia — 2 sp

Dipterocarpaceae (the winged fruit family)
    Dipterocarpus — 3 sp
    Dryobalanops — 1 sp

Ebenaceae (the ebony family)
    Diospyros — 2 sp

Euphorbiaceae (the rubber family)
    Baccaurea — 1 sp
    Drypetes — 1 sp

Fagaceae (the oak family)
    Castanopsis — 1 sp
    Lithocarpus — 3 sp

Flacourtiaceae
    Hydnocarpus — 3 sp

Gnetaceae
    Gnetum — 3 sp

Gramineae (the bamboo family)
    Dinochloa — 1 sp

Guttiferae (the mangosteen family)
    Garcinia — 4 sp

Hypoxidaceae
    Curculigo — 1 sp

Lauraceae (the laurel family)
    Eusideroxylon — 1 sp
    ? — 1 sp

Lecythidaceae
    Barringtonia gitingensis — 1 sp

Leguminosae (the pea family)
    Crudia — 1 sp
    Dialium — 2 sp
    Fordia — 1 sp
    Intsia — 1 sp
    Phanera — 1 sp
    Saraca — 1 sp
    Sindora — 1 sp
    Sympetalandra — 1 sp
    ? — 1 sp
    ? — 1 sp

Loganiaceae (the strychnine family)
    Strychnos — 2 sp

Magnoliaceae
    Michelia — 1 sp
    Talauma — 1 sp

Meliaceae (the mahogany family)
    Amoora — 1 sp
    Aglaia — 1 sp
    Dysoxylon allineceum — 2 sp
    ? — 1 sp
    ? — 1 sp
    Lansium — 1 sp
    ? — 1 sp

Moraceae (the fig family)			Rutaceae (the citrus family)	
Artocarpus	4 sp		Glycosmis	1 sp
Ficus	7 sp		Luvunga	1 sp
Prainea	1 sp		Merope	1 sp
Myristicaceae (the nutmeg family)			Sapindaceae (the lychee family)	
Myristica	1 sp		Euphoria	2 sp
Knema	1 sp		Nephelium	5 sp
Myrtaceae (the eucalyptus family)			Pometia	1 sp
Eugenia	3 sp		?	1 sp
Orchidaceae (the orchid family)			Sapotaceae (the gutta-percha family)	
Eria	1 sp		Ganua	1 sp
Coelogyne	1 sp		Palaquium	1 sp
Oxalidaceae			Planchonella ferina cv. microcarpe	1 sp
Sarcotheca	1 sp		Simaroubaceae	
Palmae (the palm family)			Irvingia	1 sp
Calamus	1 sp		Sterculiaceae (the cocoa family)	
Phamnaceae			Pterospermum	1 sp
Ziziphus	2 sp		Theaceae	
Proteaceae			Ternstroemia hocei	1 sp
Helicioptus cv. rudifidula selum	1 sp		Tiliaceae (the jute family)	
Rosaceae (the rose family)			Microcos	1 sp
Parinari of oblongifolia	1 sp		Vitidaceae	
Prunus	1 sp		Leea	1 sp

Ingestion of Proteins:
Invertebrates/Vertebrates

Worms, snails, slugs, maggots
Cockroaches, beetles, flies, mosquitoes
Ants, grasshoppers, butterflies, moths, bees, ants, spiders
Rats, mice, squirrel, peafowl, doves, small birds, lizards, slow loris
(Note: many of the above-named species have been noted to have been ingested also in the wild.)

Sources: Adapted from MacKinnon (1971) and from commmunication by Dr P.S. Ashton 'Notes of food eaten by maias to the Curator of the Sarawak Museum, 14.6.1963, displayed in the Sarawak Museum; and from Markham (1986) on zoo observation of predatory behaviour.

Appendix 2:
Shared morphologies among hominoids

	Pan	Gorilla	Pongo	Homo
1. Distal humerus/proximal radius delayed ossification	x	x	x	x
2. Subnasal plane variably stepped–down	x	x	x	x
3. Subnasal plane truncated	x	x	x	x
4. Nasal aperture trapezoidal	x	x	x	x
5. Ulnar-triquetral articulation variable	x	x	x	x
6. Infraorbital foramina removed from zygomaticomaxillary suture	x	x	x	x
7. Palatine fenestrae reduced in size	x	x	x	x
8. Distal ulna/metacarpals delayed ossification	x	x	x	x
9. Restriction enzyme *Ava* at position 10, mtDNA	x	x	x	x
10. Morphological correlates of knuckle walking	x	x		
11. Restriction enzyme (mtDNA position); *Hinc*II,*Bam*HI(15),*Bgh*I(65),*Xho*I(10)			x	x
12. Low-cusped cheekteeth			x	x
13. Molar enamel thick			x	x
14. Upper molars lacking cingula			x	x
15. Lower M_3 smaller than M_2			x	x
16. Single Incisive foramen palatally			x	x
17. Foramen lacerum			x	x
18. Scapula short, vertical vertebral border, small superior fossa			x	x
19. Proximal humerus/distal radius delayed ossification			x	x
20. Ischial callosities unkeratinized, infrequent			x	x
21. Superficial venous system in forelimb, medial vein present			x	x
22. Highest oestriol levels during menstrual cycle			x	x
23. Mammary glands widespread, c. axillary			x	x
24. Longest gestation periods			x	x
25. Female genitalia lack tumescence			x	x
26. Copulation not confined to specific part of menstrual cycle			x	x
27. Longest copulation bouts			x	x
28. Longest hair			x	x

Source: Adapted from and based on Schwartz (1984) incl. discovery by Thiranagama *et al.* (1991).

Appendix 3:

Vocalisation

Name of Vocalisation	Description of Sound	Situation
DISTRESS CALLS		
1. Crying, screaming	Long high-pitched screams inter-spersed by choking intakes of air	Young animals when frightened or in pain
2. Frustration scream	Long wavering screams lacking choking sound	Young animals when food withheld
3. Fear squeak	Small short squeak	Young animal when frightened
4. Soft hoots	Pout-face hoots	Young animals when worried, either emitted by infant or also expressed by mother to infant
INTRUSION, FEAR, THREAT		
5. Kiss squeak	Sharp intake of air through trumpet lips causing long kiss sound	Excitement; part of intruder display, fear
6. Raspberry	Sharp expulsion of air through liquid lips again extended	Similar occasions to kiss squeak
7. Chomping	Sharp raising of lower jaw forces air out of mouth cavity in an internal gulp; mouth can be closed for this noise	Intruder display
8. Lork noises	Loud repetitive noises	Made by animals frustrated by my persistent observation
9. 'Ahoor' calls	Loud long exhalations	Threatening intruder
10 Barks	Single sharp exhalations	Warning call?
11. 'Grumphs'	Deep throaty gunts and gulps, head often turned away; following kiss squeak	Part of display
12. Complex calls	Long strings of deep guttural noises sometimes repetitive, combination of several noises above	Threat display
OTHER CALLS		
13. Long calls	Very loud series of long groans	Function not quite clear, may be to keep males spaced apart or to let receptive females know of their whereabouts
14. Fast call	Similar to long call but shorter in duration	Sometimes in reply to other calls
15. Mating cries	Loud piercing shrieks	Female during mating
16. 'Rape'	Deep grunt	Female during rape
17. Play grunts	Huffy 'haah' noises	Noises made in high intensity play
18. Infant/juvenile sound	Very low-pitched purr	Noises made when resting, heard only when next to juvenile

Source: Adapted from MacKinnon, with added sounds reported by Galdikas, Kavanagh and Kaplan and Rogers (14, 16 and 18 above respectively).

Appendix 4:

International organisations associated with the orang-utan

International Union for Conservation of Nature and Natural Resources (IUCN)
- established 1948
- international, non-government organisation
- over 110 countries participating with over 500 members
- headquarters Gland, Switzerland
- tasks of monitoring, planning, promoting and offering assistance to governmental bodies
- consists of six commissions, among them the Species Survival Commission (SSC)

The IUCN/SSC Primate Specialist Group
- the SSC is subdivided into more than 60 specialist groups. The largest of these groups is the Primate Specialist Group
- The Primate Specialist Group has about 120 members from 25 different countries
- main task is to maintain the current diversity of the order of primates, includes such things as acting to ensure survival of endangered and vulnerable species and protection for primates in areas of abundance, minimising loss where possible

The World Wildlife Fund (WWF) — now known as the World Wide Fund for Nature
- founded in 1961
- private international conservation organisation
- major funding body for wildlife studies with funding support to thousands of projects
- supports the establishment of and sometimes creates national parks and does active work to help rescue species from extinction
- headquarters shared with IUCN in Gland, Switzerland

The Ecosystem Conservation Group (ECG)
- part of the United Nations
- works together with the World Health Organisation on issues of biomedical research of non-human primates

The Orangutan Foundation International (OFI)
- charitable organisation
- founded 1986
- headquarters in Los Angeles
- branch also in Australia (OFA), founded in 1992
- task to support study and conservation of the orang-utan in its natural environment
- provides funds specifically for the Orang-utan Research and Conservation Project in Tanjung Puting, Kalimantan (Indonesian Borneo)
- runs lectures, publications and public seminars on orang-utans

Other important groups

International Primate Protection League
- charitable organisation
- Summerville, South Carolina, USA

The L.S.B. Leakey Foundation
- Oakland, California, USA

Rainforest Action Network
- San Francisco, California, USA

Bibliography

Alford, C.F. 1989, *Melanie Klein and Critical Social Theory,* Yale University Press, New Haven.

Andau, M. 1993, Clarification by orang-utan centre, *New Straits Times,* 14 July, p.15.

Andrews, P. 1987, Aspects of hominoid phylogeny, in *Molecules and Morphology in Evolution: Conflict or Compromise*, C. Patterson (ed), Cambridge University Press, Cambridge, pp.23–53.

Annett, M. & Annett, J. 1991, Handedness for eating in gorillas, *Cortex*, vol.27, pp.583–593.

Aruguete, M., Ely, E.A. & King, J.E. 1992, Laterality in spontaneous motor activity of chimpanzees and squirrel monkeys, *American Journal of Primatology*, vol.27, pp.177–188.

Asano, M. 1967, A note on the birth and rearing of an orang-utan *Pongo pygmaeus* at Tama Zoo, Tokyo, *International Zoo Yearbook*, vol.7, pp.95–96.

Aveling, R.J. 1982, Orang-utan conservation in Sumatra, by habitat protections and conservation education, in *The Orang-Utan: Its Biology and Conservation*, L.E.M. de Boer (ed), W. Junk, The Hague, pp.299–315.

Aveling, R.J. & Mitchell, A. 1982, Is rehabilitating orang-utans worthwhile?, *Oryx*, vol.XVI, pp.263–271.

Avise, J.C. 1991, Matriarchal liberation, *Nature*, vol.352, p.192.

Baldwin, J.D. 1986, Behaviour in infancy: Exploration and play, in *Behavior, Conservation, and Ecology*, vol.2, part A of *Comparative Primate Biology*, G. Mitchell & J. Erwin (eds), Alan R. Liss, New York, pp.295–326.

Balog, J. 1990, Personal vision of vanishing wildlife, *National Geographic,* vol.177, no.4, pp.84–103.

Bard, K.A. 1990, 'Social tool use' by free-ranging orang-utans: A Piagetian and development perspective on the manipulation of an animate object, in *'Language' and Intelligence in Monkeys and Apes: Comparative Developmental Perspectives*, S.T. Parker, & K.R. Gibson (eds), Cambridge University Press, Cambridge, pp.356–378.

Bard, K.A. 1992, Intentional behaviour and intentional communication in young free-ranging orang-utans, *Child Development,* vol.63, pp.1186–1197.

Bard, K.A. 1993, Cognitive competence underlying tool use in free-ranging orang-utans, in *The Use of Tools by Human and Non-human Primates*, A. Berthelet & J. Chavaillon (eds), Oxford University Press, Oxford, pp.103–117.

Bard, K.A., Hopkins, W.D. & Fort, C.L. 1990, Lateral bias in infant chimpanzees (*Pan troglodytes*), *Journal of Comparative Psychology*, vol.104, pp.309–321.

Bard, K.A., Platzman, K.A., Lester, B.M. & Suomi, S.J. 1992, Orientation to social and nonsocial stimuli in neonatal chimpanzees and humans, *Infant Behavior and Development*, vol.15, pp.43–56.

Beale, B. 1994, The jungle book, *Good Weekend*, 19 March, pp.46–49.

Beccari, O. 1904, *Wanderings in the Great Forests of Borneo. Travels and Researches of a Naturalist in Sarawak*, Archibald Constable & Co, London.

Beck, B.B. 1974, Baboons, chimpanzees, and tools, *Journal of Human Evolution*, vol.3, pp.509–516.

Beck, B.B. 1980, *Animal Tool Behavior: The Use and Manufacture of Tools by Animals*, Garland STPM Press, New York.

Beeckman, D. 1714, *A Voyage to and from the Island of Borneo,* republished 1973, Dawsons of Pall Mall, Folkestone & London.

Bennett, J. 1992, A glut of gibbons in Sarawak — Is rehabilitation the answer?, *Oryx*, vol.26, no.3, pp.157–164.

Bennett, J. 1993, Orang-utan ethnozoology in Malaysia: The story of Jaloh, *Pongo Quest*, vol.5, no.1, pp.8–9.

Benson, D.F. & Geschwind, N. 1985, Aphasia and related disorders: A clinical approach, in *Principles of Behavioral Neurology*, M.M. Mesulam (ed), F.A. Davis, Philadelphia, pp.193–238.

Bermúdez de Castro, J.M.B., Bromage, T.G. & Jalvo, Y.F. 1988, Buccal striations on fossil human anterior teeth: Evidence of handedness in the Middle and early Upper Pleistocene, *Journal of Human Evolution*, vol.17, pp.403–412.

Bihrle, A.M., Brownell, H.H. & Gardner, H. 1988, Humor and the right hemisphere: A narrative perspective, in *Contemporary Reviews in Neuropsychology*, H.A. Whitaker (ed), Springer, New York, pp.109–126.

Boesch, C. 1990, First hunter of the forest, *New Scientist*, 19 May, pp.20–25.

Boesch, C. 1991, Teaching among wild chimpanzees, *Animal Behaviour*, vol.41, pp.530–532.

Boesch, C. 1993, Aspects of tool-use in wild chimpanzees, in *Tools, Language and Cognition in Human Evolution*, K.R. Gibson & T. Ingold (eds), Cambridge University Press, Cambridge, pp.171–183.

Boesch, C. & Boesch, H. 1990, Tool use and tool making in wild chimpanzees, *Folia Primatologia*, vol.54, pp.86–99.

Borner, M. 1979, *Orang Utan. Orphans of the Forest*, Allen & Unwin, London.

Bradshaw, J.L. 1989, *Hemispheric Specialization and Psychological Function*, Wiley, Chichester.

Bradshaw, J.L. & Rogers, L.J. 1992, *The Evolution of Lateral Asymmetries, Language, Tool Use, and Intellect*, Academic Press, San Diego.

Brandes, G. 1939, *Buschi. Vom Orang Säugling zum Backenwülster,* Verlagsbuchhandlung Queele und Meyer, Leipzig.

Brandt, E.M. & Mitchell, G. 1971, Parturition in primates: Behavior related to birth, in *Primate Behavior*, vol.2, L.A. Rosenblum (ed), Academic Press, New York, pp.177–223.

Braswell, L.D. 1994, Oral findings in captive orangutans, in *Abstracts, International Orang-utan Conference: 'The Neglected Ape', 5–7 March, Fullerton*, Anthropology Department, California State University, Fullerton, p.12.

Brésard, B. & Bresson, F. 1983, Handedness in *Pongo pygmaeus* and *Pan Troglodytes, Journal of Human Evolution*, vol.12, pp.659–666.

Brewer, S.M. & McGrew, W.C. 1990, Chimpanzee use of a tool set to get honey, *Folia Primatologica*, vol.54, pp.100–104.

Brinkman, C. 1984, Determinants of hand preference in *Macaca fascicularis*, *International Journal of Primatology*, vol.5, pp.325.

Bronskaya, S.D., Veselovskaya, A.V., Panteleev, A.A. & Novikova, I.V. 1986, Conditions for the joint keeping of the male and female orangutan and observation of their behavior, *Byulleten' Moskovskogo Obshchestva, Ispytatelei Prirody Otdel Biologicheskii*, vol.91, no.5, pp.11–16.

Burroughs, E.R. 1912, *Tarzan of the Apes*, 1939 edition, Ballantine Books, New York.

Byrne, R.W. & Byrne, J.M. 1991, Hand preferences in the skilled gathering tasks of mountain gorillas (*Gorilla g. berengei*), *Cortex*, vol.27, pp.521–546.

Cain, D.P. & Wada, J.A. 1979, An anatomical asymmetry in the baboon brain, *Brain, Behaviour and Evolution*, vol.16, pp.222–226.

Cameron, C. (ed) 1992, *The Great Apes*, Occasional papers of the Archaeological Research Facility, California State University, Fullerton, no.6, Museum of Anthropology, Fullerton.

Cant, J.G.H. 1985, Locomotor and postural behavior of orangutan pongo-pygmaeus in Borneo and Sumatra, 54th Annual Meeting of the American Association of Physical Anthropologists, *American Journal of Physical Anthropology*, vol.66, no.2, p.153.

Cant, J.G.H. 1986, Locomotion and feeding postures of spider and howling monkeys: Field study and evolutionary interpretation, *Folia Primatologica*, vol.46, pp.1–14.

Cant, J.G.H. 1987, Positional behavior of female Bornean orangutans pongo-pygmaeus, *American Journal of Primatology*, vol.12, no.1, pp.71–90.

Carpenter, C.R. 1938, A survey of wildlife conditions in Atjeh, North Sumatra, *Neth. Comm. Int. Prot.*, no.12, pp.1–33.

Cavalieri, P. & Singer, P. (eds) 1993, *The Great Ape Project. Equality Beyond Humanity*, Fourth Estate, London.

Central Borneo: A Bibliography 1988, special monograph, *The Sarawak Museum Journal*, vol.XXXVIII, no.59, December.

Charles, D., Dickson, D., Joyce, C., Lewin, R. & Pain, S. 1991, Chimp learns stone age use of tools, *New Scientist*, February, p.11.

Chen, Z.W., McAdam, S.N., Hughes, A.L., Dogon, A.L., Letvin, N.L. & Watkins, D.I. 1992, Molecular cloning of orangutan and gibbon MHC Class I CDNA. The HLA-A and B Loci diverged over 30 million years ago, *Journal of Immunology*, vol.148, no.8, pp.2547–2554.

Cheney, D., Seyfarth, R. & Smuts, B. 1986, Social relationships and social cognition in nonhuman primates, *Science*, vol.234, pp.1361–1366.

Cheney, D.L. & Wrangham, R.W. 1987, Predation, in *Primate Societies*, B.B. Smuts, D.L. Cheney, R.M. Seyfarth, R.W. Wrangham, & T.T. Struhsaker (eds), Chicago University Press, Chicago, pp.227–239.

Chevalier–Skolnikoff, S. 1982, A cognitive analysis of facial behaviour in Old World monkeys, apes and humans, in *Primate Communication,* C. Snowdon, C.H. Brown & M. Petersen (eds), Cambridge University Press, Cambridge.

Christman, S.D. & Hackworth, M.D 1993, Equivalent perceptual asymmetries for free viewing of positive and negative emotional expressions in chimeric faces, *Neuropsychologia*, vol.31, pp.621–624.

Citino, S.B., Bush, M., Phillips, L.G., Montali, R.J., Wang, K.P. & Ravich, W.J. 1985, Eosinophilic enterocolitis in a juvenile orangutan pongo hybrid, *Journal of the American Veterinary Medical Association*, vol.187, no.11, pp.1279–1280.

Codner, M.A. & Nadler, R.D. 1984, Mother–infant separation and reunion in the great apes, *Primates*, vol.25, no.2, pp.204–217.

Coe, C. 1990, Psychobiology of maternal behavior in nonhuman primates, in *Mammalian Parenting, Biochemical, Neurobiological, and Behavioral Determinants*, N.A. Krasnegor & R.S. Bridges (eds), Oxford University Press, Oxford, pp.157–183.

Cole, M., Devison, D., Elridge, P.J., Mehren, K.R. & Rapley, W.A. 1979, Notes on the early hand-rearing of an orangutan (*Pongo pygmaeus*), and its subsequent reintroduction to the mother, *International Zoo Yearbook*, vol.19, pp.263–264.

Collet, J.-Y., Galdikas, B.M.F., Sugardjito, J. & Jojosudharmo, S. 1986, A coprological study of parasitism in orangutans (*Pongo pygmaeus*) in Indonesia, *Journal of Medical Primatology*, vol.15, no.2, pp.121–130.

Collins, D.C., Graham, C.E. & Preedy, J.R.K. 1975, Identification and measurement of urinary estrone, estradiol-17ß , estriol, pregnanediol and androsterone during the menstrual cycle of the orang-utan, *Endocrinology*, vol.96, pp.93–101.

Colmenares, F. 1990, Greeting behaviour in male baboons, I: Communication, reciprocity and symmetry, *Behaviour*, vol.113, no.1–2, pp.81–116.

Corner, E.J.H. 1949, The Durian theory and the origin of the modern tree, *Annals of Botany*, NS, vol.XVII, no.52, October.

Crawford, C. & Galdikas, B.M.F. 1986, Rape in non-human animals, An evolutionary perspective, *Canadian Psychology*, vol.27, no.3, pp.215–230.

Crelin, E.S. 1988, Ligament of the head of the femur in the orangutan and Indian elephant, *Yale Journal of Biology and Medicine*, vol.6, no.5, pp.383–388.

Crompton, R.H. 1983, Age differences in locomotion of two subtropical Galaginae, *Primates*, vol.24, pp.241–259.

Cunningham, D., Forsythe, C. & Ward, J.P. 1989, A report of behavioral lateralization in an infant orangutan pongo-pygmaeus, *Primates*, vol.30, pp.249–254.

Czekala, N.M., Shideler, S.E. & Lasley, B.L. 1985, A comparison of hominoid female reproductive physiology, 54th Annual Meeting of the American Association of Physical Anthropologists, *American Journal of Physical Anthropology*, vol.66, no.2, pp.161–162.

Davenport, R.K. 1967, The orangutan in Sabah, *Folia Primatologica*, vol.5, pp.247–263.

Davies, G. 1986, The orangutan pongo-pygmaeus in Sabah, *Oryx*, vol.20, no.1, pp.40–45.

Davis, W. & Henley, T. 1990, *Penan. Voice for the Borneo Rainforest*, Western Canadian Wilderness Committee, Kuala Lumpur.

de Boer, L.E.M. (ed) 1982, *The Orang Utan. Its Biology and Conservation*, Papers from the 'Workshop on the conservation of the orang utan', Rotterdam, October 1979, W. Junk, The Hague.

De Silva, G.S. 1970, Training orang-utans for the wild, *Oryx*, vol.10, pp.389–393.

De Silva, G.S. 1972, The birth of an orangutan at Sepilok Game Reserve, *International Zoo Yearbook*, vol.12, pp.102–103.

Deryagina, M.A. 1983, Manipulation activity of primates, *Proceedings of the 3rd All-Union Conference on Animal Behavior*, vol.2, Behavior of animals in communities, Izdatel' Stvo Nauka, Moscow, pp.200–202.

Diamond, J. 1992, *The Third Chimpanzee. The Evolution and Future of the Human Animal*, Harper Collins, New York.

Dienske, H. & Griffin, H. 1978, Abnormal behaviour pattern developing in chimpanzee infants during nursery care, A note, *Journal of Child Psychology and Psychiatry*, vol.19, pp.387–391.

Dimond, S. & Harries, R. 1984, Face touching in monkeys, apes and man: Evolutionary origins and cerebral asymmetry, *Neuropsychologia*, vol.22, no.2, pp.227–233.

Dossaji, S.F., Wrangham, R. & Rodriguez, E. 1989, Selection of plants with medicinal properties by wild chimpanzees, *Fitoterapia*, vol.60, no.4, pp.378–381.

Drescher, K. & Trendelenburg, W. 1927, Weiterer Beitrag zur Intelligenzprüfung von Affen (einschließlich Anthropoiden), *Zeitschrift für vergleichende Physiologie*, no.5, pp.613–642.

Duplaix, N. & Grady, L. 1980, Is the international trade convention for or against wildlife?, *International Zoo Yearbook*, vol.20, pp.171–177.

Edwards, S.D. 1982, Social potential expressed in captive group-living orangutans, in *The Orangutan, Its Biology and Conservation*, L.E.M. de Boer (ed), W. Junk, The Hague, pp.249–255.

Eudy, A.A. 1994, The impact of socioeconomic decisions on the status of the orang-utan and other East Asian fauna, *Abstracts, International Orang-utan Conference: 'The Neglected Ape', 5– 7 March, Fullerton,* Anthropology Department, California State University, Fullerton, p.13.

Fiennes, R. 1979, *Zoonoses of Primates*, Weidenfeld & Nicholson, London.

Fischer, R.B., Meunier, G.F. & White, P.J. 1982, Evidence of laterality in the lowland gorilla, *Perceptual and Motor Skills*, vol.54, pp.1093–1094.

Forestry in Sabah 1989, compiled by Sabah Forestry Department, Kota Kinabalu.

Forsythe, C. & Ward, J.P. 1988, Black lemur (*Lemur macaco*) hand preference in food reaching, *Primates*, vol.29, pp.369–374.

Fragaszy, D.M. & Adams-Curtis, L.E. 1993, An exploration of manual preference and performance in crab-eating macaques, in *Primate Laterality: Current Behavioral Evidence of Primate Asymmetries*, J.P. Ward & W.D. Hopkins (eds), Springer-Verlag, New York, pp.75–105.

Francis, J. 1958, *Tuberculosis in Animals and Man*, Cassell & Co, London.

Freeman, D. 1977, *Love of Monkeys and Apes*, Octopus Books, London.

Freeman, D. 1979, *The Great Apes*, Rigby Ltd, Australia & Bison Books, London.

Frost, G.T. & Armstrong, E. 1986, A comparative assessment of the orangutan thalamus, Fifty-Fifth Annual Meeting of the American Association of Physical Anthropologists, *American Journal of Physical Anthropology*, vol.69, no.2, pp.201.

Furness, W.H. 1916, Observations on the mentality of chimpanzees and orangutans, *Proceedings of the American Philosophical Society*, vol.5, pp.281–290.

Galdikas, B.M.F. 1978, Orangutan adaptation at Tanjung Puting Reserve, Central Borneo, PhD thesis, University of California, Los Angeles.

Galdikas, B.M.F. 1979, Orangutan adaptation at Tanjung Puting Reserve: Mating and ecology, in *The Great Apes*, D.A. Hamburg & E.R. McCown (eds), Benjamin/Cummings, Menlo Park, pp.194–233.

Galdikas, B.M.F. 1981a, Orangutan reproduction in the wild, in *Reproductive Biology of the Great Apes: Biomedical and Comparative Aspects*, C.E. Graham (ed), Academic Press, New York, pp.281–300.

Galdikas, B.M.F. 1981b, Wild orangutan studies at Tanjung Puting Reserve, Central Indonesian Borneo, *National Geographic Society Research Reports*, vol.13, pp.1–10.

Galdikas, B.M.F. 1982a, Wild orangutan birth at Tanjung Puting Reserve, *Primates*, vol.23, pp.500–510.

Galdikas, B.M.F. 1982b, Orang-utan tool-use at Tanjung Puting Reserve, Central Indonesian Borneo Kalimantan Tengah, *Journal of Human Evolution*, vol.10, pp.19–33.

Galdikas, B.M.F. 1984, Adult female sociality among wild orangutans at Tanjung Puting Reserve, in *Female Primates: Studies by Women Primatologists*, M. Small (ed), Alan R. Liss, New York, pp.217–235.

Galdikas, B.M.F. 1985a, Adult male sociality and reproductive tactics among orangutans at Tanjung-Puting Borneo Indonesia, *Folia Primatologica,* vol.45, no.1, pp.9–24.

Galdikas, B.M.F. 1985b, Orangutan sociality at Tanjung-Puting, *American Journal of Primatology*, vol.9, no.2, pp.101–119.

Galdikas, B.M.F. 1985c, Subadult male orangutan sociality and reproductive behavior at Tanjung Puting, *American Journal of Primatology*, vol.8, no.2, pp.87–99.

Galdikas, B.M.F. 1988, Orang utan diet, range, and activity at Tanjung Puting, Central Borneo, *International Journal of Primatology*, vol.9, no.1, pp.1–35.

Galdikas, B.M.F. 1989, Orang utan tool use, *Science,* vol.243, no.4888, p.152.

Galdikas, B.M.F. 1992, How monkeys see the world, *Behavioral and Brain Sciences*, vol.15, no.1 March, p.156.

Galdikas, B.M.F. 1994, Keynote address, *Abstracts, International Orang-utan Conference: 'The Neglected Ape', 5–7 March, Fullerton,* Anthropology Department, California State University, Fullerton.

Galdikas, B.M.F. & Insley, S.J. 1988, The fast call of the adult male orangutan, *Journal of Mammalogy,* vol.69, no.2, pp.371–375.

Galdikas, B.M.F. & Shapiro, G.L. 1994, *Tanjung Puting National Park, Kalimantan Tengah (Central Borneo), Indonesia,* Penerbit PT Gramedia Utama, Jakarta and the Orangutan Foundational International, Los Angeles.

Galdikas, B.M.F. & Teleki, G. 1981, Variations in subsistence activities of female and male pongids: New perspectives on the origins of hominid labor division, *Current Anthropology,* vol.22, pp.241–256.

Galdikas, B.M.F. & Wood, J.W. 1990, Birth spacing patterns in humans and apes, *American Journal of Physical Anthropology,* vol.83, no.2, pp.185–192.

Gallardo, E. 1993, *Among the Orangutans. The Birute Galdikas Story,* Chronicle Books, San Francisco.

Gardner, H., Brownell, H.H., Wapner, W. & Michelow, D. 1983, Missing the point: The role of the right hemisphere in the processing of complex linguistic materials, in *Cognitive Processing in the Right Hemisphere,* E. Perecman (ed), Academic Press, New York, pp.169–191.

Gardner, R.A. & Gardner, B.T. 1969, Teaching sign language to a chimpanzee, *Science,* vol.165, pp.664–672.

Gaulin, S.J.C. & Konner, M. 1986, On the natural diet of primates, including humans, in *Nutrition and the Brain,* vol.1, R. Wurtman & J. Wurtman (eds), Raven Press, New York, pp.1–86.

Geschwind, N. & Levitsky, W. 1968, Human brain: Left–right asymmetry in temporal speech region, *Science,* vol.161, pp.186–187.

Ghiglieri, M.P. 1987, Sociobiology of the great apes and the hominid ancestor, *Journal of Human Evolution,* vol.16, no.4, pp.319–358.

Gibson, K.R. 1990, New perspectives on instincts and intelligence: Brain size and the emergence of hierarchical mental constructional skills, in *'Language' and Intelligence in Monkeys and Apes,* S.T. Parker, & K.R. Gibson (eds), Cambridge University Press, New York.

Goeltenboth, R. & Kloes, H-G. 1987, Infections of the laryngeal pouches in the orangutan and chimpanzee, *Anatomia Histologia Embryologia,* vol.16, no.3, pp.283–288.

Golding, W. 1973, *The Inheritors,* Faber & Faber, London.

Gonzalez-Kirchner, J.P. & de la Maza, M.S. 1992, Sticks used by wild chimpanzees: A new locality in Rio Muni, *Folia Primatologica,* vol.58, pp.99–102.

Goodall, J. van Lawick 1968, The behaviour of free living chimpanzees in the Gombe Stream Reserve Tanzania, *Animal Behavior Monographs,* vol.1, pp.161–311.

Graham, C.E. 1981, Menstrual cycle of the great apes, in *Reproductive Biology of the Great Apes: Biomedical and Comparative Aspect*s, C.E. Graham (ed), Academic Press, New York, pp.1–43.

Graham, C.E. & Nadler, R.D. 1990, Socioendocrine interactions in great ape reproduction, in *Socioendocrinology of Primate Reproduction; Symposium from the XII Congress of the International Primatological Society*, T.E. Ziegler & F.B. Bercovitch (eds), Brasilia, Brazil, pp.33–58.

Graham-Jones, O. & Hill, W.C.O. 1962, Pregnancy and parturition in a Bornean orang, *Proceedings of the Zoological Society of London*, vol.139, pp.510–530.

Grand, T.I. 1984, Motion economy within the canopy: Four strategies for mobility, in *Adaptations for Foraging in Nonhuman Primates: Contributions to an Organismal Biology of Prosimians, Monkeys and Apes*, P.S. Rodman & J.G.H. Cant (eds), Columbia University Press, New York.

Greenfield, P.M. & Savage-Rumbaugh, E.S. 1990, Grammatical combination in *Pan paniscus*: Processes of learning and invention in the evolution and development of language, in *'Language' and Intelligence in Monkeys and Apes: Comparative Developmental Perspectives*, S.T. Parker, & K.R. Gibson (eds), Cambridge University Press, Cambridge, pp.540–578.

Gribbin, J. & Gribbin, M. 1988, *The One Percent Advantage: The Sociobiology of Being Human*, Basil Blackwell, Oxford.

Groves, C.P. 1987, Monkey business with red apes, *Journal of Human Evolution*, no.16, pp.537–542.

Güntürkün, O. 1991, The venus of Milo and the dawn of facial asymmetry research, *Brain and Cognition*, vol.16, pp.147–150.

Hall, B. 1931, *Travel in India, Ceylon and Borneo*, H.G. Rawlinson (ed), Routledge, London.

Hamilton, C.R. & Vermeire, B.A. 1983, Discrimination of monkey faces by split-brain monkeys, *Behavioural Brain Research*, vol.9, pp.263–275.

Hamilton III, W.J., Buskirk, R.E. & Buskirk, W.H. 1978, Omnivority and utilization of food resources by chacma baboons (*Papio ursinus*), *American Naturalist*, no.112, pp.911–924.

Handbook of British North Borneo 1890, compiled from reports of the Governor and Officers of the Residential Staff in Borneo, William Clowes & Sons, London.

Hannah, A. & McGrew W.C. 1987, Chimpanzees using stones to crack open oil palm nuts in Liberia, *Primates*, vol.28, no.1, pp.31–46.

Harcourt, A.H. 1987, Options for unwanted or confiscated primates, *Primate Conservation*, vol.8, pp.111–113.

Harris, L.J. 1993, Handedness in apes and monkeys: Some views from the past, in *Primate Laterality: Current Behavioral Evidence of Primate Asymmetries*, J.P. Ward & W.D. Hopkins (eds), Springer-Verlag, New York, pp.1–41.

Harrison, G.A., Tanner, J.M., Pilbeam, D.R. & Baker, P.T. 1988, *Human biology: An Introduction To Human Evolution, Variation, Growth and Adaptability*, 3rd edn, Oxford University Press, Oxford.

Harrisson, B. 1960, A study of orang-utan behaviour in semi-wild state, 1956–1960, *The Sarawak Museum Journal*, vol.IX, no.15–16, new series, pp.422–447.

Harrisson, B. 1961, Orang-utan. What chances of survival?, *The Sarawak Museum Journal*, vol.X, no.17–18, new series, July–December, pp.238–261.

Harrisson, B. 1963a, Education to wild living of young orang-utans at Bako National Park, Sarawak, *The Sarawak Museum Journal*, vol.XI, no.21, pp.220–258.

Harrisson, B. 1963b, Report of censuses in sample habitat areas of North Borneo, *World Wildlife Fund Report,* unpublished.

Harrisson, B. 1969, The nesting behaviour of semi-wild juvenile orang-utans, *The Sarawak Museum Journal*, vol.XVIII, no.34–35, July–December, pp.336–384.

Harrisson, B. 1987, *Orang-utan,* Oxford University Press, Oxford.

Harrisson, T. 1955a, Orang-utan (Maias) v. man (and woman), *The Sarawak Museum Journal*, vol.VI, no.6, new series, pp.600–632.

Harrisson, T. 1955b, Orang-utans in the London Zoo, *The Sarawak Museum Journal*, vol.VII, no.7, new series, pp.226–228.

Harrisson, T. 1957, The Great Cave of Niah: A preliminary report on Bornean prehistory, *Man*, vol.57, article no.211, pp.161–166.

Harrisson, T. 1960, A remarkably remote orang-utan: 1958–1960, *The Sarawak Museum Journal*, vol.IX, no.15–16, new series, pp.458–451.

Hatta, T. & Dimond, S.J. 1984, Differences in face touching by Japanese and British People, *Neuropsychologia,* vol.22 no.4, pp.531–534.

Hauser, M.D. 1993, Right hemisphere dominance for the production of facial expression in monkeys, *Science*, vol.261, pp.475–477.

Hayes, K. 1992, The conservation of the orangutan with particular emphasis on the problems of rehabilitation, in *Proceedings of the Australasian Society for Human Biology,* no.5, 1991, N.W. Bruce (ed), Canberra, p.280.

Heestand, J. 1986, Behavioral lateralization in four species of ape, Unpublished doctoral dissertation, University of Washington, Seattle, cited in Morris *et al.* (1993).

Heilbroner, P.L. & Holloway, R.L. 1988, Anatomical brain asymmetries in new world and old world monkeys: Stages of temporal lobe development in primate evolution, *American Journal of Physical Anthropology*, vol.76, pp.39–48.

Hemelrijk, C.K. 1990, Models of, and tests for, reciprocity, unidirectionality and other social interaction patterns at a group level, *Animal Behaviour*, vol.39, pp.1013–1029.

Hendel, C.W. 1937, *Citizen of Geneva: Selection from the Letters of Jean Jacques Rousseau*, Oxford University Press, New York & London.

Hill, W.C.O. 1966, *Primates: Comparative Anatomy and Taxonomy,* Edinburgh University Press, Edinburgh.

Hill, W.C.O. 1972, *Evolutionary Biology of the Primates*, Academic Press, London.

Hladik, C.M. 1977, Chimpanzees of Gabon and chimpanzees of Gombe: Some comparative data on diet, in *Primate Ecology*, T.H. Clutton-Brock (ed), Academic Press, New York.

Hochberg, F.H. & LeMay, M. 1975, Arteriographic correlates of handedness, *Neurology*, vol.25, pp.218–222.

Holloway, R.L. & de LaCoste-Lareymondie, M.C. 1982, Some preliminary findings on the palaeontology of cerebral dominance, *American Journal of Physical Anthropology*, vol.58, pp.101–110.

Homma, T. & Sakai, T. 1991, Hand muscles of the orangutan, in *Primatology Today; XIIIth Congress of the International Primatological Society*, Nagoya and Kyoto, Japan, 1990, A. Ehara (ed), pp.487–490.

Hooijer, D.A. 1960, The Orang-utan in Niah Cave prehistory, *The Sarawak Museum Journal*, July–December, vol.9, no.15–16, pp.408–421.

Hopkins, W.D. 1993, Posture and reaching in chimpanzees (*Pan troglodytes*) and orang-utans (*Pongo pygmaeus*), *Journal of Comparative Psychology*, vol.107, pp.162–168.

Hopkins, W.D. & Bard, K.A. 1993, Hemispheric specialization in infant chimpanzees (*Pan troglodytes*): Evidence for a relation with gender and arousal, *Developmental Psychobiology*, vol.26, no.4, pp.219–235.

Hopkins, W.D., Bard, K.A., Jones, A. & Bales, S.L. 1993a, Chimpanzees hand preference in throwing and infant cradling: Implications for the origin of human handedness, *Current Anthropology*, vol.34, no.5, pp.786–790.

Hopkins, W.D., Bennett, A.J., Bales, S.L., Lee, J. & Ward, J.P. 1993b, Behavioral laterality in captive bonobos (*Pan paniscus*), *Journal of Comparative Psychology*, vol.107, no.4, pp.403–410.

Hopkins, W.D., Washburn, D.A. & Rumbaugh, D.M. 1989, A note on hand use in the manipulation of joysticks by two rhesus monkeys and three chimpanzees (*Pan troglodytes*), *Journal of Comparative Psychology*, vol.103, pp.91–94.

Hopkins, W.D., Washburn, D.A., Berke, L. & Williams, M. 1992, Behavioral asymmetries of psychomotor performance in rhesus monkeys (*Macaca mulatta*): A dissociation between hand preference and skill, *Journal of Comparative Psychology*, vol.106, pp.392–397.

Hornaday, W.T. 1879, On the species of the bornean orangs, with notes on their habits, *Proceedings of the American Association of Advanced Science*, Salem, 20th meeting, pp.438–455.

Hornaday, W.T. 1885, *Two years in the jungle. The experiences of a hunter and naturalist in India, Ceylon, the Malay Peninsula, and Borneo*, K. Paul, Trench & Co, London.

Horr, D.A. 1972, The Borneo orangutan, *Borneo Research Bulletin*, no.4, pp.46–50.

Horr, D.A. 1973, Orang-utan primary socialization: Mothers and siblings, *American Journal of Physical Anthropology*, vol.40, no.1, Abstract, p.140.

Horr, D.A. 1975, The Borneo orang-utan: Population structure and dynamics in relationship to ecology and reproductive strategy, in *Primate Behavior. Developments in Field and Laboratory Research,* vol.4, L.A. Rosenblum (ed), Academic Press, New York, pp.307–323.

Horr, D.A. 1977, Orang-utan maturation: Growing up in a female world, in *Primate Biosocial Development*, S. Chevalier-Skolnikoff & F.E. Poirier (eds), Garland, New York.

Horwich, R.H. 1989, Cyclic development of contact behavior in apes and humans, *Primates*, vol.30, pp.269–279.

Hose, C. 1988, *Natural Man. A Record from Borneo*, Oxford University Press, Singapore.

Hrdy, S.B. 1981, *The Woman that Never Evolved*, Harvard University Press, Cambridge.

Huffman, M.A. & Kalunde, M.S. 1993a, Short communication, Tool-assisted predation on a squirrel by a female chimpanzee in the Mahale Mountains, Tanzania, *Primates*, vol.34, no.1, pp.93–98.

Huffman, M.A. & Seifu, M. 1989, Observation on the illness and consumption of a possibly medicinal plant *Vernonia amygdalina* (DEL) by a wild chimpanzee in the Mahale Mountains National Park, Tanzania, *Primates*, vol.30, no.1, January, pp.51–63 .

Hunt, K.D. 1992, Social rank and body size as determinants of positional behavior in pan-troglodytes, *Primates,* vol.33, no.3, pp.347–357.

Ifune, C.K., Vermeire, B.A. & Hamilton, C.R. 1984, Hemispheric differences in split-brain monkeys viewing and responding to videotaped recordings, *Behavioral and Neural Biology*, vol.41, pp.231–235.

International Zoo Yearbook 1959–1965, volumes I–V.

Itakura, S. 1993, Emotional behavior during the learning of a contingency task in a chimpanzee, *Perceptual and Motor Skills*, vol.76, pp.563–566.

Jantschke, F. 1988, *Orang-utans in Zoologischen Gärten*, Piper & Co, Munich.

Johns, A.D. 1983, Tropical forest primates and logging — Can they co-exist?, *Oryx*, vol.XVII, pp.114–118.

Jones, S. 1992, The nature of evolution, *The Cambridge Encyclopedia of Human Evolution*, Cambridge University Press, Cambridge, pp.9–17.

Jones, S., Martin, R. & Pilbeam, D. (eds) 1992, *The Cambridge Encyclopedia of Human Evolution*, Cambridge University Press, Cambridge.

Jolly, A. 1966, Lemur social behavior and primate intelligence, *Science*, vol.153, pp.501–506.

Jungers, W.J. 1988, Relative joint size and hominoid locomotor adaptations with implications for the evolution of hominid bipedalism, Meeting on evolution and diversification of the postcranium in Primates, Held at the Fifty-Sixth Annual Meeting of the American Association of Physical Anthropologists, *Journal of Human Evolution*, vol.17, no.1–2, pp.247–266.

Kaplan, G. 1994, Irreducible 'human nature': Nazi views on Jews and women, in *Challenging Racism and Sexism: Alternatives to Genetic Determinism, Genes and Gender,* series, no.VII, E. Tobach & E. Rosoff (eds), Feminist Press at the City University of New York, New York, pp.188–210.

Kaplan, G. & Rogers, L.J. 1994, Race and gender fallacies: the paucity of determinist explanations of difference, in *Challenging Racism and Sexism: Alternatives to Genetic Determinism, Genes and Gender,* series, no.VII, E. Tobach & E. Rosoff (eds), Feminist Press at the City University of New York, New York, pp.63–92.

Kaplan, G. & Rogers, L.J. 1995, Rich imagery, neglected practice: The plight of the wild orangutan in past and present, in *Proceedings of the International Conference on Orangutans: The Neglected Ape, Fullerton Ca, March 1994,* N. Rosen (ed), in press.

Kaplan, J.R. 1986, Psychological stress and behavior in nonhuman primates, in *Behavior, Conservation, and Ecology*, vol.2, part A of *Comparative Primate Biology*, G. Mitchell & J. Erwin (eds), Alan R. Liss, New York, pp.455–492.

Kaur, A. 1993, Introduction, *Historical Dictionary of Malaysia*, Scarecrow Press, New Jersey.

Kavanagh, M. 1983, *A Complete Guide to Monkeys, Apes and Other Primates,* Jonathan Cape, London (introduction by Desmond Morris).

Kawabe, M. 1970, A preliminary study of the wild siamang gibbon (*Hylobates syndactylus*) at Fraser's Hill, Malaysia, *Primates,* vol.11, pp.285–291.

Kawanaka, K. 1989, Age differences in social interactions of young males in a chimpanzee unit-group at the Mahale Mountains National Park, Tanzania, *Primates*, vol.30, no.3, July, pp.285–305.

Kehoe, M., Phin, C.S. & Chu, C.L. 1984, Tuberculosis in an orangutan pongo-pygmaeus, *Australian Veterinary Journal*, vol.61, no.4, p.128.

Kehoe, M.M. & Chan, L.C. 1986, Fractures dislocations and contusions in the Bornean orangutan pongo-pygmaeus-pygmaeus, A review of 21 cases, *Veterinary Record*, vol.118, no.23, pp.633–636.

Kendon, A. 1991, Some considerations for a theory of language origins, *Man*, no.26, pp.199–221.

Kertesz, A. 1985, Aphasia, *Handbook of Clinical Neurology*, Frederiks, J.A.M. (ed), vol.1, no. 45, part of *Clinical Neuropsychology,* P. Vinken, G. Bruyn & G. Klawans (eds), Elsevier, Amsterdam, pp.287–331.

Kertesz, A., Polk, M., Black, S.E. & Howell, J.A. 1990, Sex, handedness and the morphometry of cerebral asymmetries on magnetic resonance imaging, *Brain Research*, vol.530, pp.40–48.

King, M-C. & Wilson, A.C. 1975, Evolution at two levels in humans and chimpanzees, *Science*, vol.188, pp.107–116.

King, V.T. 1993, *Best of Borneo Travel*, Oxford University Press, New York.

Kirkwood, J.K. 1992, *Biology, Rearing, and Care of Young Primates*, Oxford University Press, New York.

Klein, R.G. 1989, *The Human Career: Human Biological and Cultural Origins*, University of Chicago Press, Chicago.

Koebner, L. 1984, *Forgotten Animals. The Rehabilitation of Laboratory Primates*, E.P. Dutton, New York.

Köhler, W. 1921, *Intelligenzprüfung an Menschenaffen*, Springer Verlag, Berlin/Bern/Stuttgart.

Köhler, W. 1926, *The Mentality of Apes,* trans. from 2nd rev. ed., Harcourt Brace & Co, New York and Kegan Paul, Treuch, Trubner & Co, London.

Köhler, W. 1993, The mentality of orangs, *International Journal of Comparative Psychology*, vol.6, pp.189–229.

Koppe, T. & Schumacher, K.–U. 1992, Studies of the degree of pneumatization in the viscerocranium of humans and pongids, *Acta Anatomica Nipponica*, vol.67, no.6, pp.725–734.

Kortlandt, A. & Holzhaus, E. 1987, New data on the use of stone tools by chimpanzees in Guinea and Liberia, *Primates*, vol.28, no.4, pp.473–496.

Kraus, N., Smith, D.I., Reed, N.L., Willot, J. & Erwin, J. 1985, Auditory brainstem and middle latency responses in non-human primates, *Hearing Research* , vol.17, no.3, pp.219–226.

Kruper, D.C., Boyle, B.E. & Patton, R.A. 1966, Eye and hand preference in rhesus monkeys, *Psychonomic Science,* vol.5, pp.277–278.

Kuyk, K., Dazey, J., & Erwin, J. 1976, Primiparous and multiparous pigtail mothers (*Macaca nemestrina*): Restraint and retrieval of female infants, *Journal of Biological Psychology*, vol.18, pp.16–19.

Laidler, K. 1978, Language in the orang-utan, in *Action, Gesture and Symbol: The Acquisition of Language,* A. Lock (ed), Academic Press, New York, pp.133–155.

Laidler, K. 1980, *The Talking Ape,* Collins, London.

Lardeux-Gilloux, I. 1994, Rehabilitation centres: their struggle and their future, *International Conference on Orang-utans: 'The Neglected Ape', 5–7 March 1994, Fullerton,* California State University, Fullerton.

Larson, C.F., Dodson, D.L. & Ward, J.P. 1989, Hand preferences and whole-body turning biases of lesser bushbabies (*Galago senegalensis*), *Brain, Behavior and Evolution*, vol.33, pp.261–267.

Larson, S.G., Demes, D., Stern, J.T. & Jungers, W.L. 1991, The relationship between walking speed and force distribution on the fore limbs and hind limbs of the orangutan, Sixtieth Annual Meeting of the American Association of Physical Anthropologists, Milwaukee, *American Journal of Physical Anthropology,* Suppl.12, pp.112.

Leighton, M. & Leighton, D.R. 1983, Vertebrate responses to fruiting seasonality within a Bornean rainforest, in *Tropical Rain Forest: Ecology and Management; Symposium, Leeds, England, 1982,* S.L. Sutton, T.C. Whitmore & A.C. Chadwick (eds), Blackwell Scientific Publications, Palo Alto, pp.181–196.

Leighton, M. 1994, Habitat shifts in Bornean orangutans: Causes and effects, *International Conference on Orang-utans: 'The Neglected Ape', 5–7 March 1994, Fullerton,* California State University, Fullerton.

LeMay, M. & Geschwind, N. 1975, Hemispheric difference in the brains of great apes, *Brain, Behaviour and Evolution,* vol.11, pp.48–52.

LeMay, M., Billig, S. & Geschwind, N. 1982, Asymmetries of the brains and skulls of nonhuman primates, in *Primate brain evolution: Methods and concepts*, E. Armstrong & D. Falk (eds), Plenum Press, New York, pp.263–277.

Lethmate, J. 1977, *Problemlöseverhalten von Orang-Utans (Pongo Pygmaeus), Beiheft, Fortschritte der Verhaltensforschung* (Advances in Ethology), vol.19 supplement, Paul Parey, Berlin & Hamburg, pp.69.

Lethmate, J. 1982, Tool-using skills of orang-utans, *Journal of Human Evolution*, vol.11, pp.49–64.

Leutenegger, W. & Masterson, T.J. 1989, The ontogeny of sexual dimorphism in the cranium of Bornean orang-utans (*Pongo pygmaeus pygmaeus*): I. Univariate analyses, *Zeitschrift für Morphologie und Anthropologie*, vol.78, no.1, pp.1–14.

Lewin, R. 1984, DNA reveals surprises in the human family tree, *Science*, vol.226, pp.1179–1182.

Lewin, R. 1988, Family relationships are a biological conundrum, *Science*, vol.242, p.671.

Lewin, R. 1989, *Human Evolution: An Illustrated Introduction*, Blackwell Scientific Publications, Oxford.

Lewis, M. 1978, The infant and its caregiver: The role of contingency, *Allied Health and Behavioural Sciences,* vol.1, no.4, pp.469–492.

Lewis, M. & Coates, D.L. 1980, Mother–infant interaction and cognitive development in twelve-week-old infants, *Infant Behavior and Development*, vol.3, pp.95–105.

Linden, E. 1992, A Curious Kinship: Apes and Humans, *National Geographic,* vol.181, no.3, March, pp.2–45.

Linnaeus, C. 1758, *Systema Naturae. Regnum Animale* (etc), reproduced in 1894, Engelmann, Lipsia.

Lippert, W. 1974, Beobachtungen zum Schwangerschafts- und Geburtsverhalten beim Orangutan (*Pongo pygmaeus*), im Tierpark Berlin, *Folia Primatologica*, vol.21, pp.108–134.

Lockard, J.S. 1984, Handedness in a captive group of lowland gorillas, *International Journal of Primatology*, vol.5, p.356.

Lockard, J.S., Daley, P.C. & Gunderson, V.G. 1979, Maternal and paternal differences in infant carrying: U.S. & African data, *American Naturalist,* vol.113, pp.235–246.

Lovejoy, C.O. 1981, The origin of man, *Science*, vol.211, pp.341–350.

MacKinnon, J. 1971, The orang-utan in Sabah today. A study of a wild population in the Ulu Segama Reserve, *Oryx, Journal of the Fauna Preservation Society, London,* vol.XI, no.2–3, September, pp.141–191.

MacKinnon, J. 1972, The behaviour and ecology of the orangutan (*Pongo pygmaeus)* with relation to other apes, PhD thesis, University of Oxford.

MacKinnon, J. 1974a, The behaviour and ecology of wild orang-utans (*Pongo pymaeus)*, *Animal Behaviour*, no.22, pp.3–74.

MacKinnon, J. 1974b, *In Search of the Red Ape*, William Collins Sons, London.

MacKinnon, J. 1984, Reproductive behaviour in wild orangutan populations, in *The Great Apes*, D.A. Hamburg & E.R. McCown (eds), Benjamin/Cummings, Menlo Park, pp.257–273.

MacNeilage, P.F., Studdert-Kennedy, M.G. & Lindblom, B. 1987, Primate handedness reconsidered, *Behavioral and Brain Sciences*, vol.11, pp.748–758.

Mahaney, W.C. 1993, Scanning electron microscopy of earth mined and eaten by mountain gorillas in the Virunga Mountains, Rwanda, *Primates*, vol.34, no.3, July, pp.311–119.

Malaysian Government 1991, *OPP2 — The Second Outline Perspective Plan 1991–2000,* National Printing Department, Kuala Lumpur.

Manning, J.T. & Chamberlain, A.T. 1990, Left-sided cradling preferences in great apes, *Animal Behaviour,* vol.39, pp.1225–1227.

Manning, J.T., Heaton, R. & Chamberlain, A.T. 1994, Left-side cradling: Similarities and differences between apes and humans, *Journal of Human Evolution*, vol.26, no.1, pp.77–83.

Maple, T.L. 1980, *Orangutan Behavior*, Van Nostrand Reinhold, New York.

Maple, T.L. 1982, Orangutan behaviour and its management in captivity, in *The Orangutan: Its Biology and Conservation*, L.E.M. de Boer (ed), W. Junk, The Hague, pp.257–268.

Maple, T.L. & Hoff, M.P. 1982, *Gorilla Behaviour*, Van Nostrand Reinhold, New York.

Maple, T.L. & Zucker, E.L. 1978, Ethological studies of play behavior in captive apes, in *Social Play in Primates*, E.O. Smith (ed), Academic Press, New York, pp.113–142.

Marchant, L.F. & McGrew, W.C. 1991, Laterality of function in apes: A meta-analysis of methods, *Journal of Human Evolution*, vol.21, pp.425–438.

Marchant, L.F. & McGrew, W.C. 1994, Laterality of hand-use in daily activities by wild chimpanzees: First exhaustive field study, *Handbook and Abstracts of the XVth Congress of the International Primatological Society*, p.104.

Markham, R. 1986, Predatory behaviour in orang-utans at Perth Zoo, *Australian Primatology*, vol.1, no.2, pp.3–5.

Markham, R.J. 1990, Breeding orang-utans at Perth Zoo: Twenty years of appropriate husbandry, *Zoo Biology*, vol.9, pp.171–182.

Martin, D.E. 1981, Breeding great apes in captivity, in *Reproductive Biology of the Great Apes*, C.E. Graham (ed), Academic Press, New York, pp.343–373.

Masters, A.M. & Markham, R.J. 1991, Assessing reproductive status in orangutans by using urinary estrone, *Zoo Biology*, vol.10, no.3, pp.197–208.

Masterson, T.J. & Leutenegger, W. 1992, Ontogenetic patterns of sexual dimorphism in the cranium of Bornean orangutans pongo-pygmaeus-pygmaeus, *Journal of Human Evolution*, vol.23, no.1, pp.3–26.

McGrew, W.C. 1974, Tool use by wild chimpanzees in feeding upon driver ants, *Journal of Human Evolution*, vol.3, pp.501–508.

McGrew, W.C. 1992, *Chimpanzee Material Culture. Implications for Human Evolution*, Cambridge University Press, Cambridge.

McGrew, W.C. & Collins, D.A. 1985, Tool use by wild chimpanzees (*Pan troglodytes*) to obtain termites (*Macrotermes herus*) in the Mahale Mountains, Tanzania, *American Journal of Primatology*, vol.9, pp.47–62.

McGrew, W.C. & Marchant, L.F. 1992, Chimpanzees, tools and termites: Hand preference or handedness?, *Current Anthropology*, vol.33, no.1, pp.114–119.

McGrew, W.C. & Marchant, L.F. 1994, Laterality of tool-use by wild chimpanzees: New data on termite fishing, *Handbook and Abstracts of the XVth Congress of the International Primatological Society*, p.105.

McMullen, P.A. & Bryden, M.P. 1987, The effect of word imageability and frequency on hemispheric asymmetry in lexical decisions, *Brain and Language*, vol.31, 11–25.

Medway, L. 1970, *The Mammals of Borneo*, Malaysian Branch, Royal Asiatic Society.

Mershon, E. 1922, *With the Wild Men of Borneo*, Pacific Publishers, Mountain View, California.

Miles, H.L.W. 1983, Apes and language: The search for communication competence, in *'Language' in Primates: Implications for Linguistics, Anthropology, Psychology and Philosophy*, J. de Luce & T.H. Wilder (eds), Springer-Verlag, New York, pp.43–61.

Miles, H.L.W. 1986, How can I tell a lie?: Apes, language and the problem of deception, in *Deception: Perspectives on Human and Nonhuman Deceit*, R.W. Mitchell, & N.S. Thompson (eds), State University of New York Press, Albany, pp.245–266.

Miles, H.L.W. 1990, The cognitive foundations for reference in a signing orangutan, in *'Language' and Intelligence in Monkeys and Apes: Comparative Developmental Perspectives*, S.T. Parker, & K.R. Gibson (eds), Cambridge University Press, Cambridge. pp.511–539.

Miles, H.L.W. 1994, Chantek: The language ability of an enculturated orang-utan, *International Conference on Orang-utans: 'The Neglected Ape'*, 5–7 March, Fullerton, California State University, Fullerton.

Milliken, G.W., Forsythe, C. & Ward, J.P. 1989, Multiple measures of hand-use lateralization in the ring-tailed lemur (*Lemur catta*), *Journal of Comparative Psychology*, vol.103, pp.262–268.

Milliken, G.W., Stafford, D.K., Dodson, D.L., Pinger, C.D. & Ward, J.P. 1991, Analyses of feeding lateralization in the small-eared bushbaby (*Otolemur garnettii*): A comparison with the ring-tailed lemur (*Lemur catta*), *Journal of Comparative Psychology*, vol.105, pp.274–285.

Milne, R.S. & Ratnam, K.J. 1974, *Malaysia: New States in a New Nation. Political Development of Sarawak and Sabah in Malaysia*, Cass, London.

Mitani, J. 1985a, Mating behaviour of male orangutans in the Kutai Game Reserve, Indonesia, *Animal Behaviour*, vol.33, pp.391–402.

Mitani, J.C. 1985b, Sexual selection and adult male orangutan pongo-pygmaeus long calls, *Animal Behaviour* , vol.33, no.1, pp.272–283.

Mitani, J.C. 1989, Orangutan activity budgets, Monthly variations and the effects of body size parturition and sociality, *American Journal of Primatology*, vol.18, no.2, pp.87–100.

Mitani, J.C., Grether, G.F., Rodman, P.S. & Priatna, D. 1991, Associations among wild orang-utans: Sociality, passive aggressions or chance?, *Animal Behaviour*, vol.42, pp.33–46.

Mitchell, G. & Erwin, J. (eds) 1986, *Behavior, Conservation, and Ecology*, vol.2, part A of *Comparative primate biology*, Alan R. Liss, New York.

Mitchell, G. & Schroers, L. 1973, Birth order and parental experience in monkeys and man, *Advances in Child Development and Behavior*, vol.13, pp.159–184.

Monboddo, J.B. Lord 1774, *Of the Origin and Progress of Language,* vol.1, repr. 1973, AMS Press, New York.

Morris, R.D. & Hopkins, W.D. 1993, Perception of human chimeric faces by chimpanzees: Evidence for a right hemisphere advantage, *Brain and Cognition*, vol.21, pp.111–122.

Morris, R.D., Hopkins, W.D. & Bolser-Gilmore, L. 1993, Assessment of hand preference in two language-trained chimpanzees (*Pan troglodytes*): A multimethod analysis, *Journal of Clinical and Experimental Psychology*, vol.15, pp.487–502.

Munson, L. & Montali, R.J. 1990, Pathology and diseases of great apes at the National Zoological Park Washington D.C. USA, International Conference on Fertility in the Great Apes, Atlanta, Georgia, USA, 1989, *Zoo Biology*, vol.9, no.2, pp.99–106.

Nadler, R.D. 1977, Sexual behaviour of captive orangutans, *Archives of Sexual Behaviour*, vol.6, pp.457–475.

Nadler, R.D. 1983, Experiential influences on infant abuse in gorillas and some other nonhuman primates, in *Child Abuse: The Nonhuman Primate Data*, M. Reite & N. Caine (eds), Alan R.Liss, New York, pp.139–150.

Nadler, R.D. 1986, Sex-related behavior of immature wild mountain gorillas, *Developmental Psychobiology,* vol.19, no.2, pp.125–138.

Nadler, R.D. 1988, Sexual and reproductive behavior, in *Orang-utan Biology,* J.H. Schwartz (ed), Oxford University Press, New York, pp.105–116.

Nadler, R.D. & Braggio, J.T. 1974, Sex and species differences in captive reared juvenile chimpanzees and orangutans, *Journal of Human Evolution*, vol.3, pp.541–550.

Nadler, R.D. & Collins, D.C. 1991, Copulatory frequency. Urinary pregnanediol and fertility in great apes, *American Journal of Primatology*, vol.24, no.3–4,:167–180.

Nadler, R.D., Collins, D.C. & Blank, M.S. 1984, Luteinising hormone and gonadal steroid levels during the menstrual cycle of orang-utans, *Journal of Medical Primatology*, vol.13, pp.305–314.

Nadler, R.D., Herndon, J.G. & Wallis, J. 1986, Adult sexual behavior. Hormones and reproduction, in *Comparative Primate Biology,* vol.2, part A, *Behavior, Conservation and Ecology*, G. Mitchell & J. Erwin (eds), Alan R. Liss, New York, pp.363–408.

Napier, J.R. 1960, Studies of the hands of living primates, *Proceedings Zoological Society London*, vol.134, pp.647–657.

Napier, J.R. & Napier, P.H. 1967, *A Handbook of Living Primates. Morphology, Ecology and Behaviour of Nonhuman Primates*, Academic Press, London.

Napier, J.R. & Napier, P.H. 1985, *Natural History of the Primates*, British Museum, London.

New Straits Times 1991, 'Illegal Indonesian workers to help ease labour shortage' by A. Choong, Tuesday 25 June, p.1.

Niemitz, C. & Kok, D. 1976, Observations on the vocalisation of a captive infant orang-utan (*Pongo pygmaeus*), *The Sarawak Museum Journal*, vol.24, no.45, pp.237–250.

Nishida, T. 1993, Left nipple suckling perference in wild chimpanzees, *Ethology and Sociobioloy*, vol.14, pp.45–52.

Nishida, T. & Uehara, S. 1980, Chimpanzees, tools and termites: Another example from Tanzania, *Current Anthropology*, vol.21, pp.671–672.

Noback, C.R. & Montagna, W. (eds) 1970, *The Primate Brain*, Appleton-Century, New York.

O'Hanlon, R. 1984, *Into the Heart of Borneo*, Penguin, Harmondsworth.

Olson, D.A., Ellis, J.E. & Nadler, R.D. 1990, Hand preferences in captive gorillas orangutans and gibbons, *American Journal of Primatology*, vol.20, no.2, pp.83–94.

Ongkili, J.F. 1986, Political development in sabah: The emergence of a modern polity, MA thesis, Sydney University, Sydney.

Palmer, J.F. (ed) 1837, *The Works of John Hunter*, Longman, London, pp.1–19.

Parker, C.E. 1969, Responsiveness, manipulation, and implementation behavior in chimpanzees, gorillas, and orang-utans, *Proceedings of the Second International Congress of Primatology*, Karger, Basel, vol.1, pp.160–166.

Parker, C.E. 1974, The antecedents of man the manipulator, *Journal of Human Evolution*, vol.3, pp.493–500.

Parker, S.T. 1993, Chimpanzees are better at mechanics but orangs excel at optics!, *International Journal of Comparative Psychology*, vol.6, no.4, pp.230–233.

Payne, J. & Andau, M. 1989, *Orang-Utan. Malaysia's Mascot*, Berita Publishing, Kuala Lumpur.

Payne, J. & Andau, M. 1994, Censusing orangutan in Sabah: Results and conservation implications, *International Conference on Orang-utans: 'The Neglected Ape'*, 5–7 March 1994, *Fullerton*, California State University, Fullerton.

Payne, J. & Davies, A.G. 1982, *A Faunal Survey of Sabah*, World Wildlife Fund Malaysia, Kuala Lumpur.

Payne, J. & Francis, C.M. 1985, *A Field Guide to the Mammals of Borneo*, Sabah Society and the World Wildlife Fund, Kuala Lumpur.

Pearce, F. 1990, Hit and run in Sarawak, *New Scientist*, vol.12 May, pp.24–27.

Perkins, L.A. & Maple, T.L. 1990, North American orangutan species survival plan. Current status and progress in the 1980s, International Conference on Fertility in the Great Apes, Atlanta, Georgia, USA, 1989, *Zoo Biology*, vol.9, no.2, 135–140.

Peters, R.H. 1983, *The Ecological Implications of Body Size*, Cambridge University Press, Cambridge.

Petersen, M.R., Beecher, M.D., Zoloth, S.R., Green, S., Marler, P.R., Moody, D.B. & Stebbins, W.C. 1984, Neural lateralization of vocalizations by Japanese macaques: Communicative significance is more important than acoustic structure. *Behavioral Neuroscience*, vol.98, pp.779–790.

Phillips-Conroy, J.E. 1986, Baboons, diet, and disease: Food selection and schistosomiasis, in *Current Perspectives in Primate Social Dynamics*, D.M. Tabu & F.A. King (eds), Van Nostrand Reinhold, New York, pp.287–304.

Pickford, M. 1986, The evolution of intelligence: A palaeontological perspective, in *Intelligence and Evolutionary Biology*, H.J. Jerison & I. Jerison (eds), Springer, New York, pp. 175–198.

Poole, T.B. 1973, The aggressive behaviour of individual male polecats (*Mustela putorius, M. furo*) and hybrids, towards familiar and unfamiliar opponents, *Journal of Zoology*, vol.170, pp.395–414.

Poole, T.B. 1987, Social behavior of a group of orangutans pongo-pygmaeus on an artificial island in Singapore Zoological Gardens, *Zoo Biology*, vol.6, no.4, pp.315–330.

Poole, T.B. & Fish, J. 1975, An investigation of playful behaviour in *Rattus norvegicus* and *Mus musculus* mammalia, *Journal of Zoology*, vol.175, pp.61–71.

Pournelle, G.H. 1960, Observations on captive proboscis monkeys (*Nasalis Larnatus*), *The Sarawak Museum Journal*, vol.IX, no.15–16, pp.458–460.

Randolph, M.C. & Mason, W.A. 1969, Effects of rearing conditions on distress vocalization in chimpanzees, *Folia Primatologica*, vol.10, pp.103–112.

Redican, W.K. 1975, Facial expressions in nonhuman primates, in *Primate Behavior. Developments in Field and Laboratory Research,* vol.4, L.A. Rosenblum (ed), Academic Press, New York, pp.103–194.

Redshaw, M.E. 1989, A comparison of neonatal behavior and reflexes in the great apes, *Journal of Human Evolution*, vol.18, pp.191–200.

Reynolds, V. 1967, *The Apes. The Gorilla, Chimpanzee, Orangutan and Gibbon — Their History and their World*, E.P. Dutton & Co, New York.

Rijksen, H.D. 1974, Orang-utan conservation and rehabilitation in Sumatra, *Biol. Conserv.*, vol.6, pp.20–25.

Rijksen, H.D. 1975, Social structure in a wild orang utan population in Sumatra, in *Contemporary Primatology*, S. Kondo, M. Kawai & A. Ehara (eds), Karger, Basel, pp.373–379.

Rijksen, H.D. 1978, *A Field Study of Sumatran Orangutans* (Pongo pygmaeus abelli): *Ecology, Behaviour and Conservation*, Veenman & Zonen, Wageningen, Netherlands.

Rijksen, H.D. 1982, How to save the mysterious 'man of the rainforest'?, in *The Orang Utan: Its Biology and Conservation*, L.E.M. de Boer (ed), W. Junk, The Hague, pp.317–341.

Rodman, P.S. 1973, Population composition and adaptive organisation among orang-utans of the Kutai reserve, in *Comparative Ecology and Behaviour of Primates*, J.H. Cook & R.P. Michael (eds), Academic Press, London, pp.171–209.

Rodman, P.S. 1977, Feeding behaviour of orang-utans of the Kutai Reserve, East Kalimantan, in *Primate Ecology*, T.H. Clutton-Brock (ed), Academic Press, London, pp.384–414.

Rodman, P.S. 1979, Individual activity patterns and the solitary nature of orangutans, in *The Great Apes*, D.A. Hamburg & E.R. McCown (eds), Benjamin/Cummings, Menlo Park, pp.135–155.

Rodman, P.S. 1984, Foraging and social systems of orangutans and chimpanzees, in *Adaptations for Foraging in Nonhuman Primates*, P.S. Rodman & J.G.H. Cant (eds), Columbia University Press, New York, pp.134–160.

Rodman, P.S. 1988, Diversity and consistency in ecology and behaviour, in *The Orangutan*, J. Schwarz (ed), Oxford University Press, Oxford, pp.31–51.

Rodman, P.S. & Mitani, J.C. 1987, Orangutans: Sexual dimorphism in a solitary species, in *Primate Societies*, B.B. Smuts, D.L. Cheney, R.M. Seyfarth, R.W. Wrangham & T.T. Struhsaker (eds), Chicago University Press, Chicago, pp.146–154.

Röhrer-Ertl, O. 1989, On cranial growth of orangutan with a note on the role of intelligence in evolution. Morphological study on directions of growth primarily dependent on the age within a population of pongo-satyrus-borneensis; von Wurmb 1784 from Skalau West Borneo Indonesia mammalia primates ponginae, *Zoologische Abhandlungen*, vol.44, pp.155–178.

Roff, M.C. 1974, *Politics of Belonging: Political Change in Sabah and Sarawak*, Oxford University Press, Kuala Lumpur.

Rogers, L.J. & Kaplan, G. 1993, Koehler and tool use in orang-utans, *International Journal of Comparative Psychology*, vol.6, no.4, pp.234–240.

Rogers, L.J. & Kaplan, G. 1994a, A new form of tool-using by orang-utans in Sabah, East Malaysia, *Folia Primatologica*, in press.

Rogers, L.J. & Kaplan, G. 1994b, *Lateral Biases in Orang-Utans in their Natural Environment*, submitted.

Rogers, L.J. & Kaplan, G. 1995, Handedness in orangutans, in *Proceedings of the International Conference on Orang-utans: The Neglected Ape, Fullerton Ca, March 1994*, N. Rosen (ed), in press.

Rogers, L.J., Ward, J.P. & Stafford, D. 1994, Eye dominance in the small-eared bushbaby, *Otolemur garnettii*, *Neuropsychologia*, vol.32, pp.257–264.

Rollins, B.E. 1993, The ascent of apes — broadening the moral community, in *The Great Ape Project*, P. Cavalieri & P. Singer (eds), Fourth Estate, pp.206–219.

Rose, M.D. 1985, Functional anatomy of orangutan hands and feet, 54th Annual Meeting of the American Association of Physical Anthropologists, *American Journal of Physical Anthropology*, vol.66, no.2, pp.221–222.

Rosenblum, L.A. (ed) 1975, *Primate Behavior. Developments in Field and Laboratory Research*, vol.4, Academic Press, New York.

Rowell, T.E. 1984, Mother, infants, and adolescents, in *Female Primates: Studies by Women Primatologists*, M. Small (ed), Alan R. Liss, New York, pp.13–16.

Rubeli, K. 1986, *Tropical Rain Forest in South-East Asia — A Pictorial Journey*, Tropical Press, Kuala Lumpur.

Rumbaugh, D.M. & Gill, T.V. 1971, The learning skills of pongo, *Proceedings, 3rd Intern. Congress Primat., Zurich 1970*, vol.3, pp.158–163.

Rumbaugh, D.M. & Gill, T. 1973, Learning skills of great apes, *Journal of Human Evolution*, vol.2, pp.171–179.

Rumbaugh, D. M. & McCormack, C. 1967, The learning skills of primates: a comparative study of apes and monkeys, *Kongress International. Primat. Gesellschaft*, pp.269–306.

Rumbaugh, D. M. & McCormack, C. 1969, Attentional skills of great apes compared with those of gibbons and squirrel monkeys, *Proceedings of the Second International Congress of Primatology*, vol.1, pp.167–172.

Russon, A.E. & Galdikas, B.M.F. 1993, Imitation in free-ranging rehabilitant orangutans (*Pongo pygmaeus*), *Journal of Comparative Psychology*, vol.107, no.2, pp.147–161.

Rutter, O. 1985, *The Pagans of North Borneo*, reprint of 1929 edition, introd. I. Black, Oxford University Press, Singapore.

Ruvolo, M., Disotell, T.R., Allard, M.W., Brown, W.M. & Honeycutt, R.L. 1991, Resolution of the African hominoid trichotomy by use of a mitochondrial gene sequence, *Proceedings of the National Academy of Science*, vol.88, pp.1570–1574.

Sackeim, H.A. & Gat, R.C. 1978, Lateral asymmetry in intensity of emotional expression, *Neuropsychologia*, vol.16, pp.473–481.

Sackeim, H.A., Gur, R.C. & Saucy, M.C. 1978, Emotions are expressed more intensely on the left side of the face, *Science*, vol.202, pp.434–436.

Sakura, O. & Matsuzawa, T. 1991, Flexibility of wild chimpanzee nut-cracking behavior using stone hammers and anvils: An experimental analysis, *Ethology*, vol.87, pp.237–248.

Salk, L. 1962, Mother's heartbeat as an imprinting stimulus, *Transactions of the New York Academy of the Sciences*, vol.24, pp.753–763.

Sandin, B. 1967, *The Sea Dayaks of Borneo before White Rajah Rule*, Macmillan, London.

Sanford, C., Guin, K. & Ward, J.P. 1984, Posture and laterality in the bushbaby (*Galago senegalensis*), *Brain Behavior and Evolution*, vol.25, pp.217–224.

Sarawak Report Of The Maias Protection Commission 1960 (copy held at the Sarawak Museum, Kuching).

Sarawak Timber Industry Development Corporation. Five Year Review 1974–1978 (copy held at the Sarawak Museum, Kuching).

Saurez, S.D. & Gallup, G.G. 1986, Face touching in primates: A closer look, *Neurospsychologia*, vol.24, pp.597–600.

Savage-Rumbaugh, E.S., Sevcik, R.A., Rumbaugh, D.M. & Rubert, E. 1985, The capacity of animals to acquire language. Do species differences have anything to say to us?, *Philosophical Transactions of the Royal Society of London, B Biological Sciences*, vol.208, no.1135, pp.177–186.

Scantlebury, K. 1994, Orangutans, *New Traveller*, no.5, pp.51–52.

Schaller, G.B. 1961, The orang-utan in Sarawak, *Zoologica*, vol.46, pp.73–82.

Schürmann, C. 1982, Mating behaviour of wild orangutans, in *The Orang Utan, its Biology and Conservation*, L.E.M. de Boer (ed), W. Junk, The Hague, pp.269–284.

Schürmann, C. & van Hooff, J. 1986, Reproductive strategies of the orang-utan: New data and a reconsideration of the existing socio-sexual models, *International Journal of Primatology*, vol.7, pp.265–288.

Schultz, A.H. 1969, *The Life of Primates*, Universe Books, New York.

Schwartz, J.H. 1984, The evolutionary relationship of man and orang-utans, *Nature,* London, no.308, pp.501–505.

Schwartz, J.H. 1987, *The Red Ape. Orang-Utans and Human Origin*, Houghton Mifflin Company, Boston.

Schwartz, J.H. 1990, Lufengpithecus and its potential relationship to an orangutan clade, *Journal of Human Evolution*, vol.19, no.6–7, pp.591–606.

Scott, G.B.D. 1992, *Comparative Primate Pathology*, Oxford University Press, Oxford, New York.

Semendeferi, K., Buxhoeveden, D., Van Hoesen G., Ciochon, R. & Armstrong, E. 1992, Human evolution and area 13 of the prefrontal cortex, Sixty-First Annual Meeting of the American Association of Physical Anthropologists, Las Vegas, Nevada, USA, *American Journal of Physical Anthropology,* Suppl.14, pp.148–149.

Semendeferi, K., Schleicher, A., Armstrong, E., Zilles, K. & Van Hoesen, G.W. 1993, Prefrontal cortex in humans, apes and monkey: Image analysis of area 10, *23rd Annual Meeting of the Society for Neuroscience,* Washington, D.C., vol.19, pp.1–3.

Sergent, J. & Signoret, J-L. 1992, Functional and anatomical decomposition of face processing: Evidence from prosopagnosia and pet study of normal subjects, *Philosophical Transactions of the Royal Society, London*, vol.335, pp.55–62.

Shapiro, G.L. 1982, Sign acquisition in a home-reared/free-ranging orangutan: Comparisons with other signing apes, *American Journal of Primatology*, vol.3, no.1–4, pp.121–129.

Shapiro, G.L. 1992, Current issues in orangutans: Biology, behaviour and conservation, *Occasional Papers of the Archaeological Research Facility*, no.6: *The Great Apes*, Museum of Anthropology, California State University, Fullerton, Fullerton, pp.39–50.

Shapiro, G.L. & Galdikas, B.M.F. 1994, Attentiveness in orangutans within the sign learning context, *Abstracts, International Orang-utan Conference: 'The Neglected Ape', 5–7 March, Fullerton,* Anthropology Department, California State University, California, p.21.

Shapiro, J.S. 1993, Multivariate analysis of subspecific variation in the orangutan pongo-pygmaeus, Sixty-Second Annual Meeting of the American Association of Physical Anthropologists, Toronto, Canada, *American Journal of Physical Anthropology,* Suppl.16, pp.177–178.

Shively, C. & Mitchell, G. 1986, Perinatal behavior of anthropoid primates, in *Behavior, Conservation and Ecology*, vol.2, part A of *Comparative Primate Biology*, G. Mitchell & J. Erwin (eds), Alan R. Liss, New York, pp.245–294.

Shoemaker, A.H. 1978, Observations on howler monkeys, *Alouatta caraya*, in captivity, *Zoologische Gärten*, NF Jena, vol.48, pp.225–234.

Sia, E. 1991, No effective treatment yet for acute Hepatitis B virus infection, *Daily Express*, Saturday, 29 June, p.9.

Sibley, C.G. 1992, DNA–DNA hybridisation in the study of primate evolution, in *The Cambridge Encyclopedia of Human Evolution*, S. Jones, R. Martin & D. Pilbeam (eds), Cambridge University Press, Cambridge, pp.313–316.

Siegel, S. 1956, *Non-Parametric Statistics for the Behavioural Sciences*, McGraw Hill, London.

Simner, M.L. 1969, The cardiac self-stimulation hypothesis and non-nutritive sucking in human infants, *Developmental Psychobiology*, vol.6, pp.377–384.

Small, M.F. 1993, *Female Choices: Sexual Behavior of Female Primates*, Cornell University Press, Ithaca, New York.

Smits, W.T.M. & Herlyanto, W.S. 1994, A new approach to orangutan rehabilitation in Indonesia: Some first results, *Abstracts, International Orang-utan Conference: 'The Neglected Ape', 5–7 March, Fullerton,* Anthropology Department, California State University, Fullerton.

Sodaro, C.A. 1988, A note on the labial swelling of a pregnant orangutan *pongo-pygmaeus-abelii, Zoo Biology*, vol.7, no.2, pp.173–176.

Stanford, C.B., Wallis, J., Matama, H. & Goodall, J. 1993, Patterns of predation by chimpanzees on red colobus monkeys in Gombe National Park, 1982–1991, *American Journal of Physical Anthropology*, Suppl.16, pp.186–187.

Stern, J.T. 1988, *Essentials of Gross Anatomy*, FA Davis Co, Philadelphia.

Stevenson, M.F. 1994, Review: *The Great Ape Project,* P. Cavalieri & P. Singer (eds), 'Primate-talk' network information, 6 January.

Stott, K. & Selsor, C.J. 1961, The orang-utan in North Borneo, *Oryx*, no.6, pp.39–41.

Struhsaker, T.T. 1967, Behaviour of vervet monkeys and other cercopithecines, *Science,* vol.156, pp.1197–1203.

Suarez, S.D. & Gallup, G.G. 1986, Face touching in primates: A closer look, *Neuro-psychologia*, vol.24, pp.597–600.

Sugardjito, J. 1982, Locomotor behaviour of the Sumatran orang-utan (*Pongo pygmaeus abelii*) at Ketambe, Gunung Leuser National Park, *Malayan Nature Journal*, vol.35, pp.57–64.

Sugardjito, J. 1983, Selection of nest sites by Sumatran orang-utans (*Pongo pymaeus abelii*), *Primates*, vol.24, pp.467–474.

Sugardjito, J. 1994, Current conservation issues, *Abstracts, International Orang-utan Conference: 'The Neglected Ape', 5–7 March, Fullerton,* Anthropology Department, California State University, Fullerton, p.5.

Sugardjito, J. & Nurhuda, N. 1981, Meat-eating behaviour in wild orang utans, *Pongo pygmaeus*, Short communication, *Primates*, vol.22, no.3, July, pp.414–416.

Sugardjito, J. & van Hooff, J.A.R.A.M. 1986, Age-sex class differences in the positional behavior of the Sumatran orangutan *pongo-pygmaeus-abelii* in the Gunung Leuser National Park Indonesia, *Folia Primatologica*, vol.47, no.1, pp.14–25.

Sugardjito, J., teBoekhorst, I. & van Hooff, J. 1987, Ecological constraints on the grouping of wild orangutans (*Pongo pygmaeus*) in the Gunung Leuser National Park, Sumatra, *International Journal of Primatology*, vol.8, pp.17–42.

Sugiyama, Y., Fushimi, T., Sakura, O. & Matsuzawa, T. 1993, Hand preference and tool use in wild chimpanzees, *Primates*, vol.34, no.2, pp.151–159.

Sullivan, M.W., Rovee-Collier, C. & Tynes, D.M. 1979, A conditioning analysis of infant long-term memory, *Child Development*, vol.50, pp.152–162.

Sumita, K., Kitahara-Frisch, J. & Norikoshi, K. 1985, The acquisition of stone-tool use in captive chimpanzees, *Primates*, vol.26, no.2, pp.168–181.

Sureng, G.A. 1960, Six orang stories, *The Sarawak Museum Journal*, vol.IX, no.15–16, new series, pp.452–457.

Sureng, G.A. 1961, Orang-utan on Mt. Kinabalu, *The Sarawak Museum Journal*, vol.X, no.17–18, pp.262–263.

Suzuki, A. 1991, Forest fires' effects on the population of primates in Kutai National Park East Kalimantan Indonesia, *Primatology Today; XIIIth Congress of the International Primatological Society*, Nagoya and Kyoto, Japan, 1990, A. Ehara (ed), pp.51–54.

Swindler, E. 1986, *Comparative Primate Biology*, vol.1: *Systematics, Evolution and Anatomy*, Liss publishers, New York.

Takasaki, H. & Hunt, K. 1987, Further medicinal plant consumption in wild chimpanzees?, *African Studies Monographs*, vol.8, no.2, pp.125–128.

Takeshita, H., Tanaka, M. & Matsuzawa, T. 1991, Developmental of postural reactions and object manipulation in primate infants, *Primatology Today; XIIIth Congress of the International Primatological Society*, Nagoya and Kyoto, Japan, 1990, A. Ehara (ed), pp.473–474.

Tan, C.K. 1986, *Sabah, A Triumph for Democracy*, Pelanduk Publications, Petaling Jaya, Selan.

Tarling, N. (ed) 1989, *Mrs Pryer in Sabah: Diaries and Papers from the Late 19th Century*, Centre for Asian Studies, University of Auckland, New Zealand.

teBoekhorst, I., Schürmann, C. & Sugardjito, J. 1990, Residential status and seasonal movements of wild orang-utans in the Gunung Leuser National Park Sumatra, Indonesia, *Animal Behaviour*, vol.39, pp.1098–1109.

teBoekhorst, I.J.A. 1989, The social organization of the orangutan pongo-pygmaeus in comparison with other apes, *Lutra*, vol.32, no.1, pp.74–77.

Telecky, T. 1994, Indonesia bans wild-caught primate exports, *Primate Talk News,* Humane Society of the United States, 18 February.

Temerin, L.A. Wheatley, B.P., & Rodman, P.S. 1984, Body size and foraging in primates, in *Adaptations for Foraging in Nonhuman Primates*, P.S. Rodman & J.G.H. Cant (eds), Columbia University Press, New York, pp.217–248.

Teo, A.C.K. 1990, *A Guide to Sandakan, Sabah, Malaysia*, text by Junaidi Payne, Sabah Handicraft Centre, Kota Kinabalu.

Teo, A.C.K. & Sullivan, A.G. 1988, *Sabah, Land of Sacred Mountain*, Sabah Handicraft Centre, Kota Kinabalu.

Terrace, H.S., Pettito, L., Sanders, R. & Bever, T. 1979, Can an ape create a sentence?, *Science*, vol.206, pp.809–902.

The Star 1991, Raising Malay as a medium in Islamic nations, Tuesday 2 July, p.5.

The Star 1991, The second Outline Perspective Plan 1990–2000, Tuesday 18 June, pp.1–8.

The Star 1991, We can match Germany and Japan: Ghafar, Monday 1 July, p.2.

Thiranagama, R., Chamberlain, A.T. & Wood, B.A. 1991, Character phylogeny of the primate forelimb superficial venous system, *Folia Primatologica*, vol.57, no.4, pp.181–190.

Thompson-Handler, N. , Malenky, R.K. & Badrian, N. 1984, Sexual behaviour of *Pan Paniscus* under natural conditions in the Lomako Forest, Equateur, Zaire, in *The Pygmee Chimpanzee*, R.L. Shufman (ed), Plenum Press, New York, pp.347–368.

Tomasello, M. 1993, Cultural transmission or the tool use and communicating signaling of chimpanzees?, in *'Language' and Intelligence in Monkeys and Apes: Comparative Developmental*

Perspectives, S.T. Parker, & K.R. Gibson (eds), Cambridge University Press, Cambridge, pp.274–311.

Tomasello, M., Gust, D. & Frost, G.Thomas 1989, A longitudinal investigation of gestural communication in young chimpanzees, *Primates*, vol.30, no.1, January, pp.35–50.

Toth, N. 1985, Archaeological evidence for preferential right-handedness in the Lower and Middle Pleistocene, and its possible implications, *Journal of Human Evolution*, vol.14, pp.607–614.

Turner, C.H., Davenport, R.K. jr. & Rogers, C.M.1969, The effect of early deprivation on the social behaviour of adolescent chimpanzees, *American Journal of Psychiatry*, vol.125, pp.1531–1536.

Tutin, C.E.G. & Fernandez, M. 1992, Insect-eating by sympatric lowland gorillas (*Gorilla g. gorilla*) and chimpanzees (*Pan troglodytes*) in the Lopé Reserve, Gabon, *American Journal of Primatology*, no.28, pp.29–40.

Tutin, C.E.G. & McGinnis, P.R. 1981, Chimpanzee reproduction in the wild, *Reproductive Biology of the Great Apes,* C.E. Graham (ed), Academic Press, New York, pp.239–264.

Tuttle, R. 1974, Darwin's apes, dental apes, and the descent of man: normal science in evolutionary anthropology, *Current Anthropology*, no.15, pp.389–426.

Udarbe, M.P. 1982, The role of forest plantation in the diversification of the economy of Sabah, Conference on the diversification of the economy of Sabah, Kota Kinabalu, no.24–25 November, Sabah Foundation and Sabah Development Bank Berhad.

Ullrich, W. 1970, Geburt und natürliche Geburtshilfe beim Orangutan, *Zoologische Gärten*, WF, vol.39, no.1–6, pp.284–289.

Ulmer, F.A. 1957, Breeding of orangutans, *Zoologische Gärten*, vol.23, pp.57–65.

Utami, S.S. 1994, Meat eating behaviour of adult female orang-utans, *Handbook and Abstracts of the XVth Congress of the International Primatological Society,* p.336.

Van der Werfften Bosch, J.J. 1982, The physiology of reproduction of the orang-utan, in *The Orang Utan: Its Biology and Conservation*, L.E.M. de Boer (ed), W. Junk, The Hague, pp.201–214.

Van Hooff, J.A.R.A.M. 1972, A comparative approach to the phylogeny of laughter and smiling, in *Non-verbal Communication*, R.A. Hinde (ed), Cambridge University Press, Cambridge, pp.209–241.

Van Hooff, J.A.R.A.M. 1989, Social organization in primates. A question of adaptation, *Lutra*, vol.32, no.1, pp.73–74.

Van Hooff, J.A.R.A.M. 1994, The Orang-utan: A social outsider? A socio-ecological test case!, *Abstracts, International Orang-utan Conference: 'The Neglected Ape', 5–7 March, Fullerton,* Anthropology Department, California State University, Fullerton, p.25.

Van Schaik, C.P., van Noordwijk, M.A. Warsono, B. & Sutriono, E. 1983, Party size and early detection of predators in Sumatran forest primates, *Primates*, vol.24, pp.211–221.

Van Schaik, C.P. & Fox, E.A. 1994, Tool use in wild Sumatran orang-utans (*Pongo pygmaeus*), *Handbook and Abstracts of the XVth Congress of the International Primatological Society,* p.339.

Vancatova, M. 1994, Sterilization/castration of hybrid orangutans in captivity — Is it really the right way for future conservation?, *Abstracts, International Orang-utan Conference: 'The Neglected Ape', 5–7 March, Fullerton,* Anthropology Department, California State University, Fullerton, p.24.

Vandevoort, C.A., Neville, L.E., Tollner, T.L. & Field, L.P. 1993, Noninvasive semen collection from an adult orangutan, *Zoo Biology*, vol.12, no.3, pp.257–265.

Vauclair, J. & Fagot, J. 1993, Manual specialization in gorillas and baboons, in *Primate laterality: Current behavioral evidence of primate asymmetries*, J.P. Ward & W.D. Hopkins (eds), Springer-Verlag, New York, pp. 193–205.

Vauclair, J. & Fagot, J. 1987, Spontaneous hand usage and handedness in a troop of baboons, *Cortex*, vol.23, pp.265–274.

Veevers-Carter, W. 1991, *Riches of the Rain Forest. An Introduction to the Trees and Fruits of the Indonesian and Malaysian Rain Forests*, Oxford University Press, Singapore.

Vellayan, S., Achammah, M. & Hamid, A. 1983, Raising of a rejected orangutan pongo-pygmaeus baby at Zoo Negara Ulu Keland Malaysia, 28th Annual General Meeting and Scientific Conference of the Malaysian Veterinary Association, *Malaysian Veterinary Journal*, vol.7, no.4, p.272.

Visalberghi, E. 1987, Acquisition of nut-cracking behaviour by 2 Capuchin monkeys (*Cebus apella*), *Folia Primatologica*, vol.49, pp.168–181.

Visalberghi, E. 1993, Capuchin monkeys: A window into tool use in apes and humans, in *'Language' and Intelligence in Monkeys and Apes: Comparative Developmental Perspectives*, S.T. Parker, & K.R. Gibson (eds), Cambridge University Press, Cambridge, pp.138–150.

Voigt, J-P. 1984, Behavioral observations within a group of young orangutans pongo-pygmaeus-abelii, *Zoologischer Anzeiger*, vol.213, no.3–4, pp.258–274.

Vochteloo, J.D., Timmermans, P.J.A., Duijghuisen, A.H. & Vossen, J.M.H. 1993, Effects of reducing the mother's radius of action on the development of mother–infant relationships in longtailed macaques, *Animal Behaviour*, vol.45, pp.603–612.

Walker, E.P. 1964, *Mammals of the World*, vol.1, The Johns Hopkins Press, Baltimore.

Wall, C.E., Larson, S.G. & Stern, J.T. 1991, The role of the jaw opening muscles during mastication in the orangutan and the gibbon, Sixtieth Annual Meeting of the American Association of Physical Anthropologists, Milwaukee, Wisconsin, USA, *American Journal of Physical Anthropology,* suppl. 12, pp.280.

Wallace, A.R. 1890, *The Malay Archipelago,* 10th edn, MacMillan, London.

Ward, J.P. & Hopkins, W.D. (eds) 1993, *Primate Laterality: Current Behavioral Evidence of Primate Asymmetries,* Springer-Verlag, New York.

Ward, J.P., Milliken, G.W. & Stafford, D.K. 1993, Patterns of lateralized behavior in prosimians, in *Primate Laterality: Current Behavioral Evidence of Primate Asymmetries,* J.P. Ward & W.D. Hopkins (eds), Springer-Verlag, New York, pp.43–74.

Warren, C. 1983, *Ideology, Identity and Change. The Experience of the Bajau Laut of East Malaysia,* James Cook University, Townsville.

Warren, J.M. 1980, Handedness and laterality in humans and other animals, *Physiological Psychology*, vol.8, pp.351–359.

Weiss, M.L. 1987, Nucleic acid evidence bearing an hominoid relationships, *Yearbook of Physical Anthropology*, vol.30, pp.41–73.

Wells, H.G. 1971, *The Time Machine. An Invention*, first published 1894, Robert Bentley Inc, Cambridge.

Westergaard, G.C. 1991, Hand preference in the use and manufacture of tools by tufted capuchin (*Cebus apella*) and lion-tailed macaque (*Macaca silenus*) monkeys, *Journal of Comparative Psychology*, vol.105, no.2, pp.172–176.

Westergaard, G.C. & Fragaszy, D.M. 1987, The manufacture and use of tools by capuchin monkeys (*Cebus apella*), *Journal of Comparative Psychology*, vol.101, no.2, pp.159–168.

Western, S. 1994, Ape opera, *BBC Wildlife*, no.10, pp.30–36.

Williams, L. 1991, Born to be mild, *The Sydney Morning Herald Magazine*, 2 March, pp.34–35.

Wilson, S.F. 1982, Environmental influences on the activity of captive great apes, *Zoo Biology*, vol.1, pp.201–209.

Winkler, L.A. 1986, Relationships between the fatty cheek pads and facial anatomy in the orang-utan, Fifty-Fifth Annual Meeting of the American Association of Physical Anthropologists, *American Journal of Physical Anthropology*, vol.69, no.2, pp.280–281.

Winkler, L.A. 1987, Sexual dimorphism in the cranium of infant and juvenile orangutans, *Folia Primatologica*, vol.49, no.3–4, pp.117–126.

Winkler, L.A. 1988, Variation in the masticatory musculature of the orangutan, Fifty-Seventh Annual Meeting of the American Association of Physical Anthropologists, *American Journal of Physical Anthropology*, vol.75, no.2, pp.288.

Winkler, L.A. 1989, Morphology and relationships of the orangutan fatty cheek pads, *American Journal of Primatology*, vol.17, no.4, pp.305–320.

Wolf, M.E. & Goodale, M.A. 1987, Oral asymmetries during verbal and non-verbal movements of the mouth, *Neuropsychologia*, vol.25, pp.375–396.

Wolpoff, M.H. 1989, Multiregional evolution: The fossil alternative to Eden, in *The Human Revolution: Behavioral and Biological Perspectives on the Origins of Modern Humans*, P. Mellars & C. Stringer (eds), Princeton University Press, Princeton, pp. 62–108.

Woods, D. 1989, A life with orang-utans, *Geo, Australasia's Geographical Magazine*, vol.11, no.3, pp.60–67.

Wrangham, R.W. 1979, On the evolution of ape social systems, *Social Science Information*, vol.18, pp.335–336.

Wright, R.V.S. 1972, Imitative learning of a flaked stone technology — The case of an orangutan, *Mankind*, vol.8, pp.296–306.

Yamigawa, J., Yumoto, T., Ndunda, M. & Maruhashi, T. 1988, Evidence of tool-use by chimpanzees (*Pan troglodytes schweinfurthii*) for digging out a bee-nest in the Kahuzi-Biega National Park, Zaire, *Primates,* vol.29, no.3, pp.405–411.

Yerkes, R.M. & Yerkes, A.W. 1929, *The Great Apes. A Study of Anthropoid Life*, Yale University Press, New Haven.

Yerkes, R.M. & Yerkes, A.W. 1945, *The Great Apes*, 3rd edn, Yale University Press, New Haven.

Yoshiba, K. 1964, Report of the preliminary survey on the orang-utan in North-Borneo, *Primates*, vol.5, no.1–2, pp.11–26.

Zucker, E.L., Dennon, M.B., Puleo, S.G. & Maple, T.L. 1986, Play profiles of captive adult orangutans a developmental perspective, *Developmental Psychobiology*, vol.19, no.4, pp.315–326.

Zucker, E.L., Mitchell, G. & Maple, T. 1978, Adult male–offspring play interactions within a captive group of orang-utans Pongo pygmaeus, *Primates*, vol.19, pp.379–384.

Zucker, E.L., Robinett, D.S. & Deitchman, M. 1987, Sexual resurgence and possible induction of reproductive synchrony in a captive group of orangutans, *Zoo Biology*, vol.6, no.1, pp.31–40.

Zuckerman, S. 1981, *The Social Life of Monkeys and Apes*, reissue of the 1932 edn together with a postscript, Routledge & Kegan Paul, London.

Index

T

Tabin Wildlife Reserve 42, 44.
Tamarins 55.
Tanjung Puting 32, 39, 44, 64, 67, 74, 83, 133, 135, 151, 161. *See also* Camp Leakey.
Tarzan of the Apes 12.
Tawau 40.
Teeth 57, 65, 70, 84, 104, 114, 124, 126, 133, 136, 143, 148, 159.
  – Dentition 69, 70.
Termite fishing. *See* Tool use.
Territoriality 143.
Thailand 17, 19.
The Time Machine 13.
Threat display. *See* Aggressive display.
Thumb 120, 124, 131.
  – Sucking **127**.
Tool use 90, 114, 116, **131**, 132, 133, 134, 135, 136, 137, 138.
  – Leaf vessel 136, 137.
  – Nut cracking 103, 132, 135, 136, 137.
  – Social tool use 134.
  – Termite fishing 67, **70**, 132, 137, 138.
Touching 62, 80, 83, 97, 143, 146.
  – Of conspecifics 74, **127**, 137, 140.
  – Self touching 119, 120, **124**, 125, 126, 127, 130, 131.
Tourist behaviour 98. *See also* Eco-tourism.
Travel capabilities 36, 43, 48, 60, 61, 64, 65, 66, 67, 68, 69, 75, 106.
Tree nests 3, 32, 65, 78, 80, 133.
Trophy mentality 98.
Tuberculosis. *See* Diseases.

U

Ulu Segama Forest Reserve 40, 44, 70.
Upright posture. *See* Bipedalism.

V

Vervet monkey (*Ceropithecus aethiops*) 52, 143.
Vessel 27, 136, 137, 138.
Video camera 34, 37, 110. *See also* Camera equipment.
Vision 55, 56.
  – Eye 56, 95, 98, 115, 119, 124, 126, 143, 147.
  – Stereopsis 56.
Vocalisations 83, 96, 118, 133, 142, 146, 160.
  – Long call 83, 142, 143.

W

Wallace, Alfred Russel (1823–1913) 10, 13, 39, 40.
Wells, H.G. (1866–1946) 13, 14, 27.
Wild pigs 33, 35.
Wildlife Education Centre 49.
Wildlife photographers 98.
Wildlife reserves 1, 5, 40, 42, **43**, 45, 46, 91, 110.
World population of orang-utans 3. *See also* Population.
  – In the wild 2, 3.
  – In zoos 2.
World primate market 2.
World Resource Institute 25.
Worldwide Fund for Nature (formerly World Wildlife Fund) 150, 151, 161.

Z

Zoos 2, 3, 5, 17, 39, 45, 47, 54, 62, 76, 79, 89, 95, 99, 101, 102, 119, 152, 153, 154, 155.

7 Day

University of Plymouth Library

Subject to status this item may be renewed
via your Voyager account

http://voyager.plymouth.ac.uk

Exeter tel: (01392) 475049
Exmouth tel: (01395) 255331
Plymouth tel: (01752) 232323